IMAGINEERING: INNOVATION IN THE EXPERIENCE ECONOMY

IMAGINEERING: INNOVATION IN THE EXPERIENCE ECONOMY

Gabriëlle Kuiper and Bert Smit

Translated by Monique Hondelink

Originally published as:

Kuiper, G. en Smit, B. (2011) De Imagineer: ontwerp betekenisvolle belevenissen.
Bussum: Coutinho Publishers. ISBN 9789046902769

CABI is a trading name of CAB International

CABI
Nosworthy Way
Wallingford
Oxfordshire OX10 8DE
UK

Tel: +44 (0)1491 832111
Fax: +44 (0)1491 833508
E-mail: info@cabi.org
Website: www.cabi.org

CABI
38 Chauncy Street
Suite 1002
Boston, MA 02111
USA

Tel: +1 800 552 3083 (toll free)
E-mail: cabi-nao@cabi.org

Originally published in Dutch under the title *De imagineer Ontwerp beleving met betekenis* by Gabriëlle Kuiper and Bert Smit.
© Uitgeverij Coutinho b.v. 2011.

A catalogue record for this book is available from the British Library, London, UK.

Library of Congress Cataloging-in-Publication Data

Kuiper, Gabrielle.
    [Imagineer. English]
    Imagineering : innovation in the experience economy / Gabrielle Kuiper and Bert Smit; translated by Monique Hondelink.
        pages cm
    "Originally published as: Kuiper, G. en Smit, B. (2011) De Imagineer: ontwerp betekenisvolle belevenissen. Bussum: Coutinho Publishers."
    Includes bibliographical references and index.
    ISBN 978-1-78064-465-3 (alk. paper)
    1. Branding (Marketing) 2. Marketing. 3. Creative ability. 4. Customer relations. I. Smit, Bert. II. Title.

    HF5415.1255.K8513 2014
    658.4'063--dc23

                    2014002486

ISBN-13: 978 1 78064 465 3

Commissioning editor: Claire Parfitt
Editorial assistant: Alexandra Lainsbury
Production editor: Tracy Head

Typeset by SPi, Pondicherry, India.
Printed and bound by Gutenberg Press Limited, Tarxien, Malta

This is not necessarily a light bulb...

An Imagineer sees many things…

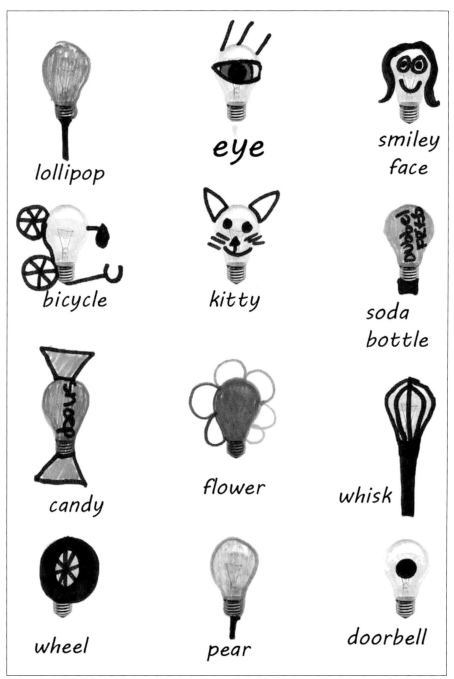

Emma van den Elshout (12 years)

Contents

Acknowledgements

The authors gratefully acknowledge:

Vincent for the trust, inspiration and belief he offers both as a professional and as a human being to the people around him.

NHTV Academy of Hotel and Facility Management and Hotel Management School Maastricht (Hogeschool Zuyd) for their trust and their contribution to this translation.

Also many thanks to Monique Hondelink and Jair Shankar who have had a bigger influence on this book than they might be able to see…

Introduction

Telling Tea Legends offers more than just an ordinary teabag – it creates an experience by offering its selection of teas with an accompanying nostalgic story, so people will not only be drinking a cup of tea but will experience the scents and aromas associated with the story. They will become aware of what kind of tea it is, and brand awareness is created.

The day I was introduced to this particular brand, the waitress who attended our table presented us with an antique looking book. The book appeared to be a tea box, filled with little booklets, each containing a different blend, while the inside of the booklet revealed the history of each particular blend.

The stories were about Chinese emperors, pirates, heroes, smugglers and other exciting adventures. From then on I started to pay attention to tea. It struck me that many tea providers try to offer their teas by adding something special, in order to try and create an experience around their product. Creating such an experience, which adds intangible value to a simple product such as tea, requires in-depth product design and marketing strategies.

An Imagineer would actually go even further than Telling Tea Legends in creating an experience. The Imagineer would fully orchestrate the ways in which the waitress actually presents the tea, her attire and the surroundings in which the tea is offered. He will also think of ways he can establish the customer's brand awareness after the initial introduction of this special tea brand.

(Continued)

Continued.

Fig. I.1 The Telling Tea Legends tea booklets.

The focus of this book is YOU:

You, who wants or needs to become more innovative in your daily professional life.

You, who would like to make the company culture more open and creative.

You, who would like to make sure that your company will be able to survive in the long run.

You, who would like to have a pleasant and stimulating atmosphere in the workplace.

You, the student who would like to master this degree.

You, the child inside, who doesn't like thinking in strict routines and rules the way professionals do.

The Imagineer in me is growing stronger day by day.

Nowadays, companies need to function in a more complex society. This complexity is due to several different factors. First, entering a market is relatively easy today and so the marketplace is inundated with a wide range of similar products. Another factor is that, due to globalization, economies and people are connected worldwide, which results in high dependency on each other. Furthermore, new technology has enabled companies to use extremely fast communication channels, which companies need to take into account when looking at communication amongst other consumers. For instance, whereas at one time it would take a few months to receive any news about the devastating effects of a natural disaster in China, today we are able to watch it in real time as events unfold.

In this economy, which is characterized by strong consumer connectivity and a change in competition pressure, companies need to start taking a different approach than in previous decades. But how can they do things differently?

For a start, in a world of abundance and oversupply one needs to be **unique**. Not just different, but **entirely** different.

UNIQUE

In a world of abundance your offer will only capture people's attention if it is unique. The word 'offer' not only means the product, but also the brand and the working environment of the employees, as well as all communication and connections that are established between stakeholders, as a consequence of which management strategies can be developed.

Standing out from the crowd is simply not enough – the offer must also be taken into consideration.

ADHESION FACTOR

Attracting attention is only useful when it 'sticks' in the long run. In order to achieve the so-called 'adhesion factor', significance or being meaningful are of vital importance. People tend to remember stories, not facts. It is relatively easy to convey the message that, as a matter of fact, using your particular detergent will result in the cleanest laundry, but when the story around your detergent stands out, it will be remembered and therefore 'stick'. A good example of such a story is the mystery of the secret ingredient of Coca-Cola, which was discovered accidently when someone added soda water to the already existing recipe. This particular story makes it authentic and easily conveyable. A good story therefore has an 'adhesion factor', which subsequently needs to be conveyed. This is the next goal.

CONVEYING THE STORY

Attention is captured by being unique – your product will be remembered because of the story that surrounds your unique product. However, interaction is necessary between those involved in communication about your product, and to make sure that meaning is given to your product by the parties involved. By giving consumers the possibility of entering the experience you created, customer involvement creates an emotional bond with the product. This bonding ensures further positive conveyance by consumers, which, in this era of social media can mean a wide range of different forums and Internet communities, YouTube, and so on. Getting the consumer himself to conveying the correct story is **the way** to stand out and ensure survival in today's complex economies.

Dan and Chip Heath, authors of *Made to Stick* (2007), show that customer communication about the product and bonding with a particular brand are the keys to SUCCESs and convey the message:

Simple
Unexpected
Concrete
Credible
Emotional
Stories

When we examine this 'formula' a little more, we can conclude that successful communication of a message is simple, but also unexpected and therefore unique. The story is concrete and consequently easy to remember. It is offered at the right moment, which means that it is relevant for the recipient, and that the recipient is open to the story. The message is credible and therefore authentic, and consists of an emotional layer by which the recipient is touched on an emotional level instead of a rational level only. This also means that the message needs to be fact based, and cause emotional recognition. In other words, the message is not only received in the left hemisphere of the brain but also in the emotions centre of the right hemisphere.

The message of communication needs to convey emotions and portray a certain atmosphere, in such a way that not only the visual or auditory senses are stimulated, but also an experience is created.

EXPERIENCE

Imagineering

To be unique requires creation of an experience around the brand – a combination of imagination and analysis. Creativity offers an unexpected perspective on stated issues. Innovation is a result of creativity and provides for differentiation and uniqueness. Creation of such a meaningful, unique experience requires a person with a set of specific skills and talents within a specific working environment; the so-called Imagineer who 'does Imagineering'.

The term Imagineering is quite well known in the USA and stands for a specific way of working. In Europe this way of working has been quite common for longer, but in Europe a different emphasis is placed on the possibilities of Imagineering as a strategic tool. An Imagineer can design and build in a rational as well as an emotional manner. He is a strategist, who possesses knowledge and insights, but is also an inspirational visionary with intuitive capabilities, who dares to dream. Above all, Imagineering means taking the liberty to dream, create, do, build, and make (Wright, 2005). In other words, he knows how to combine the analytical left hemisphere of the brain with the right hemisphere's capacities of sense of atmosphere and visuals. As a result of this combination, rational goals are achieved through a design that taps into emotions.

The Story Behind a Word

Imagineering is considered to be a 'portmanteau' word, which can be in a way compared to a compound noun. The compound noun consists of two existing nouns, which are then adapted in such a way that a new word and meaning emerge. Meanwhile it is still characterized by the meaning of the original nouns. Imagineering is thus a combination of imagination and engineering.

- **Imagination** stands for fantasy, the power of imagination and the power of representation – basically anything that can happen within your imagination. Children are quite good at imaginary play, but grown-ups seem to be unable or don't dare to create such a world.

- **Engineering** is the act of designing and further developing products or processes through technical knowledge. The term Imagineering came into existence during World War II. The first company to apply Imagineering was called the Aluminum Company of America (Alcoa). The aluminium industry formed a substantial part of the American war economy, which benefited Alcoa. Realizing that the war would not last for ever, Alcoa understood that it had to become innovative in order to keep production at the same level as during war time. Its Research and Development department was involved in creating innovative, creative and new ways of applying their goods, and described those through Imagineering as 'the fine art of deciding where to go from here' (Cullman Banner, 22 January 1942).

Fig. I.2 Advertisement in which Alcoa uses the term Imagineering.

Alcoa started the 'Imagineering programme' not only to stimulate fantasy and the imagination of its engineers, but to actively profile external communication of the company. A description of their work processes, for instance, used the word Imagineering in an advertisement in *Time* magazine, published on 16 February 1942. They emphasized that all work processes in the company were focused on the product development in terms of price and suitability, and they invented new applications for products in terms of helping people to use a product in a certain place, previously unheard of. They suggested the significance of aluminium in the current era but also in the future. Alcoa defined Imagineering as follows:

> Imagineering is letting your imagination soar, and then engineering it down to earth.

The development of new markets led to the desired results. The use of aluminium in, for example, sports goods such as tennis rackets and bicycles, developed and increased rapidly. Furthermore, the possibilities of recycling aluminium were explored and implemented. Today the company is internationally active, and in 2005 it employed 130,000 employees in 43 countries worldwide.

After Alcoa introduced the term 'Imagineering' at the beginning of World War II, others also started using it. A remarkable imitator is the brilliant futuristic illustrator Arthur C. Radebaugh (1906–1974). During World War II, Radebaugh was employed by the Design and Visualisation Department of the American Army, which designed 'weapons of the future'. After the war he became famous for his advertising campaigns for companies like Coca-Cola, as well as his excellent airbrush techniques. In 'Black Light Magic', an article from the Portsmouth Times of 1947, he labels his futuristic work 'Imagineering'.

Fig. I.3 Work by Radebaugh on a 1936 edition of MoToR Magazine.

Walt Disney Imagineering and the Imagineers

> If you can dream it, you can do it.
>
> Walt Disney

In 1952, the term Imagineering took off the moment Walt Disney introduced a separate Imagineering department (as a matter of fact, Walt Disney was such a leading company in the field of Imagineering that in the USA, only someone who had worked for the Disney Company could actually be called an Imagineer). The Disney Imagineering Department is involved in planning, creative development, design, technological development, production, project management and research, and the department is also responsible for the creation and realization of Disney theme parks, holiday resorts, hotels, water parks, cruise ships and other leisure locations worldwide. By combining knowledge of new techniques and technologies, Imagineers created new ways of telling stories that could now be experienced by large audiences. Of course Disney Imagineers have an extensive knowledge of the application and results of special effects, interactive technology, live entertainment, audio systems and technical platforms. What makes them real Imagineers is the fact that they know how to innovatively combine knowledge and keep offering unexpected experiences to theme park visitors.

Disney's theme parks appeal to the imagination of visitors and give a clear indication of what Imagineering entails – the creation and realization of a day full of fantasies, through which the participant can forget about the outside world for a while, a form of escapism. Disney therefore defined the word Imagineering as:

> Imagineering is the creation of new experiences.

Starting from the initial ideas, right through to laying the final brick of the project, Imagineering is applied in all stages and phases of project development of a new leisure location. Imagineering in this sense means telling thematic stories; this means that the atmosphere, design and visuals of the story are in detailed sync, at any given moment at any given space in the park, starting the moment a visitor enters the park, right down to the menu and door knobs of the toilets for that matter.

IMAGINEERING DEFINED

Disney uses Imagineering as a tool to create thematic stories, apply innovative techniques and theatrical elements in order to create surprising experiences. The Aluminium Company of America (Alcoa) used the term to investigate and look for innovation in application possibilities. In *Imagineering* (2002), Diane Nijs and Frank Peters describe the term as:

> Imagineering is a factual analysis, which is supplemented by imagination to develop a concept or product, that appeals to the consumer at a rational and an emotional level.

At a later date, the Imagineering lecturers of NHTV (van Gool and van Lindert, 2008) added the fact that Imagineering actually enforces business innovation from the experience perspective.

Fig. I.4 Cinderella's Castle, Disney World. (Courtesy of Bob Owen.)

While Imagineering, as defined by Disney and Alcoa, refers to imaginative, fantasy processes in specialist areas, Diane Nijs and Frank Peters seem to refer to the rational and creative side of Imagineering as a tool. Van Gool and van Lindert (2008) state that Imagineering is an innovative strategy to create and manage meaningful concepts of experience worlds for the market. In contrast to more traditional marketing strategies, by which the emphasis is on fulfilling the physical needs of the consumer, Imagineering focuses on fulfilment of emotional needs.

According to various definitions, Imagineering can be interpreted as a process, an instrument of strategy. In this book we assume that Imagineering can be used at each of the three following levels.

Strategy

Imagineering as a strategic device is usually from a management perspective. One can think of building, construction and maintenance of a brand and its social significance by offering an experience, which generates cohesion within certain groups.

Process

Such a strategy initiates a process, which is needed to find a solution for any possible detected problems within the strategic process. The development of a suitable instrument for this purpose is also considered part of Imagineering. In general, several disciplines, techniques and talents are put together in such a way that through combined powers of imagination, innovative solutions can be found. The Imagineering process continues throughout the production and execution, while the results are continuously being assessed against the original goals and adapted in case required. In this way, everyone involved in the process remains inspired and motivated in order to deliver high-quality products with an eminent level of imagination.

Instrument

The Imagineering process is applied to reach synergy and in order to reach this, both left and right hemispheres of the brain are used; ratio and analysis are combined with imagination, empathy and creativity. This could result in unexpected, innovative imagination, which meets the experience world of the users, who will be confronted with the physical results as such. This means that this particular group of users will share an emotional experience, creating a shared memory.

HOW CAN WE APPLY IMAGINEERING?

Imagineering strategically uses innovation and experience creation in order to solve challenging management issues. Imagineers develop instruments, which have the goal to bind their users at an emotional, rational and social level, for a long period of time, with the aim to carry this forward.

Imagineering can be used in different fields. It can be used as a **management tool** to deal with, and find solutions to, possible marketing challenges. Examples of this are brand loading through an experience, the introduction of a new product, the design of the physical surroundings in which the product will be used, the product design or even service design, or to find an answer to the question: 'How do people experience a visit to our restaurant?'

Human resource management issues are suitable for Imagineering. One could think of questions such as:

- How do we keep our staff?
- How do we become attractive employers?
- How can we increase productivity through intrinsic motivation?

Imagineering can be applied for **strategic purposes** in terms of deciding and developing strategies for the direction and development of new products or markets (business models). This is what the previously mentioned Aluminium Company of America (Alcoa) did.

It could also be applied in terms of **shaping a physical experience world**, in which people are stimulated and attention spans are lengthened by sharing a social moment and stimulation of the senses, which is what Disney Imagineers actually do.

When Imagineering is used as a strategic tool to solve a strategic problem, this always means the involvement of a problem holder with a business formulated interest. The Imagineer designs ways in which the problem holder can solve these formulated problems. It is the duty of the problem holder to clearly state the problem, in such a way that it gives a clear indication of needed research and design for the Imagineer. This design needs to create economic value for the problem holder. This value could mean the fact that consumers come back repeatedly, remain loyal customers, or even spend more, like to buy the product and tell their friends about it. Another possible value could be new products that are successfully introduced to the market (for example through co-creation), because they meet the consumer's needs, and guarantee customer satisfaction.

Another possible value could be the fact that there is a lower turnover of staff, because they enjoy working for the company.

TEAMWORK

An Imagineer does not work alone – there is never just one Imagineer who creates and does all the work. The Disney Imagineers work in teams, specifically constructed for the predetermined goals. This unique combination results in innovation. An example should shed some light on this – imagine that you are looking for a new type of bread and you therefore get in touch with a baker and a butcher. Chances are that the butcher comes up with a surprisingly creative idea, because he does not work as a baker and does not think like a baker, who works with yeast and flour day in and day out. The butcher might actually suggest different ingredients, which the baker wouldn't even think of. Imagineering can only be successful in terms of unique innovative ideas, when a diverse team of people, who look at things from different perspectives and with different areas of expertise, are represented and involved.

CONTENT OF THIS BOOK

This book is about the Imagineer and his working methods – called Imagineering. The book contains three parts, in which we will discuss, in detail, the Imagineer's ways of working and the theories that support these ways of working, all with the purpose of discovering and further developing the Imagineer within you.

Part I of the book discusses theory and concepts, as well as in which context and its relevance. We touch on the importance of Imagineering for providers in today's complex societies and economies. The goal of Part I is to give you, as the reader, a clear understanding of your tasks as an Imagineer in current economies.

Part II deals with the topic of the Imagineer. What kind of person, with which specific set of skills, can design within the context as described in Part I?

The Imagineer's work processes will also be discussed, in particular the importance of the composition of the team. Part II ends with the Imagineer's design methodology, in which the orchestration and creation of a successful experience is described.

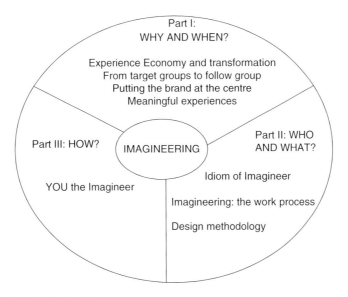

Fig. I.5 Overview of the book.

Part III, the final part of the book, forms the real inspiration for the actual work. The tools the Imagineer uses in terms of his design methodology are further explored in detail, in such a way that you, the reader, will discover the Imagineer within you, by means of a number of inspirational exercises.

The process of Imagineering starts with the first idea and ends with the physical execution of the design. Apart from previously gained knowledge about marketing and strategies, economics and communication, this book will help you to further develop products in terms of design and story writing.

The beginner will start by looking at the production phase of Imagineering, while the skilled professional will think of and develop strategies. However, anyone who reads this book will eventually be provided with tools and methodologies to combine and apply available knowledge and master Imagineering competencies, while taking Imagineering to the next level and applying it at that higher level.

LEARNING GOALS OF THIS BOOK

By reading this book, you will discover the Imagineer within yourself. You will learn techniques to further develop Imagineering to a higher level. This will simultaneously develop your self-confidence, which is essential for good craftsmanship. The concrete learning goals of this book are:

- understanding the context of Imagineering;
- understanding the economic value of Imagineering and application of economic values;
- understanding the methodology of design and application;
- to dare to become an Imagineer;
- to create a team of Imagineers.

ASSIGNMENTS

Assignment 1

Look for a typical example of Imagineering in your surroundings. Describe the experience that is being created and describe the context in which way the brand is presented. What associations do you have with the brand and how is that supported by the experiences offered?

Assignment 2

Look for video clips or pictures of products that stem from Imagineering. Think of one of the latest attractions at one of the Disney theme parks or a museum like the Centre Pompidou Paris or the Victoria and Albert Museum in London. Describe in a maximum of ten sentences why you think this is an example of Imagineering.

RECOMMENDED READING

Let your creativity be sparked by reading about the 'real' Disney Imagineers:

- The Imagineers (2005) *The Imagineering Way: Ideas to Ignite your Creativity.* Disney Editions, New York.

About making ideas stick!

- Heath, C. and Heath, D. (2007) *Made to Stick.* FT Prentice Hall, Amsterdam.

Part I

Imagineering – Where and When

To survive in today's ever more complex economies, it is important for companies to understand their consumers in terms of how and why they would like to use their products. Nowadays a brand is much more than just a quality mark that guarantees certain functional and emotional values. In society today, brands have become a part of people's lives.

In this part of the book the following chapters discuss the theory behind the ever-changing world in which companies face increasing competition:

1. Focus Shift in Western Economies.
2. From Target Group to Follow Group.
3. From Brand Marketing to Identity Branding.
4. A Meaningful Experience.
5. Thinking in Terms of Business Models.

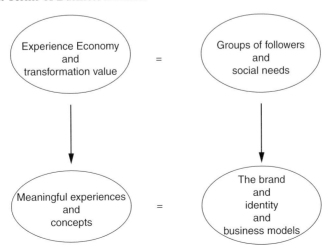

chapter 1

Focus Shift in Western Economies

Gabriëlle Kuiper

My husband recently purchased a Koga signature racing bicycle. Before the purchase we did some online research. Based on this research, the bicycle dealer and my husband assembled the bicycle step by step.

The way Koga markets itself is a good example of how products are offered and produced in an Experience Economy. They offered several options for each and every available screw and seat, right through to the colour of the handlebars and tyres. On the website, each option was explained in detail, the pros and cons were discussed as well as the financial consequences. We made conscientious choices while building his bicycle and got a thorough understanding of each and every part of it. There was even the option of putting your own signature on the frame, so that it became unmistakably his. Despite the fact that the cycle has not been delivered as yet, we feel a sense of connection to it. We know this cycle way better than our old bicycle in the shed.

In conclusion – involve the customer in the production process and he will form a connection with your product and brand.

This chapter deals with the changed focus of economic values in Western economies. In this changed focus there is a strong emphasis on offering product experiences and giving meaning to a product. We will explain what influence this has on offering products and the way these products are being offered, as well as the changed role of the consumer.

By the end of this chapter you will understand what an Experience Economy is and which developments laid the foundation for it. Furthermore, you will understand why it is becoming increasingly important and why companies need to shape, design and time their offers with great awareness. It is not only about the product but also the right timing in terms of the correct moment to buy the product, as well as the way and timing of the product purchase, which influences the social context of the consumer.

By the end of this chapter you will understand:

- what kind of new approach is needed in terms of introducing a new product to the market; and
- how the Imagineer can add value to this new approach.

1.1   TRANSITION TO A DIFFERENT ECONOMY

In order to survive, the following developments are the reasons that companies need to put their main focus on customer relationships and bonding with the customer:

1. Increased economic value of authentic experiences.
2. Oversupply.
3. A changed pattern of needs and values of the consumer due to increased prosperity.
4. The influence of emerging economies.

In this section, we will have a closer look at these developments in turn.

1.1.1   Increased Economic Value of Authentic Experiences

Companies need to survive in ever more complex societies and economies. In these economies, authentic and meaningful experiences represent the largest economic value in contrast to more standardized services or products. This is due to the fact that meaningful experiences appeal to the individual at a personal level, in other words are relevant.

How to distinguish the economic value of a product and the exact value of an authentic experience is explained below:

Pine and Gilmore (1999) distinguish different types of economic offers in *The Experience Economy*. Each type of offer has its own characteristics and corresponding ways of introducing it. They can be hierarchically sequenced based on economic values of each represented offer. They illustrate this by their famous example related to the economic values of coffee representation: the coffee bean as a basic product, which is so much cheaper in essence than paying €6 for the 'coffee experience' on the Champs-Elysees in Paris.

Having a cup of coffee on one of the most famous streets in Paris is considered to be the ultimate 'French experience'. This could be a typical story you would like to recall in your social circles ('I was in Paris, on the beautiful Champs-Elysees), you bask in the thought of ('Have a look, here I am, having a coffee at the Champs-Elysees, surrounded by successful people'), as well as the wonderful memory of your own experience ('Wow, here I am, on the Champs-Elysees; this is so French and I am really enjoying it'). Of course you are served by a real French waiter and you can sit back, relax and enjoy.

Table 1.1 Characteristics of different kinds of economic offers (adapted from Pine and Gilmore, 1999, p. 23)

Economic offer	Commodities	Goods	Services	Experiences
Economy	Agricultural	Industrial	Services	Experience
Economic function	Reap/delve	Make	Deliver	Orchestrate
Nature of offer	Exchangeable	Material/ tangible	Immaterial/ intangible	Memorable
Key characteristics	Natural	Standardized	Tailor-made	Personal
Delivery methods	Bulk	Stored piece by piece	On request	Shown during a certain period of time
Seller	Dealer	Manufacturer	Service provider	Director
Buyer	Market	User	Customer	Guest
Factors of demand	Characteristics	Qualities	Advantages	Awareness

In such a way, the economic value of a cup of coffee on the Champs-Elysees increases tremendously in comparison to the handful of coffee beans that are actually used to make that cup of coffee. The owner of the café on the Champs-Elysees is able to charge a higher price.

The increase in value and the related selection process is a natural principle. This is illustrated by the example from nature below:

> A peacock adorned with beautiful feathers is more valuable to a potential partner than a less beautiful competitor. The moment an aesthetic value is added, perhaps an arousing mating dance, the value increases further. It shifts from physical assets such as the feathers and the design of colour patterns, to a story with meaning to the specific individual by means of the mating dance. The combination creates a synergy of value: the combination is more valuable than each specific part by itself. The dance, which has a personal meaning for the potential partner, additionally has an extra added value at that particular moment.

The above example illustrates that, even in today's complicated society, the basic principle of exchange on the basis of an economic unity called money is still applicable. A product that is more beautiful or introduced in a theatrical manner arouses people's interest because of the experience that is added and thus becomes more valuable. When this added created experience has a specific meaning to the receiver, the value of the product increases for this specific receiver. Figure 1.1 depicts the 'progression of economic value' leading up to experiences.

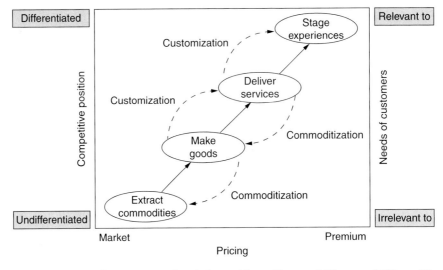

Fig. 1.1 Progression of economic value (adapted from Pine and Gilmore, 1999, p. 43).

1.1.2 Oversupply and the Consumer's Selection Process

The fact that a consumer attaches a higher economic value to meaningful experiences is the reason behind the fact that suppliers devote their attention to meaningful products and services, in order to generate more economic value. However, the effectiveness of this is impeded by oversupply in the market, a direct consequence of the fact that the market has become easily accessible to new suppliers. Technology and logistics have become much cheaper, and as a result it is possible to enter the market or even create a new (niche) market at relatively low investment costs. As a result, many suppliers, varying from a one man business to network organizations and multinationals, are active in the market.

Choosing from a wide range of supply

When there is oversupply, a noise interferes in the communication to the user. The consumer has the option to spend his money on anything, any way he likes. When he has made a choice of buying a bicycle, where should he buy it and why should he buy it there? Another factor is time constraints – there is less time in order to make a good choice.

> Imagine yourself in a large empty room. You will be able to easily hear and understand just one person talking to you; however, when there are more people talking simultaneously, it becomes increasingly difficult to listen and understand what is being said, particularly due to the acoustics. When a thousand people speak at the same time, it becomes virtually impossible to focus on what is being said by each and every one of them.

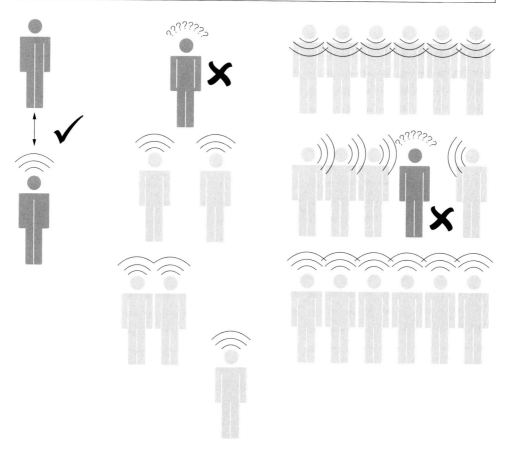

Fig. 1.2 A large room with people talking.

Something similar happens when you need to make a choice about which kind of pasta you would like to buy in a supermarket or choose a film at the cinema. We don't realize it, because we make relatively quick decisions influenced by brand name associations, which are the deciding factor in this process.

To illustrate this, imagine yourself in another country, perhaps in a French supermarket. The process of buying anything takes much longer due to the fact that you don't have many brand associations with the products. You want to buy biscuits and this could easily take up half an hour – looking at all the unfamiliar kinds and brands offered and deciding which to choose. Because you are unfamiliar with all the foreign brands and therefore have no association with the brands, you won't be able make the related quality assessment. I personally make a top three selection based on appearance, packaging and ingredients, as well as the *product promesse* I deduce.

While on holiday, you will usually have time for such activities and it can also be fun to choose the nicest or most exciting ones. On the other hand, in our daily lives we are under time pressure, and these small or big choices are made in a faster, more efficient way. The increased complexity of supply through oversupply leads, in many cases, to stress (of choice) in consumers. A wider variety of supply does not necessarily lead to better customer experiences (Prahalad and Ramaswamy, 2004).

Brand names play a vital role within the fast and effective selection process. Because brands actually decrease the undesired stress of making choices, there seems to be a need for clear brand positioning.

Brand loyalty

Another purpose of brands is the fact that the brand-related experience helps the development of long-term relationships with the consumer. In a time of oversupply, consumer loyalty is a way for the supplier to survive in the long run. Loyalty can be achieved when experiences surrounding the brand are the basis for growth of an instinctive, respectful 'friendship'.

Oversupply and emotional reasoning

Suppliers need to adapt their communication styles, because during the last century the level of prosperity in the West has increased tremendously. In the USA it has increased sixfold (Jensen, 1999).

The development of technology was responsible for the fact that basic needs became considerably cheaper; central heating or individual housing have become available to everyone. As a consequence, many people have funding available for other things, such as a second holiday home, a car, exciting long-haul holidays or designer goods. In other words, in a time of oversupply, the consumer exercises more economic power than necessary to provide for his basic needs, and so deliberations other than solely survival are taken into consideration during the selection process.

> Nowadays, the average baker sells many kinds of 'attractive' breads that, as a result, are more expensive, but provide the consumer with an experience that is in fact better, real and therefore superior (this could be true in some cases as a matter of fact). A 'deluxe' bread is not bought simply to survive; it is bought because this variety of little bread rolls looks nice on the dining table.

Less rational and more emotional deliberation is involved when buying 'deluxe' bread rolls. In other words, meaning of the product and personal added value play a role in the deliberation.

In *A Whole New Mind*, Daniël Pink (2005) relates the consequences of oversupply and the increased purchasing of the selection process and budget allocation to Maslow's Pyramid – when the needs of the lower layers of this pyramid are met, only self-actualization is left (see Section 3.2). Franzen (2004) points to the fact that at the level of Maslow's hierarchy consumers base their choice on emotional (senses) experience and meaning rather than on other criteria; what gives a good feeling is usually the deciding factor for the purchase.

1.1.3 The Changing Role of the Consumer: Prosumers and Co-creation

User value of a product

Suppliers base the price of their products on the exchange value, whereas the user focuses on the value of the product. This is particularly the case in products that are identity and self-image related, for example in symbolic brands and fashion. Such products continue to produce value during the consumption process (Humphreys and Grayson, 2008). When the consumer is involved in the production process, the product will be better suited to meeting the self-image and become of more value to the consumer. Because of this customer involvement and attached meaning, the exchange and user value increase in comparison to a standard product (Humphreys and Grayson, 2008). This is illustrated by the example below.

> A series of activities needs to be undertaken before the intended (cleaning) value is established: the cleaning cloth will only have a cleaning effect the moment something has been cleaned with it (Humphreys and Grayson, 2008).

Mass customization and prosumers

Customer involvement in the production process, as was illustrated in the example of bicycle manufacturer Koga Miyata at the beginning of this chapter, is believed to add value to a product: by investing time, the consumer and manufacturer develop value. The end product has a higher personal value for the consumer. In the 1980s, futurist Alvin Toffler predicted saturated markets for mass products, and that manufacturers who would like to keep making profits should shift to *mass customization:* mass production of tailor-made products.

When manufacturers involve consumers in the value-creating production process, the consumer becomes what is called a *prosumer*, a contraction of the words 'professional' and 'consumer' or 'producer' and 'consumer'. In both cases it relates to proactive and well-informed consumers, who are in dialogue with the supplier and involved in the production process.

Prosumers create common user value

The exchange value and the user value which we mentioned previously are the same criteria Toffler uses for his Western Economic System division into two sectors:

- Sector A is the **user value sector**, which consists of all unpaid work people do for themselves, family, friends or social circles.
- Sector B is the **exchange value sector**, in which goods and services are produced with the intention of sale or exchange.

Both sectors were strictly separated once upon a time, but Toffler understood that consumers were slowly but surely moving products from sector B to sector A.

> The upswing of Wikipedia is a good example of the transition of a product from sector A to sector B. Previously, encyclopedias were offered by the manufacturer as **exchange value** to the consumer, whereas Wikipedia is created by consumers, who create **user value** together.

Factors that made this possible are:

- information technology;
- better, as well as more education.

These factors made it possible for consumers to become more vocal, proactive and critical. Through the Internet, consumers, users and buyers connect, advise or warn each other in a complicated but highly effective network.

Co-creation and crowd sourcing

To test customer satisfaction or user friendliness of their products, suppliers often undertake market research. Based on the outcome of this research they will adapt, improve, renew and innovate these products. In fact, this is already too late as the consumer is already dissatisfied. The way to react to more vocal, critical and connected consumers is brand development that is grounded in the experiences of consumers according to Prahalad and Ramaswamy (2004). Disney, Harley Davidson and Starbucks are successful examples of this. These companies stage manage experiences from the consumer's perspectives, Prahalad claims.

In future it will become increasingly necessary to build a brand together with the consumer through a collective production process, called **co-creation,** a shared experience whereby the consumer becomes part of the production process.

Co-creation is an entirely different way of production, where consumers play an active role within the innovation process. The manufacturer gives user space in order for the consumers to shape their ideas and develop them. This is possible at any stage of the life cycle of a product: the first idea, the development, the end, and as feedback on the provided service.

Co-creation is sometimes done in small focus groups, in which a limited number of participants brainstorm new ideas. Recently, co-creation has been done via the Internet and is also called **crowd sourcing**. The advantage of the web is the ability to reach the masses; sometimes it involves thousands of participants, who generate innovation and creativity unexpectedly. Co-creation can have different goals:

- to involve consumers in product development;
- image building through users, who as part owners of the development process feel connected to the product or service;
- advantages in terms of time and cost.

Mora seeks inspiration

Snack manufacturer Mora used co-creation to activate the brand. 'How can we make the snack experience more fun?' the company asked its target group online. This generated several ideas, such as Cora of Mora – designer clothing, a toaster specially designed for quick heating of snacks, and sausages with printed texts. The question of whether these ideas actually reached the market remains, but this was not the sole purpose of Mora. They wanted to get inspiration and build a community around the Mora brand.

Dell goes for quality and cost control

Computer manufacturer Dell started an online community in which users advise each other. The website, called IdeaStorm.com, decreases maintenance costs and increases the quality of services.

The example below illustrates that coincidence can also play a vital role.

LEGO makes the best of the given situation

LEGO developed robotics to make its product more attractive and create an experience. Sooner rather than later, hackers discovered the toys. They succeeded in hacking the technique and changed it to meet their needs. Originally LEGO wanted to take serious action to prevent this from happening again, but realized in time and built an Internet community to bond with this new group of enthusiastic followers and to bind them in such way that they would change the product to something new and more valuable. The brand seems to have started a second life.

1.1.4   The Influence of Emerging Economies

In our already complex economy, emerging economies are responsible for increasing competition pressure. Countries such as Brazil, India, Russia and China (the BIRC countries) have become fierce opponents in the mature markets of the West. These emerging economies seemed to recover faster in times of the crisis of 2010 in comparison to Western economies.

Business innovations in these emerging economies will eventually change Western countries. Despite the fact that interfering technologies and business models (for example the Toyota production system) previously moved from the Far East to the West, there are three main reasons to believe that these developments will become faster, and have a greater impact.

1. Through mergers and take-overs, companies in the emerging economies **will expand at a faster rate**. In the 1990s, Japanese giants grew mainly organically, but there has been a change.
2. Emerging economies are **enormous** in comparison to Japan at a given time. The 'export machine' of emerging markets is driven by any conceivable sector.
3. Trade volume has increased substantially. Due to the low net margins of emerging economies, volume is the way to make profit. Consequently, these emerging economies are looking for markets where they are able to sell large quantities.

Western enterprises are confronted by big shifts in the economy. In 2007, international research by Accenture showed that the BIRC countries will become less dependent on the West and will move entrepreneurship to the West in order to establish further growth. Even though the number of mergers and take-overs are higher within the developed economies in comparison to the number of transactions in the emerging economies, the difference is becoming smaller (Accenture Consultants, 2007).

How will the West remain attractive despite new emerging markets, companies and professional development of people? How can distinguishability be achieved within this growing competitive market? How can the commoditization trap (Pine and Gilmore, 1999) be avoided, while the differences between offered products have become less distinguishable? Offering meaning and an experience attached to the product is a way of finding new customers and binding these customers. This will be further discussed in the next section.

1.2   FROM EXPERIENCE ECONOMY TO AN ECONOMY OF MEANING

Marketing theory is a relatively new area of expertise, but a few phases can be distinguished already:

- In the early days the main focus was on being **renowned** and the most important question asked was: How can we make sure that as many people as possible become familiar with our product?

- This was followed by an emphasis on **promise**, the position of the product in comparison to the competition. Ries and Trout further elaborated on this in their famous book *Positioning: The Battle for Your Mind* (1981).
- From this **experience** was created: staging an experience around a product by using theatrical elements, which will add more economic value and loyalty. The product offered should become an experience of the senses, and the terms 'brand activation' and 'brand entertainment' were used for this.

Nowadays, marketing is mainly 'meaning' focused. In Section 1.1 we touched on the strategic survival of companies and suppliers, via the development of innovative strategies which focus on a strong bond with the user over a long period of time.

To achieve this, companies and suppliers need to add an extra dimension to their products. This means a layer of added value in terms of experience and meaning such that consumers prefer a particular product over other products, and are willing to spend more money or time on the product.

Significance can be interpreted through:

- self-actualization;
- experience; and
- offering a social purpose.

The Imagineer can design and direct this particular added value for suppliers and manufacturers.

1.2.1   What Makes a Value Proposition Meaningful?

Meaningful experiences are memorable events that appeal to people on a personal level (Gilmore and Pine, 2007). The experience is the stimulus. Experiencing the experience is the response. Thijssen, of Saxion Hospitality Business School, describes a meaningful experience as follows (2009):

> Experience is a continuous and interactive process of doing and experiencing, action and reflection. It gives meaning to personal, social-cultural, economic, and social contexts in both the physical and virtual world. Meaningful experiences require using all our senses, while we are doing something and when we experience something. We are titillated positively or negatively by our experiences, which might lead to certain emotions such as pleasure, surprise, fear, anger, disgust, contempt or sadness. The experience gives us meaning in the form of appreciation (positive/negative), preparedness to repeat the experience, willingness to share the experience with others.

Based on this definition, Thijssen (2009) describes 12 characteristics of a meaningful experience:

1. Clear goal or motive.
2. Unique process for each individual.

3. Sense of being in control of the situation.
4. Process of doing and experiencing.
5. All senses are involved.
6. Human contact.
7. Authentic materials.
8. Changed perception of time through concentration and focus.
9. Balance between challenge and own competences.
10. Element of 'play' or 'flow'.
11. Emotionally moved.
12. Gives meaning and significance through transformation.

1.2.2 Authenticity

An experience must be authentic in order to be appreciated in such a way that a user would spend time and money on it (Gilmore and Pine, 2007). Authenticity is more than just a word: authentic must be authentic, otherwise credibility cannot be established (Heath and Heath, 2007).

The fact that a product or brand is authentic does not necessarily need to be explained explicitly. On the other hand, when you claim that your product is authentic, you need to make sure that it is actually authentic, otherwise your reputation will suffer tremendously, which means it will harm your brand name instead being profitable. The consumer is disappointed, feels cheated on, and, as a result, will remember this.

Each product has its own authenticity. Have a look at the following examples:

- Basic products such as coffee or oil have a natural form of authenticity – they are natural products and they have never been touched by humans.
- Standardized products are considered to be authentic when the design isn't a copy or imitation, but an original product.
- Services are authentic when they are executed in a good and professional way. For example, a restaurant where the waiter proactively offers a water bowl for the dog, as well as a dog snack. This creates a good experience and a warm relationship and association with the service provider; moreover it leads to long-term loyalty.

Authenticity of experiences is measured in terms of how it relates to reality. We therefore refer to it as **referential authenticity**. This term is used when history or collective memories are used as a source of inspiration; one could even think of rituals from ancient cultures.

To classify an offer in terms of authenticity, Gilmore and Pine (2007) designed the Real/ Fake Matrix. Based on two principles, four modes of authenticity can be defined. Real on the axiom of 'true to itself' means that the offer is consistent, self-steering and serious. Real on the axiom of 'is what it says it is' means that the offer is credible and true in the eyes of the users.

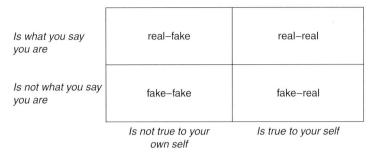

	Is not true to your own self	Is true to your self
Is what you say you are	real–fake	real–real
Is not what you say you are	fake–fake	fake–real

Fig. 1.3 The Real/Fake Matrix (adapted from Gilmore and Pine, 2007).

If a product is not what it says it is, and is therefore untrue to itself, it decreases in value – one could think of a fake iPhone, for example, which looks like a real one. The user will be disappointed when the iPhone turns out to be a fake, and as a consequence it decreases in value in the perception of the user or within the user's social context. A good example of authenticity and a meaningful experience is Amstel Brewery's Teamlink website.

Amstel Brewery's Teamlink

Teamlink enables amateur soccer clubs that are registered on the Teamlink website to have access to all games and training. This is a valuable tool for the teams concerned, as it solves a practical problem in terms of the logistics involved in sports – meetings and games. Furthermore, it provides for the social need to be connected to each other; teams can actively or passively profile themselves through Teamlink, join other amateur teams or exchange information. Amstel has created a tool that enhances the fun and experience of planning and preparing soccer games.

Amstel's concept meets the social and practical needs of its brand users and by doing so, emphasizes its image of 'the ordinary man', who likes to have a beer with a couple of friends. Amstel gains by directly binding all these friends to its brand.

1.2.3 Transformation

Meaning and experience are the central focus in a Significance Economy; however, the goal is to start a transformation by layering different experiences, for example a first layer of experiences is covered by a second layer of experience, which will effect transformation. This works as follows:

1. Experience: Experience is an intrinsic process that happens within the person who receives the experience, and is therefore relevant to that person. Due to the fact that most people are different, they also experience differently and receive it in a different way.

Because of this we can deduce that every experience is unique. The social factor – context gives meaning to the experience. By adding experience to an economic offer (a product), a memorable transaction happens. This particular memory is what is considered to be greater added economic value.

2. Transformation: An experience consists of several experiences that are linked via the interactive process of the user, who not only experiences the experience but also steers the experience. The experience causes the user to have a different view of things – it transforms the user to some extent. This transformation is also meaningful to the individual.

We speak of transformation when it has a lasting effect on the individual, it causes change within the individual which suits the personality, personal needs, values and desires. An experience, on the other hand, no matter how memorable or personal, only manifests itself at a given moment. A transformation could be compared to an individual journey. If ever you decide to go backpacking in Asia, you will see, taste, hear, smell and experience all kinds of things, mainly within a social context. You will come back a changed person, and look at the world from a different perspective.

Staged transformation is a process of a whole range of staged experiences in a sequence of time. The mutual connection, as experienced by the users, is the cause of a change in behaviour, opinion, and creates a stronger connection to other fellow users, etc.

Youplus and Menzis

Menzis youplus is a new innovative programme to increase your skills and create new possibilities. Work-related psychological and physical aspects are addressed. The programme we offer is based on the results of your personal online interview. It is a tailor-made programme.

Fast results

Menzis youplus consists of clear modules that will lead to rapid results. These modules can be done in 4 to 6 weeks. The speed is decided by the participant, depending on the time available. Individual coaching is included in some of the modules. The coach will consult you on a regular basis to discuss your personal progress by phone.

Scientific background

Menzis youplus is based on new scientific evidence in relation to improved health and proven work-related methods. The programme is developed in close cooperation with internationally leading scientific institutes. Each and every building block of the programme has been validated. Youplus is therefore able to interpret the online interview correctly and compare it to the results of others.

Source: www.youplus.nl

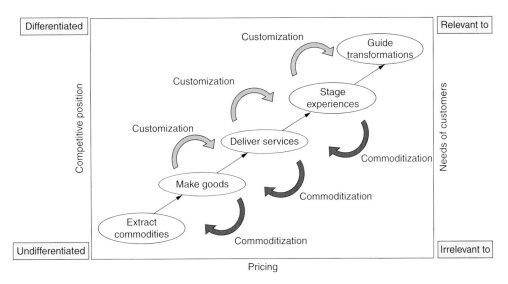

Fig. 1.4 The final stage of the progression of economic value (see also Fig. 1.1) (adapted from Pine and Gilmore 1999, p. 229).

Kees Klomp is Strategy Director Brand Experience at TWBA, one of the leading creative marketing and communication agencies in the Netherlands. He explains that brands can give meaning at three levels in the three related domains:

1. Enabling: Brand initiatives that should make consumer choice easier. This is the brand utilities domain, in other words, offering extra services or instruments by means of the brands, such as a bottle opener for a specific beer brand or a special app for an iPhone.
2. Educating: Branded initiatives that increase the knowledge of the consumer. The domain of brand courses or workshops.
3. Engaging: Branded initiatives that improve society, the domain of social responsibility and involvement.

Klomp foresees a fourth domain of **enlightening** in the near future. Marketing will play a vital role in materialization of immaterial customer happiness. Anything that contributes to this is considered to be valuable.

Transformation requires the skills of a director, who stages several experiences in a sequence of time in order to establish change. The director considers not only the user's values and needs, but also current competencies and skills, expectations and starter level of the user. Based on the above, the director stages different experiences, with the goal of changing the user and taking him to a different phase. It is the Imagineer who has the role of designer and director.

1.3 THE CONCEPTUAL ERA

The fact that more and more suppliers become aware of the fact that the total concept needs to include different factors such as time (longer periods), user value, meaning to the consumer, is why Pink (2005) began to call it the Conceptual Era.

The Conceptual Era is a direct consequence of the factors that were discussed in previous paragraphs: the emerging Significance Economy and the ever-increasing value attached to experiences, authenticity and giving meaning, but also the current oversupply of emerging economies and the related competition pressure, abundance and prosperity. Another factor is the impact this has on emotional considerations in the selection process, technological development and improved communication options, which make the consumer more expert, vocal and critical and because of this influences his involvement as consumer.

To enable competition with the emerging economies, it is not sufficient to produce high-tech products with new and exciting technologies, because the emerging economies are able to produce these faster and cheaper. In order to survive in the long term, differentiation of content by suppliers is needed in the Conceptual Era. People who have empathic and creative, as well as analytical and strategic skills will be able to help suppliers achieve this. The focus won't be solely on communication and offer, but will shift to the question 'why', as well as the philosophy and motivation and the meaning and transformation it offers.

1.3.1 High Concept and High Touch

By developing a *high concept* with a *high touch*, a higher sentimental value is added in the eyes of the consumer. To illustrate this, one could think of the difference in sentimental value between a visit to a wellness centre or having a bath in your own home (Gilmore and Pine, 2007).

In order for an Imagineer to develop a high concept with high touch, special talent and specific skills are required, which we will refer to as **high concept talent**. One component of high concept talent is the ability to create emotional, aesthetic beauty, discover patterns and chances, convey an interesting sensible story, give meaning to something and combine ideas and create something innovative (Pink, 2005), which arouses the interest of and involves the user. The other components are the analytical and rational skills needed to get an overall view of innovation and new opportunities. Pink refers to this as thinking with the right hemisphere of the brain.

1.4 SUMMARY

Suppliers have to realize that they should not only create exchange value, but a strategy that needs to be focused on user value. They can do so by designing authentic, meaningful experiences and offering transformation-inducing experiences to the user. Involving the consumer as a co-creator of the production process is a giant step in the right direction, but the conditions need to be run throughout the whole production process. Additionally, transformation over a longer period of time happens when several connected sequential experiences are experienced.

The Imagineer is the person who helps suppliers face the new challenges of the Conceptual Era. He can specifically design, develop and shape *high concepts* with *high touch* for certain types of suppliers.

In the next part of the book, the Imagineer's role and the development of the specific skills needed to take on this conceptual task are discussed.

1.5 ASSIGNMENTS

Assignment 1

Within your own environment, look for a basic product that you believe has added economic value attached to it and, as a consequence, people are willing to spend extra time and money on. Describe the product and explain how this value accumulation came about.

Assignment 2

- Choose a restaurant, pub or shop and describe in ten phrases what your expectations are of this particular place.
- Enter the establishment and write down the experiences during your visit.
- Wait one week and describe in a maximum of ten phrases what you remember of your visit.

Compare your memories to your expectations and your notes on the actual visit. You could use a grid.

Expectations	Actual visit	Memory

Are there any differences? Based on your findings, what would be your recommendation to the owner of the establishment?

Assignment 3

Have you ever experienced transformation? What did it do to you? How do you reflect on the experience that was the cause of your transformation? Do you attach value to this particular experience?

1.6   RECOMMENDED READING

The theoretical background and practical application of the discovery of meaningful experiences and the development of innovative and sustainable concepts of immaterial value:

• Boswijk, A. and Peelen, E. (2006) *Economy of Experiences*. European Centre for the Experience Economy, Amsterdam.

We live in a different kind of economy, for which a different kind of talent is needed that is not only left-brain oriented and analytical, but is also right-brain oriented and imaginative:

• Pink, D.H. (2005) *A Whole New Mind: Why Right-Brainers Will Rule the Future*. Riverhead Trade, New York.

chapter 2

From Target Group to Follow Group

Gabriëlle Kuiper

> Here we were, in the wrong street, our GPS claiming that we had reached our destination. Just as we were about to give up, a young man came to our rescue. On his iPhone he showed us our present location and with swift finger movements, barely touching the screen, he zoomed in and out, showing us the address, which appeared to be in a nearby alley. I must admit that the technology did something to him, it reflected on him. When I think of this young man, I know that he (apart from being helpful) is fashionable, innovative, and curious and that he likes nice things. He is cool!

Do you have a Blackberry® or an iPhone? Or do you still own an old-school mobile, because you only text or call people. Admit it – if you belong to the last category, the iPhone does look appealing, and it makes the user look cool. That is Apple's concept. It has an overarching effect throughout every layer in the life of the user, be it in his professional life or his personal life – moreover, it becomes part of his identity. As a user you make a statement. Of course, different categories can be identified, from light users to heavy users, who bought the iPad the moment it was introduced to the market in the USA, but who also have other Apple products such as MacBook Pro and an iPod. The brand has appropriated the letter 'i', which makes quite a statement. A strong concept such as Apple's creates a group of followers – this not only results in larger profits but also means Apple has a greater chance of long-term survival than others. This is extremely valuable in times of oversupply, where markets are inundated with products.

Why does this iPhone phenomenon occur? Why has a telephone become such a big part of consumers' lives today? The augmented reality and GPS on offer provide us with the ability to stay in touch with the outside world, within our social context. The consumer continuously knows where his friends are and how he can reach them via text messages, by telephone or through apps or the Internet. The product itself also has an influence on how society perceives the user. (Remember, I thought he was cool.) People from other target groups could say he was 'young' or 'innovative' or even 'boring' – all reactions which the provider, in this case Apple, needs to be aware of and take into account when it develops, executes and introduces new products to the market.

The Apple slogan is 'Think Different', and this is also the assignment the brand sets for itself. The brand didn't just stick to producing computers, it also developed the successful iPod, followed by the iPhone and the iPad, with software to link them together. While using the same way of thinking, different technologies and markets are targeting the same consumers. The brand not only stands for a product but also a way of doing things, in which the user recognizes and mirrors himself.

This chapter discusses how suppliers of a product or service try to tie groups of people to that product or service. These groups of people often have common characteristics and on the basis of these common characteristics, **market segments** are formed. The result of this is that congenial groups of people use the same communication and communication medium, through which the supplier sends the correct message, at the correct moment, in the correct tone of voice, in such a way that it reaches a large group of potential users. The supplier is focused on creating long-term ties with these group(s), in other words loyalty, as this will lead to repeat purchases or the purchase of a different product from the same manufacturer, positive word of mouth advertisement, etc.

This creates continuity for the supplier. Suppliers consciously position themselves opposite the competition, in order to differentiate and be recognizable to the consumer. Being renowned and brand promise are the central focus of positioning.

In Chapter 1, the term the Conceptual Era was introduced. This term indicates that we live in a world in which economic complexity, information technology, a critical consumer and the pressure of competition are such that any message that has to be communicated needs to be meaningful and aligned with the experience concept. Additionally, we explained why and how experience and meaning add to the exchange value, but also add user value, and that because of this, experience and meaning need to be added to the communication of the product or service.

An Imagineer has to have an insight into the group of users for whom he will design. He can do this in two ways:

1. In advance, he researches who this group of users is, and designs accordingly.
2. He designs a meaningful and relevant concept, which step by step ties a group of followers to its brand, and which will expand via word of mouth and (voluntary) ambassadors. A fan club will be created around the product, which steadily grows because members like to recruit

each other. For this fan club, a *tribe*, specific products and services are developed in order to meet the needs of the emerging group.

In this chapter both ways are discussed and explained. By the end of this chapter you will understand:

- what segmentation is, and how segmentation is used within a marketing strategy;
- what positioning means and how target groups are set up;
- how communication messages are processed;
- what exactly follow groups are, and how *tribal marketing* affects such a follow group; and
- how the Imagineer uses this knowledge in his designs.

2.1   UNDERSTANDING GROUPS OF USERS IN ADVANCE

To distinguish desired groups of users in advance means that homogeneous groups of people are selected before they get introduced to the product. Nowadays, this not only happens on the basis of socio-demographics (or other objectively measurable characteristics), because more subjective variables, such as shared values, have become more important.

Subjective variables influence the meaning people give to a product, or even decide whether they actually experience something as an experience. Therefore, questions such as 'What are they used to?' or 'What are their expectations?' need to be asked.

2.1.1   Segmentation

In traditional marketing, segmentation is splitting the total heterogeneous market for a certain product or service into smaller, homogeneous segments, in order to adjust, via a well-planned marketing strategy, to the wishes and needs of the distinctive segment. This makes it possible to convey the right message at the right time to the right people through the right communication channel.

This train of thought enables us to segment people, based on **segmentation criteria** (common characteristics) as a certain group, with specific behaviour, for example in the area of media usage. When a supplier focuses on a certain segment, this is considered the **target group**. The target market consists of several segments and is part of the total market:

- **Total market:** Total demand and supply of a certain product or service.
- **Potential market:** All the people who could possibly be interested in a certain product or service.
- **Available market:** A segment of the potential markets: consumers that are interested and who possess sufficient income to purchase a product or a service.
- **Legally available market:** A segment of the available market: consumers who are allowed to buy as a consequence of their age or other criteria.
- **Target market:** Consumers who will actually use the product or service.

Calculate potential markets

Imagine that in the UK, 10,000 people get their motorcycle licence annually. Of these people, 75% will buy a second-hand motor, 10% won't buy anything and will rent a motorcycle when necessary, while the remaining 15% will buy a new motorcycle. The potential market for the sales of new motorcycles will be 1500 a year.

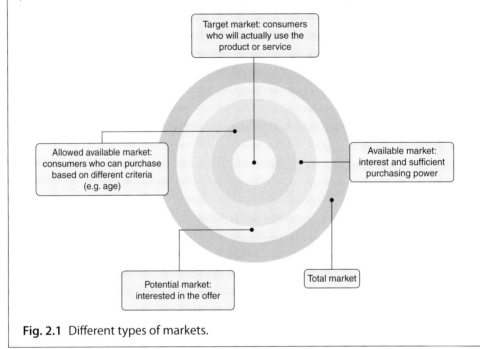

Fig. 2.1 Different types of markets.

A supplier can have two main reasons for segmentation:

- **Creation of value:** The goals and focus are consumer loyalty and satisfaction. Segmentation enables the supplier to better meet the individual wishes and needs of the consumer. Creating strong ties with the customer, via the addition of relevant meaning for the customer, is the main focus.
- **Cost reduction:** A subsidiary aim is, for example, 'being relevant'. The more targeted communication is applied for intended groups of consumers, the lower the actual cost per contact will be.

Successful segmentation-based marketing needs to meet the following criteria:

- A segment has to be **measurable, sizable** and **reachable**. Size is particularly important, as sufficient purchasing power needs to be available within the segment. Measurability is necessary to conduct specific research into the effects of marketing communication both well in advance and later on.
- Segments should **vary sufficiently in order to distinguish** and use specific communication and/or offers.

2.1.2 Segmentation Characteristics

In traditional marketing, market segmentation is generally based on different **objectively measurable characteristics**. Objective means that it can be nominated and compared based on counting, enumeration and objective data. The data can be collected through quantitative research. **Subjective characteristics** are based on data that requires interpretation, as truthful as possible. This concerns, for example, segmentation based on lifestyle or motivation. Data is usually collected through qualitative methods such as observation and/or focus groups. Subjective characteristics become more and more important in order to bind groups of people to a specific offer, as people rapidly change identity and preferences in the current ever-changing economy.

In traditional marketing different characteristics can be identified for the division of homogeneous groups. There are six types of characteristics:

1. Geographical.
2. Demographical.
3. Socio-economic.
4. Cultural characteristics.
5. Psychographic.
6. Behavioural characteristics.

The first four characteristics help to establish place, age, stage in life and cultural backgrounds, with additional considerations and priorities, such as purchasing power. Selection can be done based on relevance of a specific offer to a particular group.

Through Internet availability and increased mobility it is easier for people to try out different identities and join new social communities. Consequently, people belonging to a group that is specified based on geographical or demographical elements begin to behave less homogeneously. Because of this phenomenon, the last two characteristics of segmentation are most relevant to the Imagineer, as these indicate which expectations and assumptions the group has before starting actual usage of the product, and what will most probably give meaning to the experience of the group.

Psychographic characteristics are characteristics related to someone's lifestyle, which is measured by their activities, interests and opinions. An effective design responds to the ideal self-image of the receiver. This also includes possible benefits the user expects from the product, as well as his attitude at any specific moment towards the marketing communication method used and the average personality of the group (for example, is the group more extrovert or introvert?).

Behavioural characteristics concern usage and consumption, but also brand loyalty, media behaviour and willingness to purchase. The questions concerned are based on whether a potential buyer is actually aware of the existence of the offer, what is actually offered, as well as what is offered in comparison to competitors. Some might have the intention to actually purchase the products, whereas with others, the idea of purchasing hasn't occurred as yet. Values and norms, attitude and motivation are also considered to be behavioural characteristics.

> **Attitude**
>
> In social psychology, attitude has different functions for the individual: an instrumental function, a knowledge function, a value-expression function and an ego-defensive function (Katz, 1960). The instrumental function means that the individual is in pursuit of the largest possible reward against the smallest possible punishment. The function of value expression is mainly focused on self-expression. The knowledge function gives structure and meaning to the individual's world around him.

The values, areas of interest and convictions of an individual influence the way a communicated message is remembered by the receiver. This is called **selective retention**. The closer the message hits to home and meets the convictions of the receiver, the more easily it will be remembered. It is therefore of vital importance to the Imagineer to understand the specific convictions of the people he designs for.

An important behavioural aspect for the Imagineer is the adoption rate. This is the speed with which innovative ideas spread and are adopted within a certain group. Adoption rate within marketing is based on the social theory of Everett Rogers. Rogers shows the lifecycle of an innovation in an adoption curve, indicating in which way, and at what rate they are accepted by a certain group of people. There are always forerunners, who quickly accept a new idea and apply it, and there are people who need more time for this. Typecasting of a group gives an Imagineer sufficient information to decide how far he can go with his design, without moving ahead too fast and stepping outside the comfort zone of the users.

- **Innovators** (2.5%): dare to change and start new things, despite what anyone else thinks or says about it.
- **Early adopters** (13.5%): protagonists who are respected. They try new things, but are quite careful in what and how they make their choices.

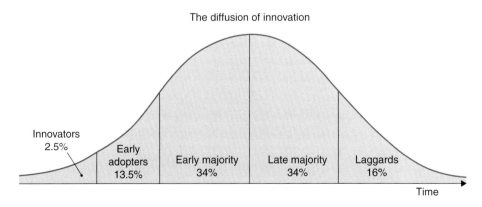

Fig. 2.2 Adoption curve (adapted from Rogers, 1962). Everett Rogers defines diffusion as the process by which an innovation is communicated through certain channels over time among the members of a social system.

- **Early majority** (34%): contemplative, somewhat anticipating people, who accept change faster than most people.
- **Late majority** (34%): sceptical people who will only use something when they are convinced it works, or when it is generally accepted because other people use it as well.
- **Laggards** (16%): traditional people who like to stick to the old, more traditional ways. They will only accept something new when it has become mainstream or traditional.

2.1.3 Value Differentiation

Social scientists developed segmentation models based on shared values. Values are fundamental views and concepts which motivate people for longer periods of time. In the long run, they remain the same, in contrast to, for instance, trends. Examples of segmentation models based on values include:

- the Values, Attitudes and Lifestyles (VALS) model of Mitchell;
- the Dutch WIN model of TNS-NIPO; and
- the Mentality™ model from Motivaction.

We will briefly discuss these models and explain our choice of Mitchell's VALS model for this book.

The VALS model by Mitchell (1983) distinguishes eight lifestyles based on two parameters:

1. Types of motivation (related to consumer values), where he distinguishes:
    - ideals (focus on knowledge and principles);
    - achievement (focus on being good and/or successful); and
    - self-expression (focus on social or physical activities).
2. The attributes of people that allow them to be innovative to a greater or lesser degree, such as energy, self-confidence, intelligence, creativity, impulsiveness, money, leadership qualities and vanity.

TNS-NIPO's WIN model reasons with the universal end values and instrumental values of the human being. This results in eight distinguishable groups with some common values from the VALS model. The model contains two parameters:

1. The way people position themselves towards others.
2. The level of conservativeness, or willingness to change.

This allows for the possibility of naming matters such as 'the level of need to discover possibilities and self-development' and 'being focused on others and the general consensus'.

In the **Mentality™ model from Motivaction** two parameters are set alongside each other:

1. Personal concepts.
2. Values that form the foundation of people's lifestyles.

Eight different environments can be distinguished from this. In the following model, different parameters are set alongside each other.

Table 2.1 Three models set alongside each other

Mentality™	VALS	WIN
Shared values	Interpersonal relationships	Personal universal values
Personal convictions/opinions versus lifestyle values	Ideals, achievements and self-expression versus available (personal) resources	Need to develop versus being focused on others

Mitchell's VALS model

Psychologist and professor Alfred Adler introduced the lifestyle concept in the 1930s. He pointed out that individuals should not be looked at on the basis of their personality traits and values, but on the basis of how they shape their lives and deal with problems and interpersonal relationships. Market researcher Mitchell adapted this view in the 1960s to what is known as the Values, Attitudes and Lifestyles (VALS) model. In 1983, international researchers SRI Consulting developed a segmentation instrument, which is still being used today. On the basis of this model eight different lifestyle segments can be distinguished: innovators, thinkers and believers, achievers and doers, experiencers and makers, as well as survivors. In this book we divide the groups on the basis of values according to the VALS model (which will be further discussed in the next chapter). On the one hand, due to the fact that it is an internationally accepted model, on the other hand because the main focus of Imagineering requires stimulation and direction of interpersonal relationships, which the VALS model addresses from this specific angle.

The box below shows how Dutch people are divided according to the WIN model and according to the Mentality™ model from Motivaction.

The WIN model

The WIN model was tested by many researchers but in particular by Schwartz and Bilsky (1987). The division into eight lifestyles seems to be universal. The ratio will most probably differ per researched 'group'. When we research the lifestyles of Dutch people above the age of 18 on the basis of the values used, the ratio appears to be as follows:

- **Broad-minded** (7%): progressive, highly educated, left oriented idealist; involved and critical.
- **Engaged** (11%): social person, who looks for harmony and stability, usually highly educated and older, feeling of freedom is of great importance.
- **Caretakers** (15%): sober, social person, a person who likes to be in the company of others and is community focused.
- **Conservatives** (16%): family and friend focused, in accordance with prevailing norms or standards.

(Continued)

Continued.

- **Hedonist** (11%): enjoyment and fun are the main focus, impulsive buying style.
- **Balanced** (21%): the majority of the population.
- **Luxury seekers** (11%): ambitious and achievement focused, do not like to procrastinate and appreciate comfort.
- **Business people** (8%): own development and ambition, highly educated, hardworking and creative, self-determination is key.

Motivaction's Mentality™ model

The Mentality™ model from Motivaction (www.motivaction.nl) looks at how people perceive the world, what motivates target groups and how trends emerge and in which broader context they operate. In total, eight different social environments can be distinguished based on common values and norms – work, relationships, leisure time, taste, dreams, aspirations and aesthetics. People who share the same social environment in terms of work, leisure time and politics show common ambitions and aspirations. Dimensions used are personal opinions and values, which are the foundation of people's lifestyles. Each and every environment has its own lifestyle and consumption patterns, which appear in, and lead to, concrete behaviour. The eight environments concern the Dutch population in the age range between 15 and 75 years.

1. Modern citizens (22%): conformist, sensitive-oriented citizens, who try to find a balance between tradition and modern values such as consumerism and enjoyment.

2. Traditional citizens (18%): moralistic, dutiful, status quo focused citizens, who cling to traditions and material possessions.

3. Upwardly mobile (13%): career-focused individualists, with a fascination for social status, new technology, risk and excitement.

4. Post-materialists (10%): society-critical idealists, who like to develop themselves, and take a stand against social injustice and stand up for the environment.

5. Cosmopolitans (10%): critical world citizens, who integrate post-modern values, such as development and experiences, with modern values such as success, materialism and enjoyment.

6. Post-modern hedonists (10%): the pioneers of the experience culture, in which experimentation and breaking moral and social conventions have become targets by themselves.

7. Convenience oriented (9%): the impulsive and passive consumer, who strives for a carefree, enjoyable and comfortable life.

8. Modern conservatives (8%): the liberal-conservative upper layer of society, which embraces technological development and resists social and cultural innovation.

2.2 MARKETING STRATEGY

There is usually a direct relationship between segmentation and positioning of a product in the so-called marketing strategy process. In this process the goals of the supplier are formulated and based on this, market research is conducted, for instance with the help of Porter's

Five Forces Model (1985). After choosing the correct marketing strategy, the segments can be decided on and researched further. Research into the segments precedes the decision over how to position the offer amongst user group(s). This is a strategic choice, in which the marketing professional works together with the Imagineer, in order to take into account the expectations and suppositions of the selected future users; in other words, what is meaningful to the group and how the product will attract attention. The ultimate goal is to reach a top of mind position with the selected group of users, responding to the need for meaningful experiences at an individual level.

The following steps can be defined in the marketing process:

- **Formulate SMART goals**: the goal needs to be described and has to be specific, measurable, acceptable, realistic, time bound (deadline for goal achievement) and output (concrete end result).
- **Define market**, through provisional segmentation.
- **Market research** on the current competition relative to the own company through a SWOT analysis (strengths and weaknesses are positioned against opportunities and threats).
- **Market potential** needs to be analysed with the help of Porter's Five Forces Model.
- **Market strategy** has to be chosen through the Ansoff matrix: market penetration (existing products and existing market), market development (existing products, new markets), product development (new products, existing market), diversification (new products, new markets).
- **Segmentation** of (potential) consumers in clearly defined homogeneous groups.
- **Broaden knowledge** about the segments through further research.
- **Target group definition**: strategic decision about which segment will be the focus of the new product, based on for example the profitability.
- **Positioning research** on which characteristics the consumer finds important and which of these need emphasis, with regard to the competition.
- **Positioning** needs to be decided (storytelling), in order to communicate in a consistent manner to gain a top of mind position within the segment.
- **Brand name** needs to be chosen, which matches the chosen story and provides correct associations.
- **Top of mind position** created with the help of the 4 Ps (product, price, place, promotion).

2.3 POSITIONING

After segment distinction, the supplier has to position himself alongside other already existing suppliers within the same segment; this could, for example, be based on purchasing power and possible profitability.

The term positioning was introduced into marketing by Al Ries and Jack Trout (1981). The goal of positioning is to reach a **top of mind position** in a selected group of future and potential consumers. The higher this position, the easier a product is purchased, the higher the profit, as well as survival chances in the long run. A top of mind position is achieved by the mind knowing and positioning a product, based on the way it is communicated and the message of communication in comparison to the communication of comparable competitors, while looking at both positive and negative aspects of the product.

Each product category had its own **positioning ladder** – on the ladder, the consumer categorizes the products within that category on different rungs. Ries suggests that this ladder can only have seven rungs. A consumer should be able to place a maximum of seven brand names in a hierarchical order (Ries and Trout, 1981). When someone is the first supplier of a certain new product, a high brain position is usually guaranteed. It is even possible that the brand name actually becomes the name for the whole product category, as has happened for example with Aspirin or Kleenex or Sellotape.

The brand supplier's strategy is focused on differentiation through communication, price, place and type of product to meet the consumer's needs. Positioning is that part of the marketing strategy that mainly deals with adding extra value to a product or service, on top of already existing instrumental characteristics of the product or service, in order to reach a higher brain position on the positioning ladder.

This position and added value have been thought of by the supplier or marketing department way in advance. In general, an expressive characteristic is added to the already existing instrumental characteristics of the product or service (Rijkenberg, 2006).

Fig. 2.3 'The Axe effect' advertisement.

The instrumental characteristics of Axe deodorant are the specific way in which the deodorant is applied, a solution to perspiration and bad body odour. However, positioning leads to 'the Axe effect', where large numbers of beautiful women pursue the man using Axe, finding him as irresistible as a bar of chocolate.

Positioning does not flow from the history of a brand or brand characteristics. It is a well thought through story, which adds expressive characteristics to the product in order to shape the relationship with the consumer, and for it to be easily distinguishable from other products.

2.3.1 The Role of the Imagineer

The Imagineer, in his role as advisor and designer in cooperation with the marketing manager or the brand manager, plays a vital role in the positioning process. The Imagineer is responsible for adding an extra emotional layer: experience and meaning.

The Nike experience

The Nike brand relates to wearing shoes, the brand experience can be experienced in 'Nike Town', whereas experience with meaning is offered through NikeID and Nike+.

At NikeID you can 'design' your own clothing through co-creation.

Nike+ is an online coaching programme through which you can monitor your own personal sporting achievements. The data can be uploaded and shared with an online community created by Nike+; this enables people to race against someone in New York, for example. Furthermore, Nike offers participants the chance to organize their own races, supported by the brand.

The above example about Nike shows the involvement of the Imagineer at different levels: the brand is built, positioned, and value and meaning are added by using a platform, as well as creating social cohesion around the product's user value.

2.4 TARGET GROUPS

2.4.1 The Communication Process with the Target Group

After choosing a segment, a target group is further researched, investigated and defined for the purpose of channelling communication via the most effective and efficient communication channels. In traditional marketing theory, this is referred to as the communication process: the sender (supplier) sends out a (information) message to the receiver (possible consumer). In the communication process the message is coded by the **sender**, i.e. it is translated into language or other symbols or experiences. The receiver needs to **decode**. Therefore the message needs to be constructed in such a way that the sender is secure in the fact that the decoding process happens as intended. Should this not be the case, then **noise is experienced** in communication.

In traditional marketing theory, the response of the receiver towards the sender is called **feedback**. Feedback plays a bigger role in current marketing and relates to the crucial interaction with the receivers during co-creation. Even when a tailor-made experience is created, interaction is needed to respond to the feeling of the participants and the experience.

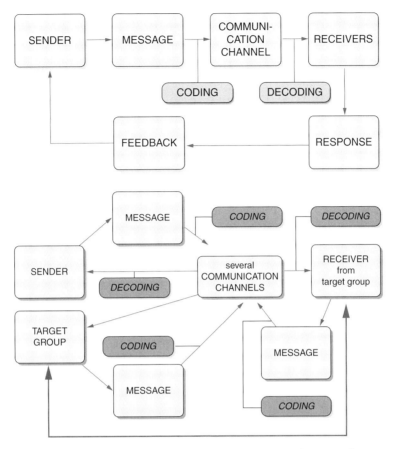

Fig. 2.4 The communication process in traditional marketing (above) and an interactive communication process (below).

2.4.2 Communication Target Group and Users Target Group

When there are several types of recipients, this is called a **communication target group**. The users target group can differ from the communication target group. The communication target group can consist of **influential** people (opinion leaders), who have social ties with the users target group, and relay the message to the possible potential users group.

The opinion leader serves as a gatekeeper, who passes on the message with his own additional commentary. Examples of these influential people are bloggers or websites such as kieskeurig.nl. **Tribal marketing** identifies and includes the influential people, because they are vital for the success of communication.

People from the communication target group can play one or several of the following roles:

1. Initiator: The person who puts the purchase on the agenda.
2. Influential person: Someone who has an opinion about the purchase, and because of his reliability in terms of his knowledge, will most probably be acknowledged in his opinion or

followed in his decision. They could also be outsiders, or people who can influence a decision through different Internet forums.

3. **Decision maker:** A person allowed to make any decision concerning the budgets.
4. **User:** The person who actually uses the product or service after the purchase.
5. **Facilitator:** The person who makes the budget available.

2.4.3   The Role of the Imagineer

The type of target group and its role are the deciding factors for the communication targets, the way the story is told and the message's relevance at a certain moment in time. Furthermore, target groups and roles determine the content of the message. Each group has different needs and the Imagineer, who designs for the sender (problem holder with communication message), has to research the target group in question. He wants to know what kind of people are in the target group, what motivates them, what expectations and emotional perception they have, as well as which media they use and what assumed knowledge they have and so on.

It is relevant to the Imagineer to know who his audience will be for his particular design and therefore an extensive description of the target group is created based on research.

To create a persona

Consequently, the Imagineer will give the target group a 'face' by creating a **persona**. A persona is a distilled graph, based on figures and objective data collection, or a visualization of the user profile of the group. The target group analysis, combined with this visualization of the user, results in a tangible idea of the people and their perception, for whom user value is created in such a way that it will be clear why a specific user value will be of value to a certain target group. A **mood board** shows which atmospheres the persona finds interesting. The rationale for a persona is the fact that it is easier to design for a 'real' person than for a graph based on data. The Imagineer will design and develop a scenario, in which he describes the experience of the concept for the specific target group, through the eyes of a persona.

2.5   PROCESSING AND INVOLVEMENT

When a target group is reached at the right moment, through the right medium, it does not necessarily mean that the conveyed message incites a certain change in knowledge or behaviour in such a way that the product will be purchased. Current marketing is less focused on the 'correct communication messaged at the right moment through the right channels', but more on the so-called change in knowledge and attitudes that will lead to product purchase.

There are different factors that may affect the way knowledge and attitude can be influenced:

- People tend to remember things better when they relate to them.
- The mood of the receiver at the moment of reception of the communication message (for example positive or depressed) has an influence on a cognitive level and evaluation (thought processing). Two examples:

○ In contrast to what you would expect, information is *better* remembered when it does *not* conform to the mood of the receiver. A cheerful message will be better remembered by a depressed receiver than a happy receiver.

○ People can process *more* information when they are in a *positive* or *neutral* mood.

The Imagineer can design his communication message in such a way that he is able to influence moods so that the communication message is relayed in a good and memorable way.

2.5.1 Emotional Involvement

In our society people need to digest many stimuli, particularly in the area of communication messages. Due to the fact that we have a selective perception, many messages will never hit base. In order to capture someone's attention (the receiver of the message), to stand out from the crowd, and to touch someone, emotional involvement is necessary. An emotionally involved person will carefully examine the message and will preferably remember it, which will stimulate him to take the desired action, according to Herremans and Rijnja (2005).

2.5.2 The Elaboration Likelihood Model

Petty and Cacioppo (1986) have already discovered that a high involvement of the receiver would not necessarily lead to a higher conviction and acceptance of the content of a message. Their Elaboration Likelihood Model (ELM) shows that motivation and the ability to process information mainly lead to a change in attitude and not just to message involvement. The ELM indicates two routes for people's information processing.

- The **central route** is high execution and in-depth processing of information by the receiver. The individual's conviction and adaptation of the attitude is led by assessment of the message's content.
- The **peripheral route** is low execution. Conviction and adaptation of attitude are possible. In such a case the receiver decides to follow a convincing situation, based and created on simple stimuli from the message.

Choice of route is based on:

- level of involvement; and
- level of conscious thought an individual gives to received information.

When a receiver is motivated to think and has the mental capacities to do so, this will result in high execution. In this execution phase, cognitive processes such as evaluation of message content, memories of previous experiences, as well as a critical evaluation based on his assessment skills, play a role.

2.5.3 The Role of the Imagineer

The Imagineer designs meaningful experiences in order to guarantee information processing of receivers through the central route. He therefore takes the following into consideration:

- The level of product involvement of the group related to the concept.
- The level of ability to process information.

When organizing a meeting for a group of unskilled people, the meeting should be simple, to the point and abstract. This group might face challenges in processing and remembering too much text and might even pull out. Practice by the participants will be the key in such meetings.

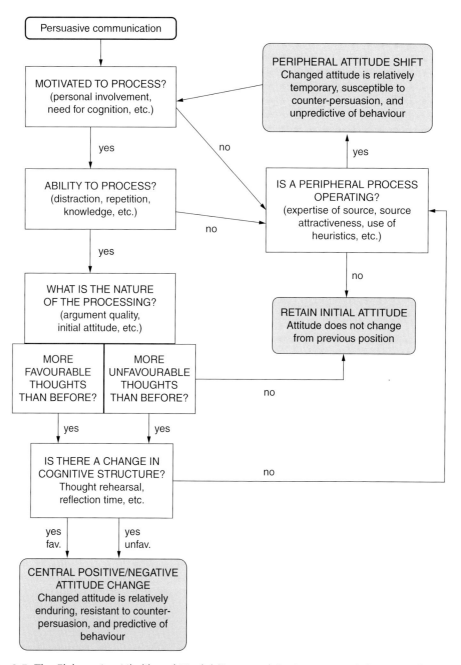

Fig. 2.5 The Elaboration Likelihood Model (Petty and Cacioppo, 1986). (Diagram by Petty and Wegener, 1999.)

2.6 FROM TARGET GROUP TO FOLLOW GROUP

Positioning and target group research is based on reasonably constant behaviour types and (re)actions of homogeneous groups. The question of how to reach these described target groups in today's society is fairly challenging:

- Mass media campaigns have become less effective as target groups can't be reached through fixed communication channels that easily any more. Target groups use ever faster new media; moreover, they switch between different media (zap behaviour). Because of this it is quite difficult to direct the message and reach the right audience.
- It is easy for people to adopt different identities. Someone could be an immigrant and experience this fact together with his parents and family, or a soccer fan and experience this with his friends. He could even have a high position in the office, where he occasionally plays golf, and negotiates with his business partners.
- Because information, similarly minded people and materials are quickly accessible and easily available online, people with several hybrid identities will be able to, and actually can, switch between these identities. Life can be filled in easily and differently.

To have an impact and to achieve a high brain position in your target groups, specific communication via a preconceived media mix, which is based on media usage for the described target group, does not seem to be the best way to tie loyal groups of consumers to your product in the long run. This way of working seems to be suitable for existing fast-moving consumer goods markets, where only little growth is possible (Rijkenberg, 2006), but despite this, the future seems to be focused on centralization of the user rather than the product.

2.6.1 Concepting

The above-mentioned complication factor can be avoided when the focus is shifted from reaching the pre-described target group not via the product, but through the user instead. The focus is mainly on profitability of the client, the lifecycle of the client (Rijkenberg, 2006), where the client is the starting point and not the product – this is called **concepting**.

The other way around

Concepting is fundamentally different from positioning, as introduced by Ries and Trout in the 1980s. Concepting starts with an investment in communication of a train of thoughts, the world of a brand (value, vision, a new concept). Those are the main focus, and only afterwards are the actual products added.

The concept is the soul of the brand and is unchanging. The product by itself is an expression of communication, which supports the value of the brand, and radiates and subscribes the vision. Subsequently, followers from different members can join and form a fan club around the concept (Rijkenberg, 2006).

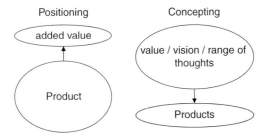

Fig. 2.6 Schematic representation of positioning in traditional marketing and concepting in new marketing. (Source: Rijkenberg, 2006, p. 53.)

No fictive value needs to be added to a product or service because it is 'marketing the other way around': it starts with the letter 'p' of promotion, after which product, price and place automatically follow. It is not an actual promotion of a product but communication, because two-way traffic with followers is possible, as well as a dialogue between followers. A lot of communication is unnecessary, but communication at the right moment is important.

According to Rijkenberg (2006), target groups no longer exist in concepting, and 'followers' of a concept are the main focus: **Anyone who feels drawn to the vision of brand X**.

The task of the concepting team is to anticipate trends and issues in society, and consequently respond to the emotional needs that emerge. They respond to the 'followers' potential, similarly minded kinsfolk. Today there is still an emphasis on what the market asks for, but not in terms of **resources level** (what kind of products do you need), but on a more **mental level** (whatever makes you feel good, what meets your norms and values). People who anticipate are called followers. In this sense it is better to think in terms of **follower groups** than target groups (Rijkenberg, 2006).

'Just do it'

Nike is one of the major brands that focuses more and more on concepting within their marketing strategy. The company has the slogan 'Just do it', which covers the range of thoughts of the brand in many different ways.

After Lance Armstrong won his seventh Tour de France, Richard Muller thought of a new campaign featuring the cyclist. The world most probably did not appreciate Armstrong that much, but Muller decided to portray him as the personification of Nike's range of thoughts. The power of the slogan 'Just do it' was subscribed by a short commercial, in which Lance was shown at a press conference a few years earlier, when he announced that he would conquer cancer and that he was convinced of a comeback.

Subsequently, anyone who subscribed to this range of thought was invited to wear a yellow LiveStrong bracelet. It became a worldwide hype: hundreds of thousands of people were wearing the bracelet subscribing to this particular range of thought.

2.6.2 Tribal Marketing

To create a group of followers, an Imagineer makes use of people's needs to be connected, and creates a product, which creates a fan club; this is in contrast to encouraging behaviour change and convincing the members of a target group of a certain product. In this context, a target group is also referred to as a **tribe** or a **fan club**. This way of working is called **tribal marketing**, a term introduced by Seth Godin (2008).

The term 'tribes' is used to indicate 'profiles' and 'patterns' of the follower group: specific clusters of characteristics, through which specific groups of people, in a specific situation, are specifically susceptible to a specific communication message. Companies use the basic need of people to be connected to other groups of people, in order to make a connection and tie these people to the product. A tribe is created around a clearly masterminded concept with values and a vision, which followers would like to identify themselves with. This is done in such a way that (newly created) social groups want to be tied to the product. Only after and on the basis of this are matching products and services developed. This product enables the members of a tribe to carry out the idea, apply it and use it as a symbol within a developing social group, etc.

From the virtual world to the physical world

Through Nike+, Nike connected many amateur sportspeople all over the world, and has been able to claim the running domain within the online communities. In order to further strengthen the social ties of the virtual runners' world in the actual physical world, the company organizes Running Experiences regularly – in this way people can run together in the physical world.

The supplier as tribe leader

Within the social group, the **community**, meaning is given to an object or subject and symbols are offered to express this among the community: for example, Facebook, the site where you can show who you are by posting photos; Spotify, where you can share music; and LinkedIn, where you can post and share your CV. Similar views and areas of interest can be shared and communicated, but although all participants are equal, a social hierarchy is possible: there is a leader, a founder or an instigator of a tribe.

In tribal marketing the supplier is the leader. The Imagineer makes sure that his design for the new group is easily accessible, and the group is able to communicate and exchange information through a specially designed communication platform: an approachable communication instrument, which enables continuous communication such as Twitter, Internet blogs or mobile phones. Apple apps or pinging with Samsung are good examples of these communication instruments.

Authenticity, leadership, transparency, interaction and experience are key words in tribal marketing (Godin, 2008). On the other hand, spreading these key words is the main focus: a need to use the product needs to be created in people, and they should preferably use the product together in a social context, where experiences can be shared. The concept of the Imagineer needs to contain concrete values and vision, which are easily conveyable and appealing to the followers. The supplier dares to be a leader, who stands for the concept and creates ties with his followers through open and honest communication.

Apple's leading position

Apple has always been an authentic brand, which actually dared to take on this leading position. The brand has many followers. At the introduction of the iPhone4 in 2010, there seemed to be a problem with the reception system of the phone. Instead of starting a dialogue with users and finding a solution together with its followers, Apple decided to close the forum discussion about the problem. In terms of tribal marketing this appeared to be a crucial mistake. By closing the communication platform, on which followers were having heated debates, the company indicated that it was not open to dialogue, which would be the basis for a fixed group of followers and would maintain this group. Apple suffered considerable image loss, but because of the goodwill of the followers it wasn't fatal for the brand.

2.7 RESEARCH IN THE NEW MARKETING ENVIRONMENT

Segmentation and positioning research are not applied in this new way of marketing, while this is based on the fact that the data collected in this way does not give enough insights into and understanding of the actual behaviour of the consumer and are therefore of unreliable quality. There are two issues:

1. In traditional marketing research, data are collected through in-depth interviews or questionnaires to investigate what people think or do. This leads to a large number of socially accepted or rational answers, and as a consequence a distorted picture.
2. Because data interpretation is channelled through a marketing specialist, his expectations will influence the outcome and therefore distort the picture.

Neuroscientists indicate that people behave and act in a less logical manner than they actually think they do, in addition to the fact that people are driven by primal instincts. This makes it difficult to describe and understand behaviour through rational marketing tools such as the 4Ps or the Aida model, in which different steps are described such as attention, interest, desire and action, which assumes that someone would go through these steps before a purchase. Marketing implies the need for other research methods, which can predict behaviour in relation to purchasing power and collect data that give a more accurate picture of the actual behaviour of a consumer and user.

2.7.1 Target Group Research

Economist and marketing expert Paul Postma (2006) designed research methods that took illogical behaviour of the consumer into consideration and for which he used behaviour observation, provocation of associations, measurements of areas in certain parts of the brain and certain behaviours from the past. The results of such research provide the Imagineer with more insights and understanding of critical success factors in relation to his concept design. Postma suggests four possible research methods:

1. **Physical biological.** Functional MRI scans show which parts of the brain are titillated by which design of a product or service. By observing in which part of the brain 'desire' is activated, a prognosis can be made of the chances and effects of the shown product.

2. **Association provocation.** By using the Zaltman Metaphor Elicitation Technique (ZMET), the brand name of a product is explained to a control group of people. After this explanation, the group is asked to collect pictures and associations for a period of a week. The results are interpreted and give a clear picture of the associations of a brand with possible consumers.

3. **Behaviour observation.** In an empathic design, an experimental subject is observed in terms of how this person relates to the product or service in his own user environment. A limitation is the fact that it has to be an already existing product or service, but the data interpretation can lead to adaptation of the product. (Postma states that when a product is stolen several times, it is coveted and therefore has a possible high success factor.)

4. **Established behaviour in the past.** Database Managed Marketing Methods (DMMM) are applicable when all commercial processes of the specific products are operational and consequently, characteristics of consumers and/or products which determine success or failure of the product. Correlations are calculated and regression analyses are carried out. Projection methods and comparing the characteristics of buyers and non-buyers can predict which part of the population is susceptible to actually buying the product. Offering certain bank products, which were rationally only suitable for higher income earners, showed that purchasing chance was not based on how high the income was, it was in fact based on the duration of the relationship with the bank.

2.7.2 Research into Dissemination Chance

One way of investigating the dissemination chance of your message among follower groups is the so-called **Net Promoter Score** (NPS). It investigates how plausible brand promotion or recommendation of a friend to a colleague is. In this type of customer satisfaction research, customer satisfaction, as well as the possibility of positive word of mouth, is taken into consideration.

NPS is based on the fact that users of a certain product can be divided into three different categories: promoters, passives and detractors. A simple question is asked – how likely are you to recommend this product to a friend or colleague? Promoters score a 9 or 10, while passives score a 6 or 7. Anyone who scores below this are unhappy users, who can actually damage the brand. The NPS is defined as follows:

Percentage promoters – Percentage detractors = Net Promoter Score

Some examples: Apple has a score of 79% and Google has a score of 73%.

The Imagineer applies different kinds of research. He can make a prototype of his design and physically test it on potential users. He can have discussions with people, use co-creation as an instrument or investigate by experiencing as if he were the user, or through role play in order to understand emotional reactions. These types of research will be discussed in the second part of this book.

2.8 THE 3CS OF IMAGINEERING

The Imagineer designs a concept, the range of thoughts which add to the meaningful experience of the user. The 3C model below represents critical success factors, which are required for each concept to become successful, and for a follower group to emerge.

- **Concept.** A clear conceptual vision needs to be developed, containing a clear vision, values, a story and playful element, which gives people the idea that they can use it autonomously, 'master' it and somehow can influence the composition of the concept.
- **Connection.** Connection serves the purpose of sharing information in order to generate a meaningful product or service or knowledge bank. Subsequently, a communication platform needs to be available to communicate the concept in such a way that it elicits dialogues between people in follower groups. This enables them to meet virtually, exchange stories and symbols, and show their identity in this area. The supplier's communication output on this platform is used to make the range of thought concrete and emotionally charged. A sense of meaning is necessary in order to touch the followers, and stimulate co-creation suited for communication strategy.
- **Consistency.** The supplier needs to be consistent in all communication, and to connect all existing and new products or services to this concept. Synergy can be created by making sure that there is consistent communication, which is integrated in all possible instruments. This way the emphasis is on continuity of the range of thought, and this then fits the range of thoughts and values of the followers (see Section 2.5).

Table 2.1 shows the 3Cs represented by key words.

Table 2.1 The 3C model

Concept	Connection	Consistency
Value	Communication platform	Integrated communication
Design	Interpersonal relations	Symphony
Vision	Empathy	Tuning
Story	Involvement	Synergy
Play	Meaning	Brand personality
Autonomy and mastery	Co-creation	Business model

2.9   SUMMARY

Traditional marketing is focused on distinguishing target groups through segmentation, and based on this marketing communication strategies are developed. Central to this process is the already developed product. Some slight changes are possible in terms of expressive characteristics such as packing, brand name or introduction and time of introduction in the market. This is based on needs, preferences and associations of the target groups. The criteria used are objective segmentation characteristics such as age or living situation. However, even in this more traditional approach, subjective criteria are used as well, and one can think of someone's value orientation.

Marketing theory has made tremendous progress and more knowledge about successful competition positioning has become available, but is no guarantee for success. The Elaboration Likelihood Model of Petty and Cacioppo (1986) shows that behavioural change only occurs through attitude adaptation. A communication message should therefore not only be received, but also needs to be actively comprehended. Whether this actually happens depends on the individual's motivation and abilities. As a result, reactions on the communication mix might vary within the target group. Consequently, the Imagineer needs to take into account how the people of his target group actually receive and comprehend information, as well as their actual motivation to do so.

The trend in new marketing is to initiate rather than to follow. The starting point is the user instead of the already developed product or service. This new way of working requires concepting and tribal marketing, for the purpose of creating groups of people that are willing to start social relationships based on a certain train of thought (idea, concept). As a result, the supplier is able to offer this group certain products or services that meet the needs of, and match specific desires and train of thoughts of, the emerged group.

The Imagineer realizes that there has been a focus shift from target group to follower groups, and that he needs to adapt this in his designs. He works for people and his designs will steer people's behaviour. He has to have an in-depth understanding and develop his approach accordingly. He needs to understand how he can possibly adapt his offer based on motivation, knowledge and abilities of his users, for whom he has to offer a vision and create user value.

2.10   ASSIGNMENTS

Assignment 1

In your environment look for what you would consider to be a group of followers.

- Describe this group in detail and investigate for which supplier, and in which way, this group of followers creates and adds economic value.
- Discuss in which way the 3Cs are related to this group of followers.

Assignment 2

Describe two products: the reception of one product's communication message through the Elaboration Likelihood Model's central route; and a product for which you have chosen the peripheral route.

- Describe the characteristics of these products, followed by how they were communicated by the supplier.
- Explain why you chose the central or peripheral route for this particular product.
- What is the difference between the two suppliers?
- What have you learned as an Imagineer?

Assignment 3

In hindsight, how do you look back at the previous question, where you chose the peripheral route for a particular product? If yes, how and why?

2.11   RECOMMENDED READING

Hope can connect a group of people who share an idea:

- Godin, S. (2008) *Tribes: We Need You to Lead Us*. Little Brown, London.

How do you stand out from the crowd of thousands of other suppliers? Seth Godin provides insights and inspiration in his book:

- Godin, S. (2005) *Purple Cow*. Penguin, London.

Strong brands such as Nike or Ben & Jerry's have been developed on the basis of in-depth understanding of consumers, combined with imagination:

- Zaltman, G. (2003) *How Customers Think: Essential Insights into the Mind of the Market*. Harvard Business Press, Boston, Massachusetts.

As a brand, the only possible way to survive is to be radically different from other brands:

- Neumeier, M. (2006) *Zag: The #1 Strategy of High-Performance Brands*. Peachpit Press, Berkeley, California.

Starting by asking 'why' in relation to your brand:

- Sinek, S. (2009) *Start With Why: How Great Leaders Inspire Everyone to Take Action*. Portfolio, New York.

chapter 3

From Brand Marketing to Identity Branding

Bert Smit

Finding a nice and suitable partner has become quite a challenge in today's society, with its abundance of online dating sites, speed dating events, blind dates, etc. The main sites, which guarantee that they have your ideal partner in their databases, are usually wrong. The other day I went on a date and there I was, stuck with a creep, who claimed to have a good sense of 'humour' and 'culture'. I am sure he was convinced that he embodied these characteristics, but a sense of culture in my view means something different than visiting a cinema and watching a very aggressive Hollywood movie.

My worst experience was a date with a senior researcher, who told me that I reminded him of someone he knew. I told him that I didn't recall ever meeting him before. Halfway through dinner he started speaking about his mother, paused…and exclaimed: 'You look like my mother!' This was the first and last date…

A friend of mine was rather successful on one of the dating sites. They used Branddating.nl, which matches people based on their most and least favourite brands. Hmm, interesting, what are my favourite brands? The Times, Hello, H&M, Abercrombie and Fitch…definitely not Wii or Primark.

BrandDating.nl was launched in 1999 and has been online ever since. It is not a dating site for brands, but for people like you and me. It is a website that matches visitors' profiles, but that are not based on personality traits such as a sense of humour or spontaneity, but based on brands you find important, or brands that don't match your personality. The current site

Fig. 3.1 BrandDating logo.
(Source: BrandDating.nl)

(2013) allows you to introduce yourself to someone else based on 25 different brands. You can indicate which brands you like and match your personality, but also indicate which brands should match your partner, brands you 'do' and brands you particularly dislike. Ten years after the site was launched, many matches were made, which even resulted in a considerable number of BrandDating babies. Why is this the case? Brands tell more about who you are than how you would describe yourself. In the old days, people would say: show me your library and I will tell you who you are. Nowadays we could say: show me your iPad, shoes, watch and phone and I will tell you who you are.

In the previous chapters we explained that suppliers have to behave differently towards users in an ever-changing economic context. This also causes a change in communication in terms of understanding what the best way of communication is. We also discussed different marketing concepts, which emerged as a response to the changing economic situation. This chapter shows how the current Western consumer creates his own identity and how brands play a role in this process. This particular knowledge is vital for the Imagineer, because he shapes and designs brand identity by linking meaning and experiences to the corporate culture and the logo.

By the end of this chapter you will have an understanding of:

- The influence of globalization and individualization on consumer behaviour.
- Why we have the need of an identity.
- How the Experience Economy responds to the need of identity.
- How brands position themselves to match a certain lifestyle.

3.1 BRANDS ARE THE NEW CHURCHES

The renowned sociologist Ulrich Beck stated: 'The problem of our post-modern society is the fact that identity is no longer fixed, but a task of each individual' (Beck, 1992). In other words: at one time it was established at birth who you were and to which social class you belonged, because the social class of your parents determined your own social class, and consequently, what your life would look like.

This is not the case today: you choose who you are and to which group you want to belong. Moreover, you **must** choose who you are and to which group you want to belong. Until recently, ordinary people would not even give a second thought to the question 'Who are you?' More than a hundred years ago, there was never any time to even think about these issues. People had to work really hard to provide for the basic needs of their families, such as food, clothing and a roof. However, following the Industrial Revolution and technological advancement, as well as the introduction of democracy, it became possible to think about these issues.

The start of the Industrial Era led to an increase in average income and consequently created the possibility of choice for many. Suddenly people had purchasing power; people had the choice between two or more kinds of the same product. More and more ordinary children were able to continue schooling after the age of 10 or 12.

3.1.1 Compartmentalization

In the early days, where one would buy groceries, for example, was determined for you. For instance, Catholics would buy their bread at the Catholic bakery, whereas Anglicans would buy their bread at the Anglican bakery. At the time, the churches had a huge influence over such things. During this time, the right to vote was first introduced, initially for men only, but later (not even 100 years ago!) women were also allowed to vote. As a result, new political groups emerged – socialists, liberals, communists, etc. Membership of such a group determined a large part of your life. It determined the newspaper you would read, which school you would attend, which union membership you would have, which sports club you would support, which shops you would go to and later, which broadcasting company you would listen to on the radio or watch on TV. This is called compartmentalization: each group had compartments and these compartments were aligned.

For many consumers, this provided them with a sense of clarity and safety; they knew what to expect. However, if someone decided to make a different choice from their parents, it came with serious implications or consequences. For example, if someone made a switch from being a Catholic to becoming an Anglican, the consequences included exclusions from the family and even the social circles associated with the family. The pressure to choose the same things as your family was thus enormous and meant that few people ever gave it much thought.

Nowadays, more than a hundred years later, the world has become more complex. Globalization and individualization were the causes of the disappearance of compartmentalization, and as a consequence, this led to the fact that shaping our identity has become a task that involves many choices. Today, we are expected to actually think about our identity and this is what Beck refers to when he states that 'identity is no longer fixed'.

3.1.2 Globalization

In this book, we define the term globalization as the disappearance of time and space as dominant factors (Levitt, 1983). Technological advancements during the last century, such as fast transport and communication, made globalization possible as the world became 'smaller'.

The invention of the steam engine, and later the steam train, for example, enabled fast transportation. The development of this particular technique (i.e. the steam engine), ultimately led to cars, large(r) ships, lorries and the aeroplane. In the end, the development of technology enabled us to fly from London to New York in a matter of hours instead of the standard ten-day journey, which made intercontinental trade so much easier and led to a boom. People and products could be transported to any corner of the world in less than a day.

Fast communication started with the introduction of the telegraph, followed by the telephone, and nowadays the Internet, which encompasses worldwide mass media. The world has become a village, where basically the same information, knowledge and products are available. (Canadian scientist Marshall McLuhan predicted this development as early as 1959, way ahead of the mobile phone, Internet and e-mail era.)

Globalization has far-reaching consequences in different areas and facets of life. Below, we will discuss the main consequences, which are important to the Imagineer.

- As a result of globalization, it is easier for people to communicate and have a better understanding of what happens in the world around them. This has an effect on the way they perceive life, their convictions, and to which groups they want to subscribe. People are no longer forced to stay in their village of birth, or no longer dependent on their place of birth, nor their family status in society. It is relatively easy and not so costly to move to another village or town, to find and get acquainted with people who are like-minded in terms of music, hobbies or religion, etc.
- Many brands have a worldwide reputation, for instance McDonalds, Harley Davidson, Toyota, Manchester United, Unilever and British Petroleum (BP), to name just a few. One of the characteristics of the growth period of these big brands is rationalization: a McDonalds hamburger tastes the same all over the world, shopping streets are the same everywhere and so are production systems.

Sociologist Ritzer (2008) called this phenomenon the **McDonaldization** of society. McDonaldization has four characteristics:

1. **Efficiency.** Particularly in terms of speed.
2. **Calculability.** Quantification overrules subjective matter such as taste and style.
3. **Predictability.** Wherever you go, the product and service are of the same standard.
4. **Control.** Whenever possible, human tasks will be standardized and later replaced by technology.

Standardization, which goes hand in hand with globalization, has an effect on people. For example, in the last decennia, people from the UK have become more and more aware of their origins. In the last decennia, consumers are more aware and have started to appreciate their local surroundings. UK residents started to call themselves Scots, Welsh, English, or even more specifically, Londoner. They are proud of their local products, history, and thus profile themselves accordingly. Suppliers respond to this via marketing and communication. A Yorkshire pudding (pub meal) with a Guinness (beer), for example, is considered to be more authentic than a McDonalds burger, which is standardized all over the world.

3.1.3   Individualization

The disappearance of influential institutions such as one's own church or political party resulted in the fact that people need to decide for themselves what to do and what not to. In the second half of the 20th century, this caused considerable social changes. This is known as 'ontzuiling' in the Netherlands, which translates to the removal of traditional religious and socio-political barriers.

Bauman (2000) notices further individualization and sees the downfall of other social, time and space institutes. For instance, sport clubs, work and families have become less of a binding factor for people. In times gone by, families would watch a programme on television together, whereas nowadays each family member can watch his or her own programme and listens to his or her own music. Individual sports, such as fitness, running and cycling, have never been as popular. More and more people work from home or have other flexible workplaces or hours instead of a number of fixed desk hours. These factors contribute to confusion for Western people, as we might wonder where we actually belong. Our sense of belonging might have got lost along the way, because there are no longer set institutions (family, religion, etc.) guiding our sense of being.

Distinguishable experience

Until recently (in the modern world), consumption was related to one's possessions, while today (in the post-modern world) the focus is now on intangible items, such as aesthetics, behaviour and personal values. Experiencing a product and the association we have with the product is more important than the product itself. Marketing professionals respond to this by 'loading' the brand with a certain feeling or experience.

> Having a computer does not provide any insights into who we are. Rather the opposite – we actually indicate who we are by our choice of brand, which is loaded with associations, such as an Apple computer. In the current time of oversupply, owning a computer does not make us distinguishable. On the other hand, by choosing an Apple, Dell or HP, we distinguish ourselves.

In summary: globalization, technological advancement and individualization are the causes of an ever-changing identity. We establish our identity based on our consumption. In the previous chapter, we discussed the same in marketing terminology, in the sense that the user value becomes more important in comparison to the exchange value. Therefore, identity has become a task and is no longer fixed or given.

3.2 THE NEED FOR SELF-ACTUALIZATION

The enormous economic growth of the West in the past 150 years produced tremendous abundance. Our social welfare states take care of our basic needs and because of this, we have more time and energy left to do other things. On average, we receive higher education in comparison to people a hundred years ago and invest more time and effort in social contacts. The question is: why have we chosen these particular things? We could have focused on other factors to fill our time with, or at the other extreme, do absolutely nothing and spend our days sleeping.

3.2.1 Maslow's Pyramid

American psychologist Abraham Maslow explains this phenomenon through his famous hierarchy of needs. Maslow's hierarchy shows us what our priorities in life are. Maslow distinguishes five different levels, with the lower two levels representing our basic needs.

1. Physiological needs. Basic needs that enable your body to function properly – oxygen, food, drink, sleep, and of course the more visceral need for sex.
2. Safety needs. This is what you need to protect yourself and to remain safe and healthy. This also includes not only physical harm, but mental harm – a house, warmth, clothing, and the money to pay for these.

The basic needs are then followed by the next three levels of Maslow's hierarchy of needs.

3. Love and belonging. This is concerned with social needs such as the need for friendship, family and intimacy or belonging to a group.
4. Esteem. This covers self-esteem, as well as respect from others in relation to who you are and what you do; you not only want to be a member of a group, you also want to be appreciated and respected by this group.
5. Self-actualization. The highest level refers to the need for self-development, to reach your full potential.

The needs of level 1 and 2 are generally easily met due to today's material abundance and social security. Therefore, we are mainly concerned with the higher levels in the model. However, futurologist Rolf Jensen suggested that we should reverse Maslow's hierarchy of needs in his book, *The Dream Society* (1999). He believes that in today's world our priorities lie on levels 5 and 4 and thus we don't need to focus on the lower levels any more.

When we look at Maslow's hierarchy through the eyes of Beck's statement ('The problem of our post-modern society is the fact that identity is no longer given, but has become an individual task'), we can draw the following conclusions:

• Levels 3 and 4 are the levels where we indicate who we are and to which social groups we want to belong, or for that matter don't want to belong to.
• Levels 4 and 5 of Maslow have become – due to individualization – the main focus: multimedia enables us to invest in ourselves, not only by looking and absorbing information, but also allows us to publish and show people, both in our network and around the world, who we are and what we do.

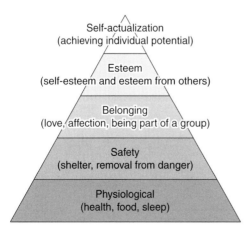

Fig. 3.2 Maslow's hierarchy of needs (adapted from Maslow, 1943).

3.2.2 Self-actualization through Transformation

In Chapter 1, 'the progression of economic value' by Pine and Gilmore was discussed. That model showed that self-development and self-actualization are very important for the consumer. The authors concluded that the final step of 'guiding transformations' is the most economically valuable one. Transformation relates to the experience that changes the consumer, which is adapted specifically to the individual. In other words – personal development.

Despite the fact that Maslow's theory is considered to be rigid by other scientists, he remains relevant for today's marketing professionals and brand designers. They can wonder at which level they want to focus on, or want to work with consumers on, and furthermore, they will also look at whether an addition of services, experiences, etc. add more economic value to their product.

Different brands of mineral water

Water appears to be a simple product. Drinking water is essential to all of us. The first thing that the International Red Cross does in any type of crisis is to provide people with clean drinking water (food and shelter are provided later on). Many households in the Western world these days have access to water from the tap and we are able to drink that tap water on a daily basis. Despite this, there are still many brands of luxury mineral water available in the supermarkets.

There are, for example, the Belgian SPA, the Canadian Gize and the German Cave H2O and more exclusive brands are emerging.

Fig. 3.3 Brands of mineral water: SPA, WELL, OGO.

The water brand OGO, from the south of the Netherlands, offers water in beautifully designed bottles, available in three different continents, at a price that is 1000 times more expensive than the regular water price. The WELL water company sells bottled water, and sends one-quarter of the total revenue to the Simavi Foundation, which uses it to invest in the digging of water wells in developing countries.

Brands increase the economic and moral value of water, but how does this work? We will elaborate on this in the next section.

3.3 THE CHANGED MEANING OF A BRAND

There are numerous definitions to describe a brand. Kotler and Armstrong (2010) define it as follows:

> A name, term, sign, symbol, design, or a combination of these five, used by the manufacturer or sales person of a product or service, which shows how a product or service distinguishes itself from the competition.

In this definition, Kotler and Armstrong do not address the meaningful experience of the brand and the value that consumers attach to the brand. This is due to the fact that Kotler and Armstrong are mainly focused on the sender, the manufacturer of the product – which means their focus is not on the consumer. They believe that consumers hardly ever look at anything other than the sticker or logo on a product, and this somehow means that the image of the product is not connected to the identity of the manufacturer.

3.3.1 Upswing of Thinking in Terms of Lifestyles

There has been a change since the 1990s. The symbolism of brands, which Kotler and Armstrong recognized, has become more important and this importance is ever increasing. As already mentioned, globalization and individualization make it more challenging for marketing professionals to send messages to different target groups in the traditional way. Due to the fact that space, environment, time and social class are all slowly disappearing, and because of the increasing scale of the brands, different ways of brand communication need to be explored. It is against this background that lifestyle thinking emerged. In Chapter 2, we discussed the fact that before communicating to the consumer, we need to consider how the consumer can use the brand to express his or her own image and identity. Table 3.1 shows the changed parameters.

Table 3.1 Differences between target group thinking and lifestyle thinking

	Target group thinking	Lifestyle thinking
Key word	To be	To want
Consumer	How many people can afford the product?	Who wants to buy the product?
How are consumers categorized?	Circumstance based	Own choice based
Dominant factors for marketing people	Income, age, social class, address, education, consumer	Component: taste, conscious or unconscious values, beliefs and norms, ambitions, life perception, status oriented
Stability	Changes per life phase	Relatively constant (as value systems are relatively constant)
Measurable	Quantitative	Qualitative product development

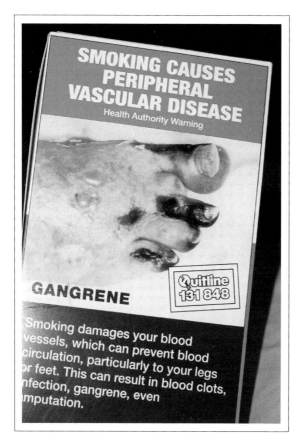

Fig. 3.4 Australia: no logos on cigarette packets. Manufacturers are furious, as smokers won't be able to communicate their identity without the logo and brands will have a harder time positioning themselves.

One of the most famous examples, from some time ago, is the cigarette brand Marlboro, which tried to create a tough image by linking their product to the traditional rural countryside with cowboys and adventures. This was in contrast to Peter Stuyvesant, which portrayed itself in a sophisticated way by using sailing yachts and jet-set parties.

Matching a certain lifestyle to a brand enables consumers to shape their own image. Marketing people choose different symbols for their brands and in this way brands become their own personalities. Expressive and emotional values are connected to a brand personality and this is essentially done to differentiate between other instrumentally similar brands. Kevin Lane Keller calls this the ability to distinguish **brand equity**.

3.4 BRAND PERSONALITY

Psychologists measure their clients' personalities based on the five dimensions of the Big Five personality test. The test consists of measuring individuals on five different categories: extraversion, agreeableness, conscientiousness, emotional stability, and openness to experience. The test results are a score scaled for each of these five categories, for example in the case of extroversion, it is an indication of extraversion versus introversion. Thus, if an individual is high on extraversion, they are extrovert, but if they score low, they would be considered an introvert. Depending on who you are and how you react to statements in the test will determine where on the spectrum you will lie. The same happens in the remaining four categories: agreeableness versus competitive, conscientiousness versus carelessness, openness versus caution, and neuroticism versus secure. The overall results, which emerge from testing the five categories, give a picture of the client's personality. Psychologists use this instrument to explain and predict their client's behaviour.

Jennifer Aaker (1997) developed a similar instrument, but it draws up a personality profile of a brand instead. Aaker defines brand personality as a set of 'human' characteristics that are being associated with a brand. As in the Big Five personality test, Aaker measures brand personality in five different dimensions:

1. Sincerity.
2. Excitement.
3. Competence.
4. Sophistication.
5. Ruggedness.

Each dimension has a number of sub-dimensions. Under 'excitement', for example, we can find 'challenging' and 'imaginative'. Brand personality can be established by asking for the consumer's opinion of the characteristics on each dimension for a specific brand. In that way, Marlboro scores high on ruggedness, while Davidoff cigarettes score high on sophistication and low on ruggedness.

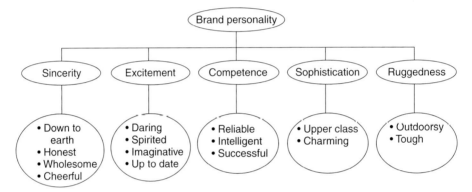

Fig. 3.5 Brand personality framework (adapted from Aaker, 1997).

Brands tell us how others perceive us

Marketing people discover more and more about how consumers can use brands to portray their identities. Not so long ago, Fennis and Pruyn (2007) illustrated that we use brands to assess the kind of person we want to come across as. Fennis and Pruyn had participants describe people based only on the photographs of a person. In one part of the test, subjects had to estimate the reliability of the person in the photograph as if the participant was dependent on information that only that person had. Participants had to imagine themselves having lost their way somewhere on the street or on a campsite. The only person available to ask for directions was the person in the photograph. In one of the pictures, a man is wearing clothing with a Hugo Boss label and in the next picture, the same man is there wearing the same clothing, however this time with an Australian logo.

After each photo, the subjects were asked to judge the person based on reliability. It might come as no surprise that the person with the Australian logo was found to be less reliable than the person with the Hugo Boss logo. This was even found when the participant was in the campsite situation. In other words: we judge people's character traits based on the brands that they use.

3.5   IMAGE AND IDENTITY

Marketing people are facing a new challenge. To create a brand image is way more challenging in today's society than, for example, 20 years ago. Today, consumers are more aware of their choices and are more critical in terms of what they consume. Creating an image for a product is simply not enough. The product and manufacturer have to 'be' the brand, they have to convey the central vision and mission behind it in anything and everything they do by linking it to the everyday lives and values of their end users.

3.5.1   The Brand as Strategic Instrument

The Internet makes it easier for users to see right through the façade of a commercial by allowing them to see what a manufacturer really stands for. The world has become more transparent and as a result, brands are no longer the sole domain of commercial and marketing professionals. Brands have become a strategic instrument, the deciding factor in the production process, human resources management, office image, etc. Brand image relates more and more to the identity of the company behind the brand. Propagating this identity has become important for companies that like to distinguish themselves based on the brand experience.

3.5.2   From Sender Perspective to Interaction Perspective

David Aaker (1991) and other brand gurus claim that the brand equals the identity of a company, and therefore image and identity are blended together. This means there can be no actual distance between image and identity. The consumer will only perceive the brand as authentic when there is congruence between the identity and image. This goes beyond Kotler and Armstrong's views on brands. The brand is no longer only about a physical presentation (logo, packaging), but also relates to behaviour, symbolism, employees and (live) communication of the brand. In other words: the relationship the brand actively pursues is with its users, as well as the representation of the brand, and 'the people behind the brand'. Thinking in terms of brands is now shifting from the 'sender perspective' to a receiver perspective, more commonly known as the 'interaction perspective'.

More interactive and more personal

Recall the powerful images of Marlboro and the message the company wanted to get across. Compare this to, for instance, the recent online communities such as MyStarbucksidea.com, in which the individual consumer or groups of users are the main focus. Starbucks adapts its products and services to the (individual) wishes of the crowd. Moreover, they also reward the crowd for their role in improving their business. This is way more interactive and personal than the tough, smoking muscular cowboys of the 1990s.

3.5.3 Brand Democracy

'Interaction perspective' means that brands are trying to genuinely start an individual relationship with their potential clients. This means that brands not only have to listen to their clients, but also are actively trying to listen to them and considering them prosumers. As in real human relationships, brands need to sometimes adapt to their partners (i.e. the consumer). This is a fundamental shift in brand thinking. Some brand gurus predict that brands will eventually adapt to the individual level of the consumers. This power shift from producer to consumer (or prosumer) is also referred to as brand democracy or brandocracy (The Future Laboratory, 2008).

The brand's ability to adapt is limited and, like in any real relationship, you could also ask too much of it. If the wishes of the consumer don't match the principles and core identity of the brand, the brand will opt for a break-up of the relationship, rather than adapting itself.

3.6 BRAND VALUE CREATION

Brand strategist Kevin Lane Keller (2007) considers identity to be the starting point when building a distinguishable brand. Brands are becoming more important and are a valuable asset to many large companies. The economic value of a brand is something that has become more valuable than all other assets combined.

What is the value of the Coca-Cola brand?

Brand consultant Interbrand publishes a yearly list of the most valuable brands and named Coca-Cola (with a turnover of US$70 billion) the most valuable brand of 2010. Interbrand bases its findings on goodwill, predicted sales, and the consumer's brand choice.

Managing the Coca-Cola brand is vital for the soda manufacturer. A dent in the consumer's trust or a production error, or even the wrong brand association, will decrease shareholder's value at the stock exchange.

The most valuable brand

Every year Interbrand (a brand consultancy firm) publishes the list of the most valuable brands in the world and in 2010 Coca-Cola topped the list (again). As Interbrand puts it, 'Coca-Cola gets almost everything right. Its brand promises fun, freedom, spirit, and refreshment, which resonates the world over and it excels at keeping the brand fresh and always evolving – all this, while also maintaining the nostalgia that reinforces customers' deep connection to the brand.'

1	Coca-Cola	70,452 (US$m)
2	IBM	64,727 (US$m)
3	Microsoft	60,895 (US$m)

(Continued)

Continued.

4	Google	43,557 (US$m)
5	GE	42,808 (US$m)
6	McDonald's	33,578 (US$m)
7	Intel	32,015 (US$m)
8	Nokia	29,495 (US$m)
9	Disney	28,731 (US$m)
10	Hewlett-Packard	26,867 (US$m)

(Source: www.interbrand.com, 2010)

Keller (2007) defines brand value (brand equity) as:

>…the addition of tangible and intangible values to a service or product by a brand.

The Imagineer is conscious of this value and will take this into account while designing a meaningful experience, with the emphasis of course on the development and addition of an intangible value. In order to do so, he can make use of Keller's Customer-based Brand Equity (CBBE) model (2007). It explains that brand development of strong brands should consist of:

1. Brand identity: This is about how many people regard a product in a positive light – is it positive enough or salient? Others call it brand awareness or brain position. The main question in this phase is: who am I?

2. Brand promise: This consists of two parts – market performance and brand imaging. Market performance is concerned with functional demands of the consumer, which consist mainly of tangible or measurable variables such as price, accessories, packaging, and reliability of the brand. Brand imaging is more abstract and is more concerned with the psychological and social needs of the consumer. More specifically, it is related to lifestyle, brand experience and the consumer's value system, which all play a role in creating the brand's image. Keller claims that it is in this part of the model than an important part of brand loyalty is established. The central question here is: what am I?

3. Brand response: This is mainly focused on feedback from consumers. A brand needs feedback, specifically in terms of the reactions and evaluations from users. Feedback can be objective and/or subjective. Keller emphasizes that evaluations and emotional feedback on brands should be differentiated. The question of this step is: what do you think of me?

4. Brand resonance: This is the relationship between the consumer and brand and the relationship between other users of the brand. This relationship determines how the consumer identifies with the brand and how loyal s/he is to the brand. In other words: how does this work for you and I?

Strong brands, which have a clear identity and are consistent in the way they work, follow certain values and principles. Brands that don't have a strong identity will be considered

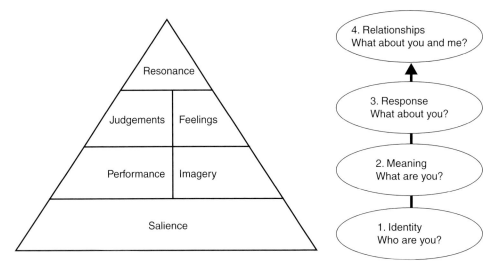

Fig. 3.6 CBBE model (adapted from Keller, 2007).

insincere and unauthentic. The consumer will then usually consider the brand less valuable. We can see evidence of this in steps 3 and 4 of the CBBE model. In the following subsections each step will be discussed separately.

3.6.1 Brand Identity: Be Different

There is only room for a few brands in our brain. To understand and make sense of all the different offers, the consumer needs to categorize the different products or services. Within the product category of 'toothpaste', for example, subconscious mind positions are ascribed. In their famous book about positioning, Ries and Trout came to the conclusion that, in general, a maximum of only seven brand names can reach a top of mind position. In general, the consumer will mention these brands spontaneously, as they are the first ones to come to mind, known as the so-called *consideration set* or *evoked set*. Ries and Trout (1981) call this a 'ladder with a maximum of seven rungs'.

The goal of each brand is to remain on the top rung or, at least, to belong to the *choice set*, meaning that they belong in the top two or three brands to reach the top of mind position. The higher in the order, the sooner a brand is actually selected in the selection process. Ries and Trout (1981) state two dominant influences of brain position:

1. Brand name: The name of the brand is the first contact with a product, service, goods or experience and its association will influence where a brand will be positioned on the positioning ladder (which rung). A brand name such as Jaguar has associations with words like wild, fast, exciting, hunting, sleek and beautiful. The choice of the brand's name is absolutely essential in reaching a high mind position.

2. The moment of entry into the market: The first supplier of a product or service usually reaches the top rung of the mind-positioning ladder. In some instances a successful marketing entry, such as a brand name like Aspirin, has ensured that the whole product category takes on that name.

Trout (2005) researched brand familiarity and compared brands in the USA in 1923 and 2005, and concluded that strong brands have longer lives. He specifically chose simple consumer products from the food and clothing industry. Amazingly, the strongest brands of 1923 are still the most renowned: Lipton Tea, Coca-Cola, Gillette, Kellogg's and Colgate are still high on both lists.

3.6.2 Brand Promise: What are you Actually?

Once a brand and position have been decided on, the next step is related to what the brand does, also known as the brand promise. This concerns objective measurable achievements, whereas subjectively, it relates to giving meaning to the brand.

Objective measuring points

Keller describes five important objective measuring points, through which brand promise is mainly determined:

1. Primary parts of a product and possible options.
2. Reliability, sustainability and low maintenance of a product.
3. Effectiveness, efficiency and empathy of the product-related service.
4. The sensory perception of a product in terms of: size, style, design, sense, etc.
5. Price.

It is this part of brand promise that the mind weighs up when deciding whether the product is useful in terms of functionality and price value. This part of brand promise is based on rationally comparing the brand to other brands.

Brand experience

The second part of brand promise, which is also important, is less measurable and tangible. This is where brand experience starts. The brand gets an identity, a personality, a value pattern, and matching expressions. Brand experience is necessary to reach brain position and for some products, it is there to maintain the already established brain position or even move up in brain position.

Brand experience relates to the experiences of the brand user. During the designing stage of the production process, a product or service can be strengthened to increase the experience value of the product. In relation to cars, it is about the 'driving experience', and in relation to washing machines, it is the 'laundry experience' (Pine and Gilmore, 1999). The target group is the main focus of brand marketing, because the target group is actively participating in the supplier's created experience.

We previously saw that Aaker could provide brands with brand personality and that it can be used to match the consumer's lifestyle. In today's society, however, it is important that the brand personality also connects to the identity of the brand and the company. Formulating brand values physically makes the design of the brand and the company behind it easier to understand and it becomes clearer what a brand 'does' or 'does not do'.

Nike or Puma?

Nike and Puma both produce good sport shoes, but different people feel attracted to either one or the other brand. This is due to the fact that both companies communicate, produce and act in different ways. Therefore, both brands have clearly developed value systems, and by actively communicating these values, try to establish a connection to the consumers who have similar value systems and wish to express these values. This is called **value fit**.

Psychologist Rokeach (1973) was the first person to design a method that made it possible to determine value systems of people. He distinguished instrumental values, which were used to reach a certain end goal or end value. For example, 'politeness' is an instrumental value, which could reach 'respect' as an end goal.

Kahle (1983) simplified the values and value system by using her so-called list of values (LOV). She classified values based on people's most common values. In contrast to the 18 instrumental and 18 end values of Rokeach, Kahle only uses nine (Kahle, 1983):

1. Self-fulfilment.
2. Self-respect.
3. Being well respected.
4. Sense of belonging.
5. Warm relationships with others.
6. Sense of accomplishment.
7. Excitement.
8. Fun and enjoyment.
9. Security.

These nine end values strongly cohere to Maslow's Pyramid. Kahle sees a correlation between self-fulfilment and self-respect from her LOV and the highest level of Maslow's hierarchy of needs model (Kahle, 1983). The sense of belonging, being well respected, and warm relationships with others are strongly correlated to the middle levels of Maslow. Excitement, fun and enjoyment, security, and sense of accomplishment are comparable to Maslow's basic level of needs and security.

Making brand values visible

How do brand values become visible? Values only become visible when they are translated into characteristics, behaviours, or in communication. Reynolds and Gutman (1984) developed the **means/end analysis**, in which values are converted to consequences and from there will be converted to concrete characteristics of a product.

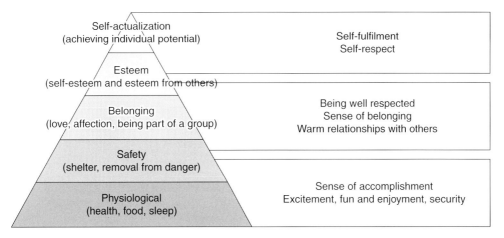

Fig. 3.7 Maslow and Kahle: the correlation between Maslow's Pyramid and Kahle's value system.

Self-respect as a core value

Self-respect is one of the core values of the brand and organization that is Apenheul Primate Park in the Netherlands. Apenheul remains loyal to its principles of nature education and conservation, which are specified in its mission statement. As a consequence of this, the park does not want to cause any damage to the natural environment. Apenheul therefore only buys ecologically produced Fairtrade coffee, green energy, and paper, disposable cutlery and crockery that are sustainable and recyclable.

Successful brands know how to convert their central values and mission into ideas that they can communicate to consumers. They have a sort of mental image or a prototype of who their users are and they know when consumers will use their products.

Lonely Planet travel books

Lonely Planet considers 'self-fulfilment' and 'warm relationships with others' an important basis for its travel books. The books contain references to places where travellers can culturally and anthropologically enrich themselves. Travellers act as co-authors of the Lonely Planet books, as Lonely Planet would like to (not only) stay up to date, but also get a better understanding of its readers' needs and interests.

There is a reason why Lonely Planet travel guides are double stitched, strong and sturdy books, which remain in relatively good shape, even after heavy usage and having been exposed to rough travelling. Lonely Planet experienced enormous growth and in 2010 it sold its billionth copy. Additionally, they are more actively online than any other travel guide publisher

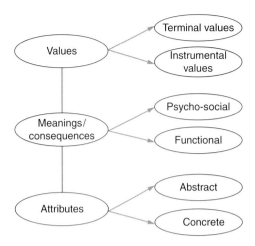

Fig. 3.8 Values–consequences–attributes (adapted from Reynolds and Gutman, 1984).

and this is a result of the fact that Lonely Planet wants to engage in a relationship with its users/co-authors. The online platforms, books, TV programmes and mobile applications they design are a direct result of their interest in the world, and the travel stories of their readers. This has all come about due to their core values and mission.

Strong brands use their history, inheritance, founders (or other heroes) and adventures to emphasize their values and mission. Think of Jamie Oliver in his parents' pub; the Guinness museum, which was built in the oldest Guinness brewery; Steve Jobs, who came to Apple's rescue yet again; and (zoo owner) Steve Irwin who rescued Australian animals, particularly crocodiles, in his own rescue shelters.

3.6.3 Brand Response

Once the brand identity and the brand promise have been created, the next step would be to focus on the consumer's response. What are the reactions of the consumers going to be? The brand feel has to show whether the expectations, which were based on brand promise, were met, or in the best-case scenario, were surpassed. In step 3 of the CBBE model, the main focus is on how consumers experience brand promise. Is the brand actually as cheap as it was advertised? Is the quality as durable and sustainable as promised? Are there any other brands that are as good, as fast, and/or innovative in the market?

Keller differentiates between an objective brand evaluation and a subjective brand feel. The objective aspects of brand evaluation relate to price, credibility, superiority and relevance. Brand resonance is the most important of all – if a consumer does not adopt your brand into his or her consideration reference frame, the product will not be chosen.

The consumer's reasons for considering a product are generally subjective. Often lifestyle or the portrayal of certain belief systems play a clear role in the purchasing process.

Lonsdale sportswear is as good as Adidas in terms of quality and price, but not many people have adopted Lonsdale in their consideration set. Lonsdale's association with extreme right-wing ideology is one of the reasons why many consumers don't want to buy the brand. The subjective brand feel has a negative effect on the adaptation process in the consideration set.

Connection between values and behaviour through VALS methodology

Previously, we showed that consumers use their lifestyles in order to express their identity and create their image. Many people prefer to match their lifestyle and image closely because it helps them express their values to the people around them. It is important for the Imagineer to really understand this, because he can use this need for self-expression. Using the VALS methodology he can have a good insight into the type of people he is designing experiences for. VALS is, amongst others, based on Kahle's value system, which Mitchell used to make a connection between consumer values and consumer behaviour. This resulted in the creation of the VALS methodology (Values, Attitudes and Lifestyles), which divides consumers into eight different types of lifestyles based on personal values, behaviour, personality and demographic characteristics.

The eight VALS types are formulated based on a combination of two dominant factors and a number of psychological and demographical characteristics of the consumer. These two dominant factors are: (i) motivation; and (ii) means.

The VALS test checks the respondent's motivation; for three different categories:

- ideals;
- achievements; and
- self-expression.

The results of the VALS test provide you a lifestyle, or a combination of lifestyles for consumers, and this is based on the personal scores on these dominant factors.

If motivation of an individual originates from ideals, the behaviour is guided by knowledge and principles. Motivation that is based on achievements is usually also expressed through products and behaviour, showing successful experiences of individuals to others (red Ferrari, Gucci jacket and being knighted by the Queen). Consumers, whose main motivator is self-expression, are usually looking for social or physical activities, whereby variation and/or risk are important factors in expressing oneself (think of rock climbing, or theatre visits, or even creative courses).

When we look at means, we not only look at financial means, we also look at education, energy level, impulsiveness, vanity, leadership needs, the need for new impulses and self-confidence as important examples in determining lifestyles. The eight lifestyles of VALS can be described as follows:

- **Innovators:** They score relatively high on all three motivation types and have an abundance of means at their disposal in order to reach their ideals, to display their success, to self-develop, and to express themselves through different activities.
- **Thinkers:** They are consumers who are in pursuit of their ideals and who have the means to do so. They value knowledge, responsibility and order. In general, they are highly educated and are heavily involved in societal developments. They base their decisions and judgements on actively gathered information. Even though they respect authority, they are open to new ideas and opportunities. Thinkers are practical and conservative consumers; they look for quality, sustainability and functionality of the products they purchase.

- **Believers:** Their ideals are their main motivator. They are conservative and conventional people who highly value family, convictions and society. Their consumer behaviour is quite predictable and they generally choose familiar products of well-established brands. Therefore they are loyal customers. Believers are not necessarily religious; they could also be vegetarians or communists.

- **Achievers:** They are focused on achievements. They are goal-oriented and their social lives revolve around their careers and family. Generally they are conservative thinkers, who value authority and society. Achievers value consensus, predictability and stability over risk taking, intimacy and personal development. Their consumption behaviour is recognizable by their prestigious products, such as second homes, sports cars and luxury watches. They are also recognizable by their time-saving gadgets.

- **Strivers:** They are trendy and are pleasure seekers. Because they are achievement focused, they value the opinion and acknowledgement of others. Having money is related to their feeling of being successful, but they don't have sufficient funds to fulfil all their desires. Strivers look at products that rich people buy and try to buy products that are similar in quality or better. Shopping is a very important activity for strivers, as it offers them the opportunity to be socially engaged in such a way that they can actually show others that they have money. They are impulsive buyers, but only when their financial situation allows them to be.

- **Experiencers:** Self-expression is the main motivator for them. Overall, they are young, impulsive consumers. They are often highly enthusiastic about new opportunities, but at the same time quickly lose interest when other people share the same interests. Experiencers enjoy variation and excitement in their lives and they continuously look for new, unconventional choices and like taking risks. They are highly energetic, which shows in their busy, sporty, and social lives. Experiencers spend a lot of time on entertainment, fashion and social activities. They like to look good and like to have cool gadgets.

- **Makers:** Self-expression is the main motivator for makers. Makers express themselves through the things they make and they enjoy manual labour. They would rather reconstruct their homes themselves, repair their own car and bicycle, and are very involved in raising their children. Self-sufficiency is important to them. They are often not connected to anything beyond their family, sports club and work. They are often suspicious of new innovative ideas or huge companies, but show respect for unions and government as long as they don't affect their gained privileges. Makers focus on simple, functional products that are sustainable.

- **Survivors:** They score low on means. As a consequence, they are mainly concerned with the fulfilment of their basic needs (lowest level of Maslow's Pyramid), which in turns means that they are not able to focus on the higher levels in the pyramid. In their consumer behaviour, they are at ease with products that they are already familiar with and they are weary of new products and services. They don't have a dominant motivator, as they lack the means to do something with it.

When comparing the eight VALS lifestyles, motivation and means are the dominant factors in predicting consumer buying behaviour. The dominant motivator is particularly indicative of whether the consumer's behaviour is influenced by their friends, by their parents, by reviews, or even the government. Achievers and strivers are most influenced by their friends and their work environment. Believers and thinkers are more conservative and thus place more value on their upbringing and convictions when choosing their brands. For Imagineers, it is crucial to know what kind of lifestyle a person has because an Imagineer is trying to connect the product and consumer on an emotional, social and rational level, and therefore must adapt the means of communication accordingly.

3.6.4   Brand Resonance

Brand response is the sum of rational and subjective reactions of a consumer to the brand promise. The characteristics and facts of the product, in combination with the motivation to use available means, form the basis of the final purchasing decision. The degree of the connection between promise and response determines the definite choice for the brand. This is the final step of Keller's CBBE model, known as brand resonance: the way the brand resonates with the consumer.

The fourth and final step of the CBBE model revolves around which brand resonates with the consumer and what kind of relationship evolves from that. Brand loyalty is extremely valuable for most brands. It is important that customers are loyal to your brand from a brand value and financial value perspective. You want your brand to take a hold and connect to your customers – in other words, you want to have brand resonance. Keller (2007) distinguishes four cumulative degrees of brand resonance:

1. Behavioural loyalty.
2. Attitudinal attachment.
3. Sense of community.
4. Active engagement.

We will discuss these below.

Behavioural loyalty

How often a consumer buys a certain branded product and how many products they actually buy can be expressed in money, which is an instrument to justify their loyalty programmes. A loyal Volvo buyer is valued at approximately €190,000. He is awarded this value by his own purchase (life-long) and through word of mouth with family and friends.

Behavioural loyalty by itself is simply not enough. In some cases, consumers only buy certain products because they are the only ones available in the store or possibly because they are the cheapest available. This means that not all consumers are necessarily loyal, because the moment they have access to another supplier, they will switch. Personal satisfaction is no guarantee of brand resonance. It requires a more personal connection.

Attitudinal attachment

Consumers who actually 'love' the brand will actually carry it out actively. A study by Xerox (copy machines) illustrated that consumers who rated Xerox a 4 out of 5 (quite a high score), are six times more likely to change brand in comparison to consumers who rated the brand a 5 out of 5 (the highest score).

Attitudinal attachment is promoted as the extent to which the brand meets the needs of a consumer. When a product or service matches the ideal picture of the consumer, the consumer will be more loyal to the brand.

Sense of community

Reaching the third level of brand resonance depends on how you can connect consumers who really like your brand (attitudinal attachment) to each other. This has of course become easier due to social media, but this is not the key to success. Reaching a community strongly depends on the consumer's need to meet other users.

Apple had user groups in all major cities of the USA and the company used these groups to strengthen the user's ties to the brand. They also made sure to get feedback and make consumers co-owners of the brand. Other examples are the Harley Davidson clubs and Star Trek conventions, which (still) take place worldwide.

Active engagement

The highest level of brand loyalty means that the consumer actually wishes (not only has the need) to participate, think and invest in 'his' brands. Brands that actually manage to have their consumers involved and co-create with them are usually met with success in the future. This is also referred to as brand democracy or brandocracy. Examples of this are LEGO or Linux, who develop their own open source software in collaboration with their users, or even YouTube, who wouldn't have any content if it weren't for its users. Sellaband.com is another example of such a collaborative relationship, where fans invest in a new CD of their favourite band, or even tenpages.com, where readers/users invest in new books.

Kevin Roberts, CEO of the world famous marketing and communication company Saatchi and Saatchi, says that brand resonance goes beyond the actual brand. He uses the term 'Lovemark' for a product, service or entity that inspires loyalty beyond reason. Lovemarks provoke emotional loyalty and score high on the so-called love–respect matrix. Lovemarks are not just respected by their consumers, they are also sincerely loved by them. This irrational love aspect for Roberts is the essential difference between a Lovemark and a normal brand. Examples of famous Lovemarks are U2, Starbucks, IKEA, and concerts/festivals such as Glastonbury (Roberts, 2005).

(Continued)

Continued.

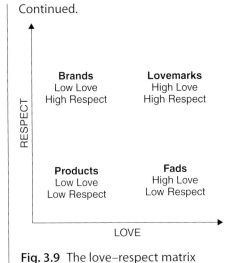

Fig. 3.9 The love–respect matrix (adapted from Roberts, 2005).

Besides provoking love and respect, all Lovemarks share three core qualities: mystery, sensuality and intimacy. Mystery is the sum of stories that are told about the product, which include the products: history, future, dreams, symbols and heroes that are the brand. Sensuality is the way a Lovemark plays with consumer senses in imagery, sounds, scent, taste and touch. Intimacy consists of the little things that create a feeling of involvement that evoke the emotions of passion, empathy and dedication. Intimacy turns consumers into emotional co-owners of the brand (and its success).

3.7 THE ROLE OF THE IMAGINEER

Imagineers understand the consumer's search for identity. They understand value systems and lifestyles and how you can connect and bind specific people by giving them meaningful experiences. Imagineers can link their creative ideas to logical and rational systems that large brands work with. Imagineers can give us the feeling that we are part of the brands we value. I feel strongly connected to my old Volvo 240 and other Volvo 240 owners. I feel at home when I visit a Citizen M hotel. I find it important that my family and friends also drink Fairtrade coffee. Imagineers are the ones that can make those connections.

The Imagineer uses each of the four steps of CBBE. They understand how to translate brand values to experiences and are able to communicate that appeal to the consumer on a personal and emotional level; they develop characteristics based on brand values; they bind people to brands because they will always look at the product's brand value and identity through the eyes of the possible user (the third step of the CBBE model). This is why AirRacing matches Red Bull and the famous soccer player David Beckham is a match to H&M.

3.8 SUMMARY

In the new post-modern world, consumerism provides us with stability: one recognizes congeners by what they consume. This could be done by looking at their clothing or the foods that they eat, but also through their political preferences, their holiday destinations, how they spend their leisure time, and/or their work environment. It will be virtually impossible to meet someone who shares your exact same preferences, but based on consumption, one can estimate whether you and this person are a match or not. Modern brands are aware of the fact that the consumer is the one with the power and not the brand. Conscious consumers choose products that portray their background or their exquisite eye for quality instead of quantity. They will choose BrewDog beer, for example, but also Iberico ham, champagne and a vintage classic bicycle. They will choose a brand with identity and history, but not for the standardized products of multinationals.

Brand managers try to add economic added value to their product or service (brand equity). How much of the economic value brand managers can add depends on the brand loyalty of consumers. In the relationship between brand and users, the users – consumers – become more and more powerful as they use their consumption to state 'who they are' and 'what they represent'. Brands anticipate by giving personality traits to the brand, which adds value in the eyes of the consumer. They try to connect to the consumers by looking for active interactions and engagement with the consumers.

The Imagineer helps to build the identity of the brand and to introduce this in all layers of the company in such a way that the image of the brand conforms to the identity of the employees, the work environment, communication, the physical and virtual contact, the user's value(s), the user's environment, and also the meaning and interaction that meet the expectations and the needs of the consumer.

3.9 ASSIGNMENTS

Assignment 1

Look around you in your own house and look for three different brands that tell us who you are. Which characteristics do these brands have and which ones are important to you?

Assignment 2

Some brand gurus claim that brands need to become more democratic, but at the same time they need to maintain their identity and core values. Which brands are you aware of that have such a strong identity? Which characteristics represent brand values?

Assignment 3

- Go to http://www.strategicbusinessinsights.com/vals/presurvey.html and do a VALS test.
- Make a list of familiar people within your direct environment and match these to the eight different VALS types (it is possible that you won't find all eight matching types). Make an inventory of which brands the experiencer, achiever and thinker use. What are the differences and what are the similarities?

3.10   RECOMMENDED READING

Jensen explains why consumers like to buy lifestyles, stories and experiences rather than just products:

- Jensen, R. (1999) *The Dream Society: How the Coming Shift of Information to Imagination will Transform Your Business*. McGraw-Hill, New Jersey.

Sinek explains that it is important to understand why a company exists rather than focusing on profit:

- Sinek, S. (2009) *Start With Why: How Great Leaders Inspire Everyone to Take Action*. Portfolio, New York.

Branding concerns the vision of a company, not marketing. This book discusses how brands can have meaningful interactions with users:

- Roscam Abbing, E. (2010) *Brand-Driven Innovation: Strategies for Development and Design*. AVA Publishing, Singapore.

chapter 4

A Meaningful Experience

Bert Smit and Gabriëlle Kuiper

It was a sad and miserable day in Paris. It was raining heavily, which prevented us from visiting all the monuments, let alone enjoying a drink on a terrace. Staying in the room with our children was not an option, so in the end we opted for the National Museum of Natural History. We usually prefer to visit the real zoo, because all the stuffed animals in a museum often gave us a dusty, scruffy feeling. The National Museum of Natural History is housed in a beautiful 19th century building, so even if the exhibition turned out to be disappointing, we would still have been able to admire the wonderful architecture of this enormous museum. There were long queues outside, because the museum only let in people in small groups in order to prevent it from getting too crowded. When we entered, we were instantly overwhelmed by the magnitude of the building and its architectural details. Impressive!

My oldest daughter noticed it first: a monkey climbing one of the pillars of the building, chasing a parrot. Further away, a leopard was attacking a totally unaware zebra, while on a different floor, an adult giraffe watched her calf. There were hundreds and hundreds of stuffed animals. The designers of the exhibition managed to show the animals in such way that they seemed to be moving. We spent a long time in the museum, and time and time again our children were in awe of what they saw. They still talk about the whale that popped up out of nowhere, located on the second floor.

(Continued)

© G. Kuiper and B. Smit 2014. *Imagineering: Innovation in the Experience Economy* (G. Kuiper and B. Smit)

Continued.

Fig. 4.1 National Museum of Natural History, Paris.

In previous chapters we have seen that as a consequence of Western economic, social and technological developments, a meaning (or experience) economy has emerged. We further discussed the consumer needs and challenges that manufacturers face as a result of this. In this chapter, we will explore the theory behind reaching strategic goals of a meaningful experience by using different suppliers from different sectors. We have now reached the core competency of the Imagineer: creating and directing an interactive meaningful experience with people to reach a predetermined strategic goal.

After reading this chapter you will understand:

- what a concept is, and why there is a need to design 'high concepts';
- the difference between perception and experience;
- which factors you need to take into consideration when creating a meaningful experience for the user; and
- what the role of an Imagineer in his capacity as designer is in all of this.

4.1   LEFT OR RIGHT HEMISPHERE OF THE BRAIN?

Daniel Pink (2005) was one of the first writers to combine the insights of communication, psychology and the design world into one theory in his renowned book, *A Whole New Mind*, in which he pleads for a new orientation in Western society. He suggests that rational, logical and systematic ways of thinking need to be changed in order to offset the growing competition of the emerging economies, to keep up with technological development, as well as the need to be distinguishable in a world of oversupply. Suppliers can only be distinguishable on emotional grounds, or in other words, by offering a meaningful experience. Western consumers are more focused on sense belonging and expressing their identity and less on satisfying their primary needs. In other words, he is more prepared to spend money on satisfying his emotional needs than on things that he really needs.

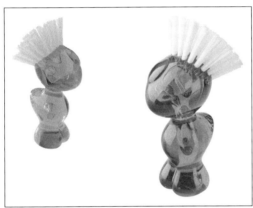

An old-fashioned Sorbo dishwashing brush no longer suffices. We actually prefer one with a better grip and one that looks more attractive. This could be a dishwashing brush from Koziol or Philippe Starck, for example. Be aware that we aren't talking about a sofa, a house or a painting. On the contrary, we are talking about fast-moving consumer goods, such as a brush.

Fig. 4.2 Designer dishwashing brushes.

4.1.1 Processing Scientific Finding

Experiencing a design has been subject to academic research for some time already. This research has supplied us with considerable knowledge on what triggers people's behaviour or associations, and to which mental and sensory stimuli these are connected. An Imagineer is able to integrate the specific knowledge of mental stimuli, associations and human behaviour into the design of a situation, where reactions and behaviours of people can be directed at an individual level. This could result in reaching a predetermined communication goal.

Prior to designing a product, the US design agency IDEO collects data through field research and prototype testing. Owner Tim Brown talks at 'Ted Talks' about a hospital research assignment to improve the patient's experiences at the first aid department. IDEO started the research by sending their own staff members to the first aid department, where they were to be checked in as patients. They made a video of everything they saw and did during their stay there. Upon evaluation of the videos, the team noticed that most of the footage was mainly of the ceiling. This was rather unexpected and provided a unique insight into new ideas about how to improve the patient's experiences and services provided by the hospital.

4.1.2   Left Brain and Right Brain Thinking

The increased awareness of meaning and design does not necessarily mean that it should be at the expense of rational goals. However, it does mean, according to Daniel Pink, that this skill requires people with complementary talents, i.e. people who are able to use both sides of the brain in their thinking processes. For some time, it has been known that the processes for rational and logical thinking happen in the left hemisphere of the brain, while emotional and associative processes take place in the right brain hemisphere. Pink points out that during the Industrial Era and the Information Era (even way before), the qualities of logical and rational thinking were considered the most valuable assets an individual could embody. However, for an Imagineer, this concept is outdated. To design a successful concept, right brain thinking is required and therefore, during the Conceptual Era or meaning economy, the qualities of the right hemisphere of the brain are increasingly being tapped into.

Table 4.1 Different qualities of both hemispheres of the brain

Logic	Feeling and empathy
Details	Big picture
Facts	Fantasy and imagination
Words, grammar, language	Symbols and pictures
Past and present	Present and future
Knowledge and comprehension	Philosophy, religion and stories
Order, structure, patterns	Spatiality
Realistic and rational	Holistic, meaningful and belief/religion
Know the name of an object	Know the function of an object
Forms strategies	Insight/understanding
Practical	Passionate
Acknowledgement	Appreciation
Safe and balanced	Risks and playful
Process oriented	Intuition and perception
Objective	Subjective
Analysis	Synthesis and synergy
Reason and argument	Aesthetic awareness
1000 words	1 picture
Qualities of the left hemisphere of the brain	**Qualities of the right hemisphere of the brain**

An Imagineer actively combines the thinking processes of both sides of the brain. By quickly shifting from rational argument to the power of imagination, meaningful and strong (in terms of content) concepts can be designed, and from there predefined goals can be achieved.

Robinson (2011) added to Pink's vision by saying that training both hemispheres is crucial and should be included and focused upon in schools. However, he observed that most school systems emphasize the development of the qualities found in the left hemisphere, such as maths, economics, physics and chemistry. These courses are focused on filling the brain with knowledge and objective information, which is accomplished in a logical and rational way. The training of the right hemisphere of the brain, using imagination, painting, drawing, building, cutting, pasting, fantasizing and playing, is by no means stimulated in a similar way. The Imagineer has to (re)discover the abilities of his right hemisphere and how they can be stimulated. We will examine this is more detail in the next chapters of this book.

4.2   HIGH CONCEPT AND HIGH TOUCH

Pink (2005) believes that some manufacturers who create functional products and services will taste defeat, in contrast to manufacturers who create an equally comparable functional product that have added experience and meaning. The rise of the Experience Economy, as coined by Pine and Gilmore (1999), is confirmed by the fact that many manufacturers offer higher economic value by consciously adding an emotional experience to the product. The aforementioned authors state that offering a transformation (not only an experience) is considered to be the most valuable economic offer. Transformation, as Pink defines it, is an experience that has meaning and a lasting effect. This is due to the fact that a learning aspect has been attached. An experience becomes meaningful when the person who undergoes the experience actually changes on a personal level (even if only minimally) (Pink, 2005).

To really resonate with, and change a person, 'high concept' and 'high touch' are necessary to achieve certain set goals. This is more than a holistic experience, just like the *staging* within the Experience Economy theory. In transformational experience, personal development and meaning are linked:

- **High concept** means the recognition of patterns and the ability to apply these patterns in new situations or to make and establish new connections (Pink, 2005). A high concept creates a story of artistic and emotional beauty, with the goal of creating something new.
- **High touch** is focused on the connection to other people. High touch can be defined as empathic ability or understanding the details of human interaction. High touch enables the concept to meet the need for pleasure and the personal development of other individuals. It becomes meaningful to some extent. High touch means that the concept meets the upper layers of Maslow's Pyramid, as discussed in Chapter 3.

The Conceptual Era is connected to an Experience Economy, because it too is focused on producing high-quality concepts that generate experience, perception, meaning and transformation. During the Agricultural Era, farmers were needed and when we transitioned to the Industrial Era, factory workers were in demand. In the Conceptual Era, however, employees with specific talents and abilities are needed, and according to Pink, these people need to be creative, empathetic, give meaning and understand patterns. We would like to call them Imagineers, because we believe these traits are the embodiment of an Imagineer.

Pink made an inventory of six qualities he believed a creative person must possess in order to design a concept that contains both 'high concept' and 'high touch'. These qualities will be further discussed in Part II, where we will also address ways an Imagineer can use these successfully in the Imagineering process.

	Design	Meaning		**Symphony**
Story				
	Play		**Empathy**	

4.2.1 The SUCCESS Formula

Pink's six essential qualities can be combined with Thijssen's 12 aspects, which are the characteristic for a meaningful experience (as previously discussed in Section 1.2.1) as well as the characteristics of the SUCCESS formula of the Heath brothers, which we discussed in the Introduction. We will now add the 'S' of subliminal (subconscious), which has led to a newly adapted SUCCESS formula in relation to 'high touch' and 'high concept'.

- **Simple** is the necessary balance between challenge and own competencies, and a symphony of different elements, which blend into a unity that is comprehensible for the user.
- **Unique** stands for authenticity, which is meaningful in the social context and in terms of offering transformation.
- **Credible** goes hand in hand with unique, because authenticity makes something credible and therefore gives meaning by offering transformation.
- **Concrete** means that there has to be a clear goal.
- **Emotional** feeling of being in control of the situation by responding to the expectations and needs of the user (empathy) touch the person on an emotional level by using all senses and offering a desirable design.
- **Story** stands for the story and positive interactivity with the user (a form of co-creation) by adding an element of 'play'.

Additionally we add an extra 'S' for SUCCESS:

- **Subliminal**, which stands for a changed perception of time through concentration and focus.

> **Schools miss opportunities to differentiate**
>
> Doing a sports instructor course, for example, or any other form of schooling that is rewarded with a diploma, are all considered transformation because a person undergoes change. However, schools and institutions also function within a market, and are therefore 'suppliers', of knowledge in this case. In this capacity, unfortunately, they hardly ever use meaning and attached experience strategically.
>
> As a consequence, they don't distinguish themselves from other suppliers. The context of the offer's design doesn't allow a more intense experience and transformation, and therefore the offer is not unique or distinguishable. Schools comply with expected conventions: long rows of tables, teacher in front of the class, assessments or exams at the end of a period. The experience, emotion and memories are mainly created by an unexpected context, offered by fellow students for example.

4.3   WHAT IS A CONCEPT?

Philosophers and scientists have used the word 'concept' since ancient times. It is derived from the Latin word 'conceptus', which is the past participle of the verb 'concipere', which means to 'invent' or to 'conceive'. The concept gives meaning to an idea and connects different elements to create a whole. Concepts are clear to most people, whether it concerns an event, such as the Red Bull Air Race, the space shuttle launch, or something more abstract such as 'democracy'. Almost everyone will have the same picture in their head while thinking of any of these concepts.

A concept is needed in order for us to see things that are made up of separate elements as a whole picture. A concept is therefore seen with the right side of the brain. If you were to only use the left side of the brain to look at the concept of a bicycle, you would only 'see' a seat, handlebars, chain and tyres. The bicycle is analysed and falls apart into its individual parts and connections and because of this the meaning is lost, in other words, there is no concept. The right side of the brain, however, which sees those same individual components as a whole, sees a bicycle. A similar example of this is the so-called visual perception of Geursen's flower.

Gestalt psychology is named after this phenomenon, which is the fact that people automatically see a pattern or a whole form (Gestalt) while looking at individual parts. A successful concept uses this phenomenon and automatically appeals to people's imagination.

A concept is only successful when the predetermined effect is achieved. It should be easily recognizable (distinguishable) and because of that be:

- easily conveyable to participants;
- easy to communicate;

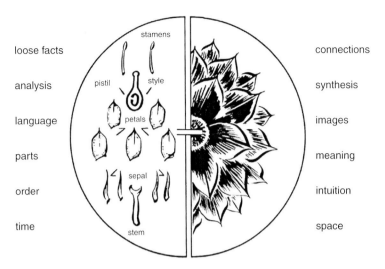

loose facts

analysis

language

parts

order

time

stamens

pistil   style

petals

sepal

stem

connections

synthesis

images

meaning

intuition

space

Fig. 4.3 Geursen's flower (reprinted with permission).

- meaningful; and
- sustainable (durable).

This also specifies the differences between a concept and an 'idea'. A concept is overarching and because of this, it is persuasive, and applicable for a longer period of time. All strong concepts are based on the (subjective) views of a person or company. The persuasiveness of the people behind the vision is responsible for the concept being born, distinguishable and meaningful. The goal of a concept is to indirectly and visually communicate the predetermined vision to the user. Therefore, Geursen suggests that a concept should consist of different layers.

'Sesame Street concept'

Sesame Street is a TV programme in which people and dolls experience all kinds of adventures (which translates to the primary interpretation or first layer). When you pay attention and listen carefully, however, you will notice that the dolls and people are making jokes, show emotions such as sadness, fear and happiness, and share things with each other (which are the secondary interpretation or second layer in the model). If you were to delve deeper and pay closer attention, you will see the third layer, the essence or vision of Sesame Street. The third layer revolves around the importance of fantasy stimulation, tolerance and honesty. Without the second and third layer, Sesame Street would not have been a strong concept and additionally, it wouldn't have lasted this long.

(Continued)

Continued.

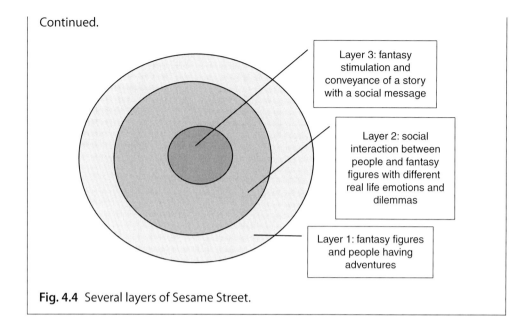

Layer 3: fantasy stimulation and conveyance of a story with a social message

Layer 2: social interaction between people and fantasy figures with different real life emotions and dilemmas

Layer 1: fantasy figures and people having adventures

Fig. 4.4 Several layers of Sesame Street.

4.3.1 The Verb Concepting

Rijkenberg (2006) discusses various opportunities and possibilities for communicating a vision in his book *Concepting*. He describes concepting as introducing a train of thoughts, through a brand, to the market, with the purpose of inspiring and motivating consumers. These consumers form a group of like-minded people, who are intrinsically motivated to further carry out the vision behind a product or service. In this way, consumers create a way of expressing their identity and expressing themselves.

The experience of a brand and the meaning behind it are valuable for concepting. It is more valuable than the product or service itself. Disney's theme parks are a good example of this.

The Disney theme park experience

Disney theme parks are not only about the individual rides the parks have to offer, they are magical places where everything is possible. Disney adds rides, fairy tales, stories and merchandise to its concept to support, strengthen and carry out the concept. Carrying out its vision through symbols is particularly important, as visitors will bring home souvenirs (merchandise) to remember the fantasy experience (memory and brand loyalty), which they then can show to people in their social circles (identity) and tell about their experience (creating a new group of Disney followers).

4.3.2 Imagineer: Designer and Director of High-quality Concepts

In this book, we focus on high concept with high touch, and we believe that it requires an Imagineer to design and direct these during the creation of a concept. Within Western society, this role will become more eminent, mainly because of increasing economic value, which represents meaning, emotional attachment and transformation. In the USA, the job title Imagineer is reserved for people who work or have worked for the Disney Company. They are individuals who have shown the ability to design new attractions for the park. In Europe, however, the interpretation of an Imagineer will be focused on designing and directing high concepts with high touch to strategically connect brands and suppliers to various stakeholders and subsequently, offer transformation when needed. Imagineering uses innovation and experience to reach strategic goals. Imagineers develop instruments that connect manufacturers to users on an emotional, rational and social level with a long-lasting effect in mind. Imagineers are the ones who bind employees and consumers to a company.

4.3.3 The Concept as Umbrella

The Imagineer designs a concept that is more than just an idea by itself. It is a way to strategically realize a predefined vision and goal, by tapping into the imagination and emotions of a group of people that he tries to connect to. The concept works like an umbrella: the binding factor between all the predetermined goals, requirements, conditions, needs, starting position and expectations of people that become a part of the concept. In this way, new ideas and old surroundings in new contexts are combined to become something new, with clear emotional and content-based layers added on.

The outcome of the concept produces a transformation for the participating group of people, which is not only a one-off experience, but also represents a lasting effect. This type of concept creates a picture in the future, a dot on the horizon, which motivates all employees to create a concept with the intention of reaching high standards, because they want to be part of the success. The concept 'to put someone on the moon' makes you want to be part of this experience and thus you are actually participating in giving meaning to something. Furthermore, the concept is also concerned with the stories after the event: you can say that you were there or that you helped achieve this concept. Even though you were only responsible for copying, you were part of the vibe, the flow, the whole picture. The concept is somehow a kind of an agreement, a set of rules for the participants or consumers to follow.

> When Disney tells us that we are on a Pirate Island, it actually feels like it, and we 'dare' to enter the fantasy and become a pirate ourselves and even end up treating dressed up pirate dolls as fellow pirates. Arr…!

The concept serves as a social script that participants abide by. This could be quite subtle (i.e. we don't speak during someone's speech), or even very obvious like the air of playfulness that is allowed in theme parks. Adjusting this social script leads to surprise and that is what creates an experience. Adjustments can be made by unexpectedly offering something that goes against existing conventions.

4.4   A MEANINGFUL EXPERIENCE

The word **experience**, if you look it up in a dictionary, has many connotations. Experience is linked to conscious learning or practising (gaining experience in or with …), to discovery (which links to curiosity, experimenting and subconscious learning), and to perceptions in everyday life (how you experience things). The first two have an active impact on memory. The latter is very much related to **perception**. When we refer to designing experiences in this book, we focus on the two connotations that are learning and memory.

We define experience as: a moving experience, where the individual attaches meaning and emotions to the experience which leads to both an emotional response and rational thinking processes. An emotional response can manifest itself in three ways (Pieters and Van Raaij, 1992):

- **Activation** refers to the intensity of the activated emotion.
- **Impression** refers to inner feelings or emotions.
- **Expression** is the visible, physical expression of emotions.

4.4.1   Strategic Goals

An experience leads to a combination of thoughts, behaviours, cognitive processes, perception, memory, fantasy and emotions. This can actually be designed in advance and directed during execution. You can opt for a specific combination of behaviours, cognitive processes and emotions, which will steer the user's experience in relation to the brand from beginning to end, which is based on a predetermined strategic goal.

Disney's strategic goal

Disney wants all its visitors to leave the park with a memory of a fun-filled day full of fantasy, which enables them to forget about the outside world with all its worries and its daily routines. Disney wants to inundate its visitors with fantasy, with the purpose of increasing its brand value ('wow this is awesome, Disney is so much fun'), increase in revenue ('let's buy some souvenirs and have another bite'), and loyalty ('we had a wonderful day, let's do this again sometime soon'). This designed experience serves a strategic purpose.

4.4.2   Perception

Perception is the process by which stimuli that come from our surroundings are received and interpreted by the brain. In other words: interpretation of a message is mainly based on how it is perceived. This is an individual process, because the decoding process is influenced by our desires, needs, expectations, and other patterns that are already located in the brain of the receiver.

Individuals generally have selective perception due to the number of stimuli our senses are able to cope with. Selective perception is a by-product of evolution and serves as a strategy for our survival. As a consequence of this, human beings tend to reinforce existing concepts with available information from the environment, as well as neglecting information that undermines existing concepts. As a result of this, conscious and subconscious decisions are made with information that will or will not be used and therefore affect the interpretation of said information.

4.4.3   Experience or Participation

Due to its popularity and *en masse* use of the word experience, its meaning has somehow eroded: 'the London experience', 'experience the musical', 'herbal tea experience', 'experience the new Audi'. 'Experience' is no longer a 'touching experience', but has become the synonym of 'participation', more or less. The purpose of this participation is to form masses: Come and join, don't miss it! When we speak about experiences and creating and designing experiences, we explicitly speak about the other meaning of the word: a touching experience, which includes a personal learning aspect for the participant and thus creates transformation. This does not necessarily mean that moving experiences cannot be orchestrated for the masses, because sometimes groups are needed in order to make something a touching or moving experience. This does mean, however, that the designed experience must have individual meaning and effect on an individual. Touching (meaningful) experiences are therefore harder to design and direct. It is up to the Imagineer to combine his knowledge of experiences and psychology to achieve this.

4.5   THEORIES ABOUT EXPERIENCE

Each and every day, we are busy with interpreting the stimuli that are found in our surroundings, which are interlinked to experience. Our brain has a selective process for stimuli that are important and to which we need to pay attention, for example a truck that does not stop for a zebra crossing. Other stimuli, such as the street tiles near the zebra crossing, will not be the focus of our attention. Our brain uses a lot of its capacity in assessing and filtering of stimuli – what is relevant and what is not, what is beautiful or ugly, what is soft or hard, what is considered a bad smell or a sweet smell, etc. Our brain combines all the received input with the already existing information from previous experiences, and from that estimates the results of actions that could be undertaken. Based on this process, a person can react either consciously or subconsciously to a possible situation that is occurring. It is important for the Imagineer to understand how the brain processes sensory information and experiences in order to design a concept. Therefore, you need to be able to make a good estimate of how a user will react and which buttons need to be pushed in order to further influence this. For decades, many scientists have been researching this phenomenon and have created different theoretical models to describe individual experience and experiences of groups in social contexts. However, only the most important models will be discussed in this section.

4.5.1 Framework of Product Experience

Desmet and Hekkert (2007) researched how products are experienced, specifically focusing on the emotions of the users while interacting with a product. Based on their research, they distinguished three types of experiences that lead to a core emotion for a specific product:

- **Aesthetic experience:** The characteristics of a product that pleasantly arouses our senses. One can think of smell, sound, taste, colour, texture and shape.
- **Experience of meaning:** The symbolic value and usage of a product can be the expression of our wealth, our interests, or what we find important. For instance, using organic vegetables to express one's ethical view of the world.
- **Emotional experience:** Your personal connection to, or personal attachment to, the product elicits certain emotions, for example souvenirs or inherited items. However, the emotion does not need to always be positive, it could also be frustration experienced in relation to the introduction of new software.

According to Desmet and Hekkert, a combination of the three types of product experience will eventually lead to a product evoking a core emotion. The question of which stimulus in our surroundings leads to the actual core emotion remains difficult to answer, as it is often a subconscious process. Russell (1980) created a model, whereby he put these core emotions along two dimensions. The first dimension was the degree to which the product elicits pleasure and the second dimension was the degree to which the product activates or stimulates emotion in an individual.

In their work, Desmet and Hekkert (2007) show that product experience has a very personal aspect, which is a consequence of the meaning factor and the emotion factor given to

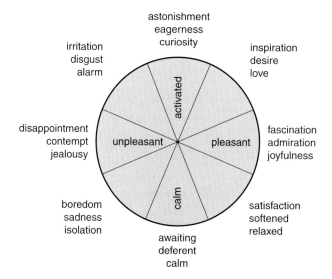

Fig. 4.5 Circumplex model of core emotions (adapted from Russell, 1980).

the product by the user when they use the product. Even though their research is focused on the experience of products, a comparison to other forms of consumption can easily be made. A trip to the jungles of Thailand or a family outing to a Disney theme park are easily translated to the three types of experiences that Desmet and Hekkert identified.

4.5.2   Flow: Experiencing Time

In the 1970s, American psychologist Csikszentmihalyi researched work experience as part of his research on what people consider to be a happy life. By conducting numerous interviews, he tried to discover the cause of boredom and anxiety in the workplace. He noticed that people who were passionate about their work were happier in their lives than people who weren't. This phenomenon is called *flow*. Typical of people who experience flow is the fact that they lose track of time and don't notice physiological signals such as hunger and thirst. In some cases, people only notice that their work day has come to an end when they notice that the sun has already set – they have forgotten to have lunch and their coffee has gone cold. A common characteristic of these people is the fact that they are intrinsically motivated in relation to their work. For them, work as a separate entity was more rewarding than the extrinsic motivation: the salary. The feeling of flow was not necessarily something they experienced on a daily basis, but some experienced it more often than others. Csikszentmihalyi (1990) showed that being in the flow positively affected 'being happy'. He did further research on this phenomenon and discovered that flow more frequently occurred during work rather than during leisure time and that flow had a positive effect on happiness.

We are all familiar with the phenomenon of time passing by extremely slowly, while at other times it seems that an hour or a day can pass by so quickly. Recent research shows that strategy games such as Sims and World of Warcraft can cause flow, as the players lose themselves in the game. Sports people and musicians also experience flow and can regularly be found in this state.

Once you lose your sense of time, this does not necessarily mean that you are in flow, as flow requires an active role of the individual. Should you lose your sense of time while watching a TV programme, this could be the result of your brain operating in a lower mode of consciousness.

Csikszentmihalyi (1990) formulated three basic requirements needed to get into a state of flow:

- The person has to be engaged in an activity that has a clear direction, structure and goal.
- The person must have a good balance between observed challenge and his own observed skills. The person must be confident that he is able to successfully complete the task.
- The task has to provide the person with fast and clear feedback (direct or indirect), so that it enables the person to adapt to the requirements of the task and remain in the flow.

Subsequently, Csikszentmihalyi made a conceptual two-dimensional flow model, based on his observations and interviews. The two dimensions are: the observed degree of challenge that a task embodies, and the person's own skills.

The model shows that flow is caused by a high degree of challenge and a high estimation of the person's own skills. The interesting part of the model is the fact that you can gain a lot

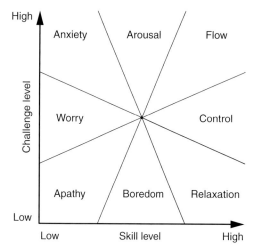

Fig. 4.6 Flow: mental status measured by level of challenge and skills.

of insight into how a person feels when the work is considered less challenging or when a person believes that his skills are insufficient for a given task. When both dimensions are low, this leads to apathy (left bottom corner), which is in essence the opposite of flow.

Flow is not age related. Flow can occur in children, who are trying to discover and make sense of the world around them, but also in an 80-year-old taking a course in art history. As long as there are clear goals, as well as a balanced level of challenge and required skills, flow can basically happen to anyone. Over time, it gets more difficult to remain in a state of flow, due to the individual constantly developing their skills, so that the individual must find bigger or new challenges to overcome.

Csikszentmihalyi also refers to flow as the psychology of optimal experience, which is important to Imagineers, because they design meaningful experiences. Flow releases chemicals that bring us to a state of happiness, which is also addictive, and is therefore a good way to pull participants into the experience. To create such an optimal experience and flow, you must make sure that the task offers sufficient challenge for your consumers, gives them feedback, and make sure that there is a balance between the challenge and consumers' skills and means.

4.5.3 The Four Realms of Experience

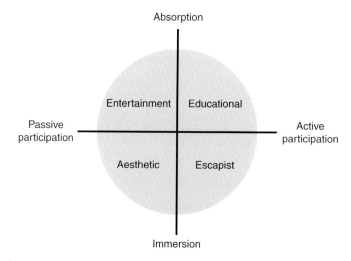

Fig. 4.7 The four realms of experience (adapted from Pine and Gilmore, 1999, p. 51).

Pine and Gilmore (1999) distinguish four experience realms, arranged along two dimensions: absorption versus immersion in an experience, and active versus passive participation in an experience. The grid provides us with four quadrants:

- **Passive and absorption:** In this quadrant, we find experiences that we refer to as entertainment. You basically pick up the experience, but you are passive. You have no influence on the experience, e.g. watching a film in a cinema.
- **Passive and immersion:** These are experiences within a certain context. However, you don't play an active role in the experience. Pine and Gilmore refer to this as aesthetic. One could think of an organized bus safari with a driver.
- **Active and absorption:** This type of experience requires you to play an active role and you take in the experience. Pine and Gilmore refer to this quadrant as educational. An educational experience is, for example, a lecture or presentation on a certain topic, or participating in a general knowledge quiz on television, or when you actively try to figure out who is the killer in a game of Cluedo.
- **Active and immersion:** This quadrant relates to the experiences that require active participation and a complete immersion in your surroundings – in essence one is escaping reality. This is why it is called escapism. To illustrate, you can think of computer games that require so much of your focus and concentration that you forget about the world around you.

To reach flow within your participants, you must target the two active quadrants of the four realms model. In both cases you must carefully consider a balance between the skills level of your participants and the challenge offered.

To ensure that a participant reaches flow, the Imagineer must choose which quadrant will ensure that the target group can experience flow. The Imagineer must begin by looking at the two dimensions and decide in which direction he wants to go on either dimension. For instance, does he want his participant to be active or passive? Once this has been decided, he can move onto the next dimension – should the participant be absorbed or immersed in the experience? The decision is made based on a clear balance between the skill level of the participant and the challenge offered. Using this process, the correct quadrant can be chosen to ensure that the participant experiences flow.

4.5.4   Service Experience and Service Design

What is very important in Csikszentmihalyi and Desmet's work is that experience is closely connected to subjective factors such as emotions, motivations and expectations. The more you focus on individual qualities and wishes when designing an experience, the higher the chances are of creating an optimal experience. Marketing professionals who occupy themselves with service design see this as the quest for the Holy Grail. It is therefore understandable that they are interested in measuring services and client satisfaction. In the 1980s and 1990s, many marketing researchers spent a lot of time and energy on measuring this. One of the first methods used, which was developed for service evaluation, was the SERVQUAL model (Parasuraman *et al.*, 1988). However, the model received a lot of critique as it uses very subjective (and therefore unreliable) factors in measuring experience (perception of services), which goes against the tenets of a marketing researcher who only works with objective data.

On the other hand, the model is valuable to an Imagineer, for experience is something subjective and personal. SERVQUAL does not serve the purpose of measuring client satisfaction, as it is difficult to divide satisfaction into separate entities and variables. However, SERVQUAL can actually give us insights into how service delivery is experienced by the consumer. SERVQUAL helps us to analyse a concept, but doesn't show the cause and effect relationship between the components of the service and consumer satisfaction.

The SERVQUAL model is also called the gap model, as it clearly shows that there can be gaps between expected service, service experience (perception) and actual service. The core terminology of the model is perception, expectation and interpretation. Gaps 1 to 5 show us moments where the information is turned into interpretation. An interpretation is always a condensed version of the actual intentions, hence the moments when noise appears. In this model, Parasuraman *et al.* (1998) show that consumers do not necessarily experience an offered service in the way it is intended. The expectations of a consumer are based on his needs or previous experiences and any other relevant factors that might influence the consumer. The management tries to measure these expectations, but it is based on their

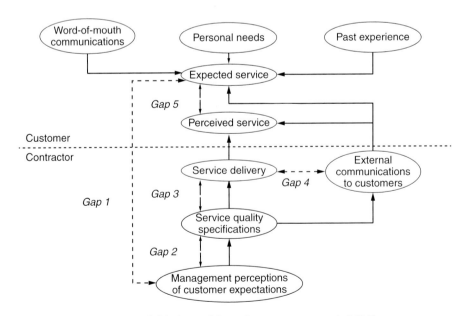

Fig. 4.8 The SERVQUAL model (adapted from Parasuraman *et al.*, 1988).

perception and interpretation of customer expectations that they design their processes, communication and final services.

Obviously, it is crucial that these expectations and the interpretation of expectations are as closely related as possible. The SERVQUAL model shows that that is often not the case.

The sixth gap

A common mistake that many companies make is that they evaluate their services based on the perception the client has of the offered service and not the predetermined expectations of the consumer (gap 5). Companies that are solely interested in the quality of their services will never be able to understand whether they have actually met the expectations of the client or not. The only thing they will find out is whether the client has just *settled* on the offered service in comparison to what they had actually wanted. Pine and Gilmore (1999) developed a formula for this:

> Guest satisfaction = Client's expectations – Client's perception of offered service

A professional manager understands how to close gap 5 by adapting service to meet the client's expectations. A professional Imagineer understands that a lot more is needed to achieve optimal service experience. The Imagineer tries to influence the interaction between provider and customer. The Imagineer understands that the arrow between 'service delivery' and 'service experience' is in actual fact gap 6, in which the experience is actually taking place and where a service provider is able to adapt his offer to meet the exact wishes of the client. This requires interaction! The Imagineer understands that the expectations of the client and what the client really wants do not always coincide, and through interaction he is able to look ahead and address these issues by bridging the gap. Pine and Gilmore (1999) refer to this gap as 'customer sacrifice'. Their formula illustrates why narrowing the gap is important:

> Client sacrifice = What the client really wants – What the client actually settles for

The perfect service experience

Designing a perfect service experience for each specific individual customer is somewhat like the Holy Grail experience for many service marketers. They try to minimize the difference between the expectation and perception of the consumer and on top of that the difference between desire and expectation. They try to design a service environment in such a way that both interaction between client and physical environment, as well as client and employee, will lead to an optimal result. As it is difficult to adapt hardware (shop interior) to each and every individual, they create flexibility in the service experience by training employees and creating software that enables the gathering of as many characteristics and client behaviours as possible. Marie Jo Bitner (1992) used all these elements in a clear model (Fig. 4.9).

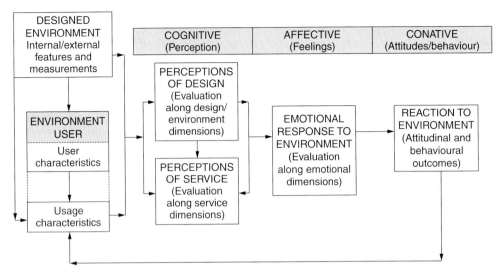

Fig. 4.9 Servicescape physical environment–response model (adapted from Bitner, 1992).

The best way to understand this model is by starting at the end: the behaviour and attitude of the client. The main focus when designing a *servicescape* is the expected behaviour. Your focus could be on guests choosing to visit your restaurant or your clients buying a certain product. According to Bitner, the deciding factor for behaviour is the affective response to the service environment. That affective response is triggered by a guest's perception of the physical environment and the perception of the service performed in it. This response is evoked due to the design of that environment and the way it can be used by the potential user. In this evaluation process, subjective factors such as taste play a role, but also more objective factors, such as budget and physical condition, influence the overall outcome of the process. Imagine visiting a supermarket in a wheelchair or wearing a blindfold; this will change how you actually experience the *servicescape*.

4.5.5   Interactive Experience and its Three Contexts

According to Desmet and Hekkert (2007), there are three levels an Imagineer should take into consideration when creating an experience: emotional, aesthetic and meaning. He can imagine how to generate the optimal experience, or in other words, how to have people reach flow, by offering a feasible task with sufficient challenges for the participant. The effect of the concept can be analysed beforehand through the SERVQUAL model. However, all these theoretical models are concerned with steering individual experiences, while the Imagineer designs for groups of people, who have a common experience, but to which has subjective meaning for each individual.

Experience is always subjective and is perceived individually. It is therefore crucial to have a thorough understanding of this when designing an experience for a group of people. When we send 100 people on a sailing boat excursion and have them go through the exact same

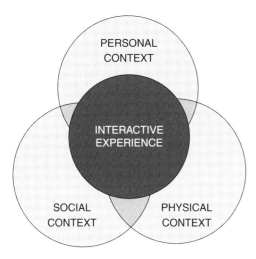

Fig. 4.10 The interactive experience model (adapted from Falk and Dierking, 1992).

programme, in the end, all 100 people will have a different (memory of this) experience. This is because they have experienced different family environments, education, sailing experience or personal interests, and look at the same situation from different perspectives. In other words: each person gives different meaning to and experiences different emotions within a group. Naturally, a consensus is reached within the group dynamics in terms of how the group experiences the event as a whole, while informal leaders will influence that general opinion.

The interactive experience model

The next model, by Falk and Dierking (1992), takes the personal interpretation mentioned above into account in their interactive experience model.

Falk and Dierking (1992) developed their model based on a museum experience and their ideas on how such an experience can be designed successfully. The model consists of three contexts: personal, social and physical. These three contexts put together form an interactive experience. Experiences are processes that individuals have, in which they filter and interpret based on their own personal and social context. The individual is mainly responsible for the experience through interaction with the physical and social environment. This understanding is crucial for experience designers, as it shows that their design only partially influences the end result of the experience. Professional designers know how to elicit the desired interaction between the individual and his surroundings. To achieve this, the designer must obtain a thorough understanding of the three contexts of Falk's interactive experience model. We will briefly discuss the three contexts below.

- **The personal context.** This consists of all the personal characteristics of an individual: individual motivation, emotion, expectations, interests, knowledge, history, culture, and the memories of history and culture. The personal characteristics mentioned all determine the interaction and in which way they will interact, what will be remembered of the experience, how it will be remembered, and which meaning he will attach to the experience. All sensory input is filtered based on this. It is therefore important that individual choice is built into the experience, for instance choices about what to do, how to do it, and where and when to participate. In this way, the participant stays in control of the experience and is able to choose experiences that best meet his personal needs.
- **The social context.** This is concerned with the social structure in which you find yourself. Most experiences are shared experiences, particularly when we look at free-choice

learning. We actually learn a lot through interactions with others. Interaction is possible with the people you come with: your family, your friends or your colleagues. Additionally, there is interaction with employees and other visitors. The social context has a big influence on your behaviour. The group you belong to and the other people in your environment will determine the social scripts that are used are appropriate for the situation. You use a different kind of register when talking to your mother compared to when you are talking to your friends. Another example is that while dancing, it is easier for some people when there are already people dancing on the dance floor. Such social scripts also determine why we are quiet in a library or why we scream on a roller coaster.

- **The physical context.** This emphasizes the meaning of presented ideas. They are the physical characteristics of a situation, the feel of the location, and the sensory stimuli people are exposed to, etc. There is also the setting behaviour, for example the way participants are prepared for a meaningful experience, which influences physical context. In order to prevent this, all of our attention is needed to discover how everything works and to figure out the purpose of the service or product. For this to occur, participants need to receive information in advance. This serves the purpose of enabling a balance between controlling the situation and spontaneity. There must be a sufficient number of new items to arouse the consumer's curiosity; however there should not be too many items, because that can become distracting. On the one hand, variety is necessary to maintain the feelings of happiness in a person and on the other hand, there should be some form of cohesion between all the individual items in order to create a meaningful coherent context.

The uncontrollable social context

Experience is determined by the individual's interaction of his own personal context with the other two contexts. In an ideal situation, the three contexts should form an authentic holistic experience for the individual; the holistic experience we previously discussed in the service design of Bitner (1992). Falk and Dierking (1992) add a valuable dimension to Bitner's service views, the relatively uncontrollable social context, i.e. people who are not trained to be part of the experience (for instance other visitors to the museum).

4.5.6   Experiential Learning

Learning and experimenting are important elements of a meaningful experience and learning also plays a key role in a consumer experiencing transformation. The Imagineer must have a clear understanding of how experiences can be used to offer learning development and simultaneously offer meaning to the participants.

Many things happen throughout the day, but not everything that happens is automatically translated into a meaningful experience. First of all, for experiences to be meaningful they need to capture our attention, we need to be able to observe and think about them. It is only through reflection that we can link cause and effect, which are links between what happened and the effect it had on the individual. This is what we consider *giving meaning to something*.

Consequently, it is through reflection that the concrete experience is moved to a more abstract level, where mental rules are formulated and fixed based on the links between cause and effect.

The individual continues his learning cycle by testing the concept's new rules in new situations. By being exposed to more experiences, we further develop and create more rules, while existing rules are further expanded and adapted.

Kolb's learning cycle

David Kolb described the cycle of experimental learning in his book *Experiential Learning* (1984), which gives insights into how people learn from experience. Kolb's cycle (Figure 4.11) connects conscious learning with subconscious learning. This cyclical learning process consists of an exchange of experience, reflection, conceptualization and experimentation. Reflection on the experience enables you to deduce generally accepted rules from specific situations you have experienced. These can be conceptualized via deduction into an abstract concept, which can be later applied in other realms (to experiment).

Kolb's learning cycle shows that there are four layers that can be built into the concept of a meaningful experience in order for the user, consciously or subconsciously, to further develop and create meaning. We will now discuss these four layers.

1. To experiment: There is room for experimentation or interaction (game/play).
2. To experience: You undergo an experience by seeing it or by it being presented to you (design, symphony, empathy).
3. To reflect: Having time to reflect (quiet time or significance).
4. To conceptualize: Abstract comprehension by a story (story).

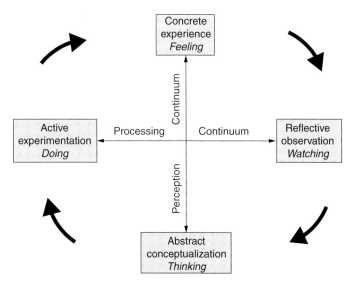

Fig. 4.11 Kolb's learning cycle (adapted from Kolb, 1984).

> When asked to organize a workshop, you must know your audience, because their previous experiences determine what level they can achieve. In addition, you also need to know the expectations of the individual participants in terms of which level they would like to reach.

Understanding and researching the expectations of people you will be working with is crucial in terms of experience design. This is the topic of the next subsection.

4.5.7 The Influence of Expectations on Intrinsic Motivation

As an Imagineer you can design fantastic experiences, but the moment your audience isn't motivated, you will never be able to move them in the broadest sense of the word.

People who visit a theme park like Disneyland have already gone through an extensive decision-making process. Because of this, they are motivated to actually 'experience Disney' and are open to receiving more of the experience and to really undergo the experience. When a man in a Mickey Mouse costume approaches, they might actually shake hands and enjoy the moment with one of the stars of Disneyland.

Visitors to a Disney theme park will most probably enjoy seeing a person dressed in the costume of their favourite Disney character. However, this will most probably not be the case when visitors to a local supermarket, who want to quickly do their grocery shopping, are confronted with a dressed up comic figure. The context and expectations don't match and as a result the experience will be endured differently and may be rejected.

Operant learning

Skinner, one of the most famous behaviourists, claimed that behaviour is the product of an interaction between the history of the person and the context the person is in. He found there is a relationship between the behaviour and rewarding that behaviour and calls this operant learning. Skinner is famous for his experiments with pigeons, where he taught them to play table tennis and how to jump through hoops using a reward system. His pigeons started displaying this behaviour because they were rewarded for it (Skinner created expectations).

By positioning the expectations (the individual learning history) at the correct level prior to the situation, motivation can be increased and the shown behaviour during the experience can be positively influenced. Skinner uses the following formula for this:

Motivation for the purpose of optimal experience = Expectation × Context

Expectancy theory

The expectancy model by psychologist Victor Vroom (1964) describes the effect of motivation and the behaviour it results in. In this theory, behaviour is the result of a conscious choice between alternatives, whereby human beings try to maximize pleasure and minimize pain. According to Vroom, individual factors such as personality, knowledge, skills, previous experiences and our own capacities (personal context) influence our targets and the behaviour related to this. The Imagineer needs to understand that the person he wants to motivate has to believe that:

- putting in effort leads to a good performance;
- a good performance will be rewarded; and
- a reward satisfies an existing need, which makes the effort worthwhile.

Vroom formulates this as follows:

> Motivation = Expectancy × Instrumentality × Valence

whereby:

- Expectancy is the expectation that effort leads to good performance (the level of the challenge of the task, self-effectiveness perception (self-confidence), control of end result).
- Instrumentality refers to the expectation that a good performance leads to the desired outcome (trust/control/formalize a reward system).
- Valence is the value given to the outcome by a person in relation to his needs.

The role of motivation in learning

The priorities of different needs are sequenced in Maslow's hierarchy (see Section 3.6.2). These priorities, however, do not tell us much about the power of motivation to actually fulfil these needs. It is quite obvious that someone who is hungry will be highly motivated to do activities that will provide him with food. On the other hand, how high is motivation for self-development of a person who already enjoys a comfortable life? Vroom's expectancy theory provides insights into the different degrees of how needs are satisfied. The value of the outcome/reward particularly plays a role in the outcome of the individual. This value and appreciation are a given and is something the Imagineer can consciously design.

To intrinsically motivate people

Motivation plays an important role in cognitive processes such as learning, problem solving and creative tasks. Research at the Massachusetts Institute of Technology (cited in Pink, 2005) shows that extrinsic motivation does not contribute to a favourable result in these types of processes. In order to have success and make progress, people need intrinsic motivation, and this requires three conditions:

- **Autonomy:** Self-steering in terms of how, when and where certain tasks can be executed.
- **Mastery:** Further and better development of the knowledge and skills related to these tasks (examples such as Linux and Wikipedia, where many highly educated and well-paid people freely invest their leisure time in building and maintenance of these systems, as it results in something meaningful rather than a 'cold' financial reward).

- **Proof:** Having a feeling of meaning and significance, actually knowing that executing a task using your skills will contribute to a meaningful goal. Apple founder Steve Jobs's goal was to 'put a ding in the universe'. Skype's founder stated 'our goal is to be destructive but in the cause of making a better world'. These are significant goals that serve as motivation for themselves and their followers.

Active cognitive processes can occur in the mental state of *flow*. The three conditions to intrinsically motivate people, as was discovered by MIT, are beneficial in reaching flow for the participants, provided of course that the expectations have been predetermined. Pine and Gilmore (1999) imply that the phase *after* design needs to be taken into consideration too.

Mastery, as described by MIT, agrees with the definition of transformation in the Experience Economy. Transformation entails directing a number of experiences that are sequenced in time. The mutual connection, as experienced by the user, influences a change in behaviour, opinions, and a stronger sense of group with other users, etc. This can be illustrated by a University of Applied Sciences, in terms of the product it offers: the user (student) experiences experiential learning and, in time, will undergo transformation. As a reward he will receive a diploma.

4.6 SUMMARY

In this chapter we have further investigated concept development, experience, significance and design. We explained what a good concept is and how to recognize bad concepts. We have introduced left and right brain thinking, discussed the importance of both and why this is useful information for an Imagineer. Imagineers develop high concepts with high touch in order to reach a strategic goal.

While using this concept, he additionally takes into account the critical success factors from the extended SUCCESS formula, as well as the understanding of how individual and group experiences come about and become meaningful. A good overarching concept:

- is simple, achievable but challenging and cohesive;
- is unique, therefore it offers transformation;
- is credible, due to the fact that it is authentic and concrete goal focused;
- is emotionally charged and emphatic in terms of interaction between supplier and user;
- is conveyable as a story and therefore interactive; and
- has a subconscious influence by generating focus and influence on perception.

We have discussed different theories and models that describe individual experiences and have further looked at how these individual experiences can be designed and directed within a concept that is focused on large groups. The Imagineer needs this knowledge together with his imagination to design, analyse or direct experiences.

Additionally, an experience is meaningful when it has a subconscious learning aspect. Learning is only possible when a participant is intrinsically motivated, hence open to the offered information. Therefore, the concept should have a layer that actually elicits this intrinsic motivation. There must be mastery (becoming better at something), a sense of autonomy, and relevance. The expectation of the users beforehand is of influence too – the Imagineer has to design and shape the early stages right up to the start of the experience. The concept further needs to take into account the different learning styles of individuals, and because of these different styles, different learning development levels need to be offered. There has to be time for reflection, experimentation, experience and conceptualization.

The Imagineer uses the knowledge of the models discussed in this chapter to design and direct individual meaningful experiences within a concept that is focused on groups. As such, the Imagineer knows how to combine the qualities of their left hemisphere of the brain (analysis) with their right hemisphere of the brain (imagination) to create a concept.

4.7   ASSIGNMENTS

Assignment 1

Link the theory of this chapter to real-life examples of Kile Ozier, Arjan van Dijk and Red Bull. Which theory and models do you recognize in their real-life working methods?

Assignment 2

Visit a restaurant in your area and bring along Bitner's servicescape model. Assess the service experience of the restaurant according to the model. What do you notice?

Real-life experience Kile Ozier

The Imagineer works intuitively. He somehow feels what works and what doesn't – the theoretical models about experiences and behaviour can be used as an explanation. Kile Ozier is a concept developer in New York who has earned his spurs. He identifies five points that are required in order for a meaningful experience to be successful. These are:

Research on assumptions: Ozier starts the design process with an internal investigation based on his own expectations and assumptions of what is necessary and possible. He is aware of the pitfalls of having wrong assumptions. After this inquiry, he will research what the public and participants' expectations are, and whether their social-cultural context will influence their expectation patterns. How will they undergo the experience?

Convictions and expectations: Kile Ozier also wonders whether existing expectations and convictions can be overcome or changed without alarming the audience that this

(Continued)

Continued.

is the target group. It should never be presented literally. When participants understand the intentions of the product or service, part of the magic will be lost. It is important to never feed the existing convictions, but to surprise people and have them on the edge of their seats to adopt a new way of looking at things.

Comfortable disorientation: This is where you try to catch the audience's attention unexpectedly. The Imagineer must slowly but surely lead them into a more unfamiliar situation and context, while offering a sense of safety by creating a safe environment.

Sequential revelations: The Imagineer should never show the whole experience at once. The story needs to be told step by step, also known as 'gasp and grasp': have your audience gasp for air in shock, but also get them to immediately try to grasp the product or service. It is like a symphony, which leads you from one moment to the next. Then there should be a quiet moment of peace so that everyone can catch his or her breath.

Subconscious engagement: Engage the audience to create their own experience without too much emphasis, as this would break the magic. For example, making masks for the audience, so that the audience becomes part of the story. The personal context becomes part of the physical context, as well as the social context, and this occurs simultaneously (Falk and Dierking described this in their model).

Real-life experience of Arjan van Dijk

In 2010, Arjan van Dijk won a Golden Giraffe for being 'Event Personality of the Year'. As founder of a successful event organization, the Arjan van Dijk Group, he earned his credits as a designer of experiences. He describes the following critical success factors for designing an experience:

- Make it attractive and exciting, and it should arouse curiosity with 'nothing'.
- Anticipation: the constant threat that something is about to happen, but in the end it doesn't. (Am I going to be wet in this ride or not? This type of excitement gives pleasure.)
- Understand your audience and give people room to believe that something exists.
- Create an environment that stimulates. Offer stimuli and create a situation in which you remove boundaries, explore boundaries, and are playful.
- It is not about the act by itself, but the story and predetermined message.
- Cohesion: everything should match and become coherent.
- Check the story for elements that might cause noise, confusion, or blur the mind.
- Short attention span.
- When people enter an experience, you should provide a 'cooling down' period: a tunnel (support programme) to enable them to move into another world.

(Continued)

Continued.

- Basic needs need to be met: food, warmth, shelter, etc.
- New combinations lead to new innovations: linking and building bridges between different disciplines or realms.

Real-life example of Red Bull experimental marketing: building a category and brand through meaningful 'touch points'

Tomasito Bobadilla is the Managing Partner at Momento Marketing Group LLC, New York. Momento Marketing Group is responsible for Red Bull's marketing department. Red Bull is an 'experimental marketing brand/company', which means that the product is secondary to the brand. The brand is built to offer a unique experience to existing users. In this way they will be challenged to bring new users to the brand. The whole brand and the company are focused on offering this unique experience. Marketer Bobadilla looks for experiences that will dumbfound the (core) users, touch them on an emotional level, and activate their brains and mind. The brand holds 'brand own' events that are unique, personal activity and interaction, which is done so that there is room for the new lifestyles of existing and new users. Tomasito Bobadilla suggests the following elements for a strategically used experience:

- Sense
- Feel
- Thought(-provoking)
- Act (call-to-action)
- Relate

Four critical success factors of experience are:

- Focus on experiences of the core user.
- Improving and expanding product usage (competition analyses related to usage, design and communication, etc.)
- Existing users are emotionally motivated, because the user experiences are fantasy, emotion, and fun driven.
- Ideology that is used appropriately and is diverse and versatile. Don't just use one methodology.

4.8 RECOMMENDED READING

Mihalyi Csikszentmihalyi describes how to recognize a state of consciousness called flow:

- Csikszentmihalyi, M. (1990) *Flow: The Psychology of Optimal Experience*. Harper Collins, New York.

A clear overview of issues that are a result of services marketing of intangible products:

- Zeithaml, V., Bitner, M.J. and Gremler, D.D. (2002) *Services Marketing. Integrating Customer Focus Across the Firm*. McGraw-Hill/Irwin, New York.

This is one of the first books written from a museum visitor's perspective, and so a must read on how to design a museum in order to fascinate and engage the visitor. It is also a valuable book to use other domains:

- Falk, J.H. and Dierking, L.D. (1992) *The Museum Experience*. Howells House, Washington, DC.

Background on techniques and methods of service design and design thinking are described in this inspiring book:

- Schneider, J. and Stickdorn, M. (2011) *This is Service Design Thinking*. BIS Publishers, Amsterdam.

chapter 5

Thinking in Terms of Business Models

Bert Smit

> My grandmother used to say: 'There is no such thing as a free lunch, my boy.' Nowadays, this is no longer the case. Once you have a computer and Wifi, all Internet sources are easily accessible for free. All the information you can imagine can be found using the Google search engine and is just one mouse click away. Facebook is now keeping track of my agenda. Texting has been replaced by Twitter, Ping and Whatsapp, and this is all for free! How do companies survive, exist or make a profit when I don't pay for anything…?!
>
> Really? Do they really earn that much money by selling all my personal details that they have collected based on my Internet usage and preferences for certain sites?

In previous chapters, we discussed how an Imagineer can respond to the experience and identity of user group(s), the product and the brand. When Imagineering is used as a strategic tool, the understanding of how business models work is of vital importance. In this chapter, we will explain what business models are and the role of the Imagineer in constructing a business plan, where the relationship with the consumer as a value is taken into account.

By the end of this chapter you will understand:

- what a business model is;
- what the value chain of a company is and how a consumer can influence this;
- the influence of co-creation on the making of a business model;
- how a modern business model is constructed; and
- the role of the Imagineer in the making of business models.

5.1   WHAT IS A BUSINESS MODEL?

A business model describes how a company translates technology, skills and revenue to euros and dollars. Traditionally it means the following:

1. **Value proposition**: which products and which services are offered.
2. **Target group**.
3. **Positioning**: who is the competition and how to face them.
4. **Value chain** of the company: gaining an understanding of the production process of a product. The added values of different departments during that process (purchase, production, marketing, research and development) is also investigated.
5. **Value network**: networks of suppliers, companies and people that contribute to the final production and sales of the product.
6. **Profitability**: the actual cost of making the product in relation to its final selling price.

By creating a business model, a company indicates what value they create for their consumers, the process of how they will execute this, and how they will earn money doing this.

In a less complex economy, this was a perfect way of determining how to turn the product into money. In the 1980s and 1990s, however, most companies were focused on the value chains and value networks, because they wanted to reduce costs and make higher profits. Competition was found in production costs and distributions. Most companies considered value networks and propositions as equals, but this was all about to change.

Dell gets its competitors into problems by using an innovative business model.

In the 1990s, most PC manufacturers focused on product features, such as speed and memory of their PCs. Many of these companies almost went bankrupt when Dell's new business model was introduced, in which innovation wasn't shown in the new product's features, but in the distribution instead (value network). Dell started delivering customized PCs directly to its customers at low cost. This nearly killed the competition. For instance, competitors like IBM couldn't afford to do something similar, because they had very high overhead costs, such as distributors, shops, etc. Due to its innovative business model, Dell became one of the market's biggest players in no time.

This example clearly shows how an innovative business plan can actually support positioning of a company in relation to the competition, as well as its survival.

5.1.1   The Influence of Co-creation and Prosuming on the Value Chain

Dell was one of the first companies to no longer focus solely on production and the traditional distribution costs, but also tried to understand how consumers could actually participate in creating the value chains. What Dell did was make the consumer part of its value network, so to speak. As a consequence of this, the business model changed in other areas too. When a consumer (as part of the value network) decides the value propositions, the entire value chain will change and so does the profitability and positioning.

> When a consumer wants to purchase a Dell computer and to understand which parts and features a Dell computer consists of, he will no longer need a shop with employees to do so. This reduces the cost of the PC and enables keen competition in terms of price, consumer satisfaction and loyalty. (We should not forget that Dell was one of the first companies to have end users actively engaged in brand proposition.)

As a matter of fact, Dell was one of the first companies to introduce and use online co-creation between the consumers and the producers. This example also shows that co-creation influenced the business model and the value chains. Co-creation and prosumerism have been further influenced, and therefore changed, other parts of the value chain too.

To illustrate this change, we believe it is useful to take a closer look at the value chain of a company. One of the most renowned traditional value chain models is by Porter (1985, p. 11–15), which clearly shows the cost structure of a product. The value chain can be divided into two parts:

- **Primary activities:** The direct link to production and distribution of a product or service.
- **Supporting activities:** The direct relationship to five primary activities (see Fig. 5.1).

Finally, a margin is added to determine the selling price.

When Porter developed this model, he believed that all companies had to realize that it was only through optimal tuning of all activities that the lowest possible costs could be achieved. When a purchase prognosis is correct, the correct number of materials will be purchased, the

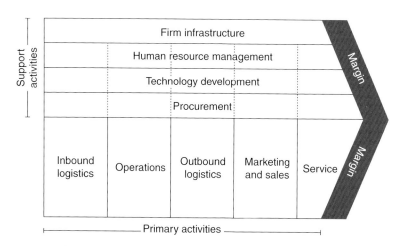

Fig. 5.1 Porter's value chain (adapted from Porter, 1985).

correct number of employees will be hired, etc. Porter, in this sense, is an extreme left-brain (analytical) thinker: in order to become as efficient as possible, everything should be understood and calculated through extensive processes and procedures. In the 1980s and 1990s, however, companies forgot to research this extreme focus on efficiency (making the same process faster and cheaper) and forgot to address whether the same process could be reorganized in a different manner involving the end-user.

> Dell changed its way of operating to respond to the individual wishes and needs of the consumer and, by doing so, changed other primary activities. It took the competition, still fixed in their old ways, quite a number of years before they were able to create a similar business model to Dell's.

5.1.2   Recent Developments

Due to the development of modern technology, mainly in terms of communication offered to us by the Internet, many other parts of the company's value chains were changed – co-creation and direct interaction with individual users in particular have had a huge impact on the business models of manufacturers.

> **Facilitating cooperation**
>
> Service departments offer a lot of their services online via websites and forums. Users can ask questions on these forums, inquiring whether or not someone has had the same problem with a product and how they solved said problem. Users can also provide other users with advice and tips on how to solve common problems without interference from professionals. It is then sufficient for companies to facilitate cooperation by offering a platform.

As a result, the field of marketing has changed as well. In Chapter 2, we discussed the fact that more brands are trying to connect to a community of users that share similar/ the same views. In turn, these user communities try to create awareness of the brand with other people, but are also actively involved in the creation of new products and service development.

> By the end of 2010, Apple announced that 10 billion apps had been downloaded from the Appstore. The majority of these apps had been designed by and for the users. Instead of mainly focusing on their 'own' products, Apple created an environment where users can design apps themselves.

We can see similarities between Apple and the examples of Koga Miyata and NikeID in the previous chapters.

Meanwhile, co-creation with and by consumers has become part of the business models of many companies. Consumers have become part of the production, marketing and service process and this has a fundamental influence on the value proposition. The consumer's influence changes the experience of the rendered service and consequently the price the consumer is willing to pay for said service. Obviously this has an effect on the profitability of the company. In some cases, the experience of the provided service has become more valuable than the product itself (see NikeID example in Section 2.3).

Existing literature meanwhile identifies five different basic types of co-creation:

- **Co-branding:** Two or more brands join together to introduce a new product or service onto the market that is based on the shared brand values. Well-known examples of this are Senseo (Philips and Douwe Egberts), SMART (Swatch and Daimler) and Red Bull Air Racing.
- **Crowd sourcing:** A broad audience is approached to engage and cooperate in solving a problem or problems in the production process of a new product. Famous examples of this are Linux Software, MyStarbucksIdea.com and ReDesignMe.com.
- **Crowd funding:** A large group of people are asked to invest a small amount of money in new products or services. In this way, no banks or other investors are required to start up a company. Famous examples are TenPages.com and Kickstarter.com.
- **Community building:** A platform is facilitated for users, where they can ask questions, give advice, or create the final product. The core idea in this process is that users or community members have a shared interest or hobby. There are many examples of this, however Facebook, LinkedIn and Myspace are perfect examples of frequently used platforms where communities are created. Another nice example emerged from the cooperation between Apple and Nike. They designed an App, which enables runners to run against other people on the other side of the world and share their achievements, track records, etc. with others in the community.
- **Prosuming:** The consumer creates his own 'unique' product within the indicated framework of the manufacturer. NikeID and Koga Miyata are examples of this. You can also think of designing your own wallpaper and having it printed by an online printing company or look into Lulu.com, where you can print and publish your own book or magazine in different quantities, from one to one million copies.

Co-creation changes the companies' business models drastically, because other parties, such as consumers or other brands, become involved and influence the outcome, and in the case of community building, other parties determine the value of your product.

This has such a big impact on companies that the traditional business models are no longer applicable. In the traditional model, a company was in control of its processes and development, where standardization and efficiency were the key ingredients for achieving the best results. In a left-brain world, this is perfectly logical. Whereas using right-brain thinking, which is thinking in terms of emotions and imagination, is becoming more and more the determining factor in cultivating customer relationships with the manufacturer. Customization requires space, in such a way that it enables consumers to consume their own ideas and identity.

LEGO (based on Schultz and Hatch, 2003)

LEGO, the famous interlocking bricks manufacturer, was one of the first companies to radically change its business model in order to enable co-creation with its consumers. Despite the fact that LEGO was a renowned and reliable brand during the 1990s, its production experienced tremendous pressure. The pressure came from changing trends in the toy industry, computer games gaining in popularity, and emerging brands such as Spiderman, Star Wars and Harry Potter. Under threat of losing its interlocking bricks patent, LEGO's management decided that it was time for drastic changes in order to survive in the 21st century. LEGO understood that it could not maintain its profits by improving its production process, because their Asian competitors were able to produce the same product at lower costs. LEGO returned to its core mission of producing quality products that are modular, elicit play, stimulate creativity, and have a unique design. LEGO named the concept LEGO DNA, and the company uses this as its foundation. The mission statement of LEGO is nurturing and cherishing the child in every person.

When the company decided to transform its business model, LEGO DNA survived, and based on the philosophy behind it, LEGO started to investigate how it could create added value. Four sub-brands were created:

- **EXPLORE:** where the emphasis is on young children discovering the world.
- **MAKE & CREATE:** where consumers are engaged in building and creating their own LEGO universe (while using old LEGO as the foundation).
- **STORIES & ACTION:** which is a response to the emergence of big brand names or products, for example Harry Potter or Star Wars, where children are able to re-enact the stories.
- **NEXT:** where new innovations in construction toys come together, such as robotica, and audio/visual additions.

Together with publishers who focus on children's books, LEGO EXPLORE started publishing picture books based on LEGO figures and animals. These books and LEGO sets helped children better understand and make sense of the world (co-branding).

LEGO's MAKE & CREATE has done a great job of engaging consumers and including them in the production process. Via the LEGO website, users are invited to share their designs, but also give other users the opportunity to order these new designs straight away. This is completely different from the old standard sets LEGO used to make in the old days. LEGO

(Continued)

Continued.

outsources part of its product development to consumers, while it simultaneously binds the consumers to the company (i.e. loyalty). Of course LEGO needs to create frameworks to enable this (prosumer and community building).

LEGO's STORIES & ACTION offers the consumers new possibilities for play that involves their favourite heroes by cooperatively developing with other brands (co-branding).

LEGO's NEXT not only provides physical parts for robot building, but also provides a platform for consumers to think about and have them help with programming the software related to the robot sets. LEGO challenges users to share their software via online platforms, because it is only through this that the robot's abilities can increase substantially (crowd sourcing).

By strengthening LEGO DNA in cooperation with its consumers and further expanding via websites and software, LEGO distinguishes itself from other brick manufacturers worldwide. LEGO remains visible, by focusing on its core mission and DNA, and additionally by actively co-creating with its consumers, which results in an endless stream of new ideas.

5.2 BUSINESS MODEL GENERATION BY OSTERWALDER (AND 470 OTHERS)

The LEGO case study is a good example of LEGO not only creating the physical bricks, but also the experience that is felt when using the bricks. LEGO has adapted its strategies in order to co-create new products with parents and children, and as a result of this, the relationship between LEGO and its users is considered to be of more value than the bricks alone: the users feel connected to LEGO and because of this the users show loyalty.

At the beginning of this chapter, we discussed the elements of Porter's traditional business model. Obviously there is hardly any room for this standard model in today's Experience Economy and the relationship between manufacturer and consumer. The model is focused on production and efficiency and not on value creation with the consumer, which does not ensure success in today's Experience Economy.

Alexander Osterwalder (Osterwalder and Pigneur, 2010) understood this. He observed that renowned strategists were having trouble adapting their business models to compensate for the new generation of consumers and it was this lack of success that was sending shock waves through the business world. There was also a lack of adaptation to the technological developments that were occurring at the time, for instance the Internet and its related different kinds of communication channels, or the relationship with consumers and the relationship the consumers have amongst themselves. It was because of this that Osterwalder, together with Yves Pigneur, started an online community where strategists were given a platform to discuss these topics. This context-driven community became an instant success.

Starting with only 150 members, the platform expanded rapidly and so did the number of participants. Osterwalder was leading the discussions and started a new vision of business models in cooperation with 470 of the platform members. In 2010, this led to the first online co-created book: *Business Model Generation*.

The core element of this new vision of business models is the **Business Model Canvas**. The canvas is the foundation that defines a business model. The canvas consists of nine standard blocks:

1. Key partners.
2. Cost structure.
3. Key activities.
4. Key resources.
5. Value proposition.
6. Distribution channels.
7. Customer relationships.
8. Customer segments.
9. Revenue streams.

Osterwalder considers the canvas to be a kind of jigsaw puzzle. Each and every company makes a different puzzle and consequently creates a different picture, depending on how the nine puzzle pieces are shaped. The canvas is (usually) used in the following sequence:

1. Determine which customer segment(s) the company wants to serve.
2. Determine the value proposition.
3. Determine through which channels the value proposition will be delivered to the customers.

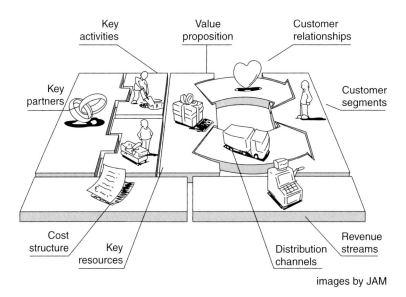

images by JAM

Fig. 5.2 Business model canvas (Osterwalder and Pigneur, 2010) (reprinted under Creative Commons licence).

4. Determine customer relationships, and how they are established and maintained.
5. Determine how customer segments are to pay for a rendered product or service.
6. Determine which key resources are essential for value position creation.
7. Determine the organization's key activities.
8. Determine key partnerships.
9. Determine cost structure.

We will further discuss what these nine blocks entail.

Step 1: Determine customer segments

This step is concerned with: 'Who are our most valuable customers?' and 'Which customer segment will we serve (niche market or masses)?'

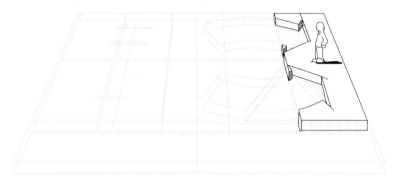

Fig. 5.3 Customer segments.

Step 2: Determine the value proposition

The central focus of this canvas is the value proposition. On the left, all the necessary elements are there to create proposition. On the right is how the money is earned and how the value proposition reaches different customer segments. The value proposition could be, for example, not only a product or service, but also an experience or a train of thought that can play a central role in formulating the value proposition. Core values of a product or service are equally as important as the actual product itself. The brand, feeling, user value (convenience, design, uniqueness, etc.), and price are all part of the value proposition.

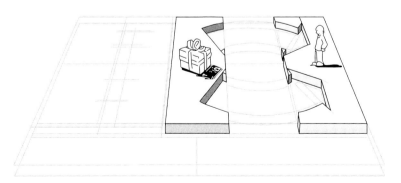

Fig. 5.4 The value proposition.

Steps 3 and 4: Through which channels will we deliver the value proposition and what kind of customer relationships do we establish and maintain with our customer segments?

Once the value proposition has been established, two closely connected elements are determined. On the one hand, research is done into how customer segments want to buy and receive the value proposition, as well as which channels are needed to accomplish that (shops, mail, online, door to door). On the other hand, what kind of customer relationship is desired with the concerned customer segments (initial contact, after-sales service, customization, etc.). The desire and need to have a relationship determines the choice of distribution channels and the other way around – some distribution channels offer various possibilities for building and maintaining relationships.

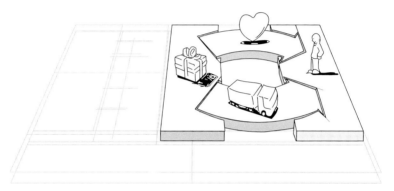

Fig. 5.5 Distribution channels and the relationship with the customer segment.

Step 5: Determine how customer segments will pay for a product or service

The first four elements determine the revenue streams of the business model. Customer segments will pay a certain price for the value proposition, relationship and distribution. How they will actually pay that price is the next step that needs to be determined. Customer segments can pay in various ways (per product, per subscription, or via a membership). It should be noted that Osterwalder does not always consider payment in terms of monetary means. Most people who search the Internet using a search engine, such as Google, don't pay by means of money, but by 'Internet behaviour/usage'. Google uses this behaviour for their own value proposition, i.e. customized advertising.

Customized advertising by Google

Google enables companies to use target advertising. For instance, Google can offer advertisements for local kitchen shops or restaurants to someone who regularly visits cooking websites. When a cooking fan clicks on one of the advertisements, Google will receive a few cents from the shop or restaurant concerned.

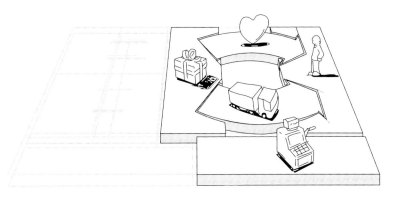

Fig. 5.6 Determine how customer segments will pay for a product or service.

Steps 6 and 7: Determine which key resources are essential to create a value proposition and what are the key activities of the organization

The moment the previous steps have been determined, the customer side of the value proposition can be arranged. First of all, we need to determine which key resources are essential for value proposition so that we can organize distribution, enable desired customer relationships, and payments (money or some other method(s)). The essential resources can be tangible, for example factories and trucks, or non-tangible, such as the brand, websites and software. Staff and intellectual property are also considered to be key resources. The organization needs to have an understanding of key activities in order to determine what the essential resources are. This is why steps 6 and 7 are done simultaneously. Available resources will partially determine how the activities are arranged and organized. However, this is not always the case because for some key activities, resources need to be obtained or created.

Of these activities, creating value proposition, enabling distribution, relationships and payment (production, service, sales, etc.), companies need to determine whether they will be executing these activities themselves or outsourcing them to partners.

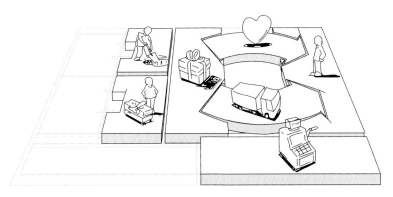

Fig. 5.7 Determine key resources and key activities.

Step 8: Determine key partners

To enable value propositions, choices concerning the key resources and key activities determine the key partners.

Companies might have various reasons for choosing strategic partnerships. They could have the desire to remain flexible, or they might not possess the sufficient knowledge or skills to accomplish their mission, or even guarantee certainty of products or services.

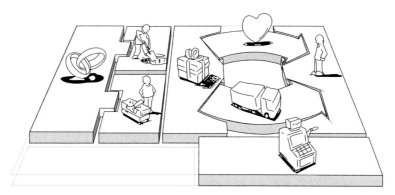

Fig. 5.8 Who are the key partners?

Amazon.com promised to make speedy deliveries to its customers and so they decided to outsource the distribution method of their products. To accomplish this goal, cooperation between Amazon and mail companies was and is essential. On the other hand, Amazon must also have a fast and efficient relationship between their wholesalers and publishers in order to enable their speedy delivery.

Step 9: Determine cost structure

By choosing key resources, key activities and key partners, a cost structure emerges. Cost structures are:

- the ratio between fixed and variable costs;
- the means related to key activities and key resources; and
- which parts are essential for key partnerships.

Companies that frequently outsource, computerize and pursue the lowest prices are known as cost-driven companies. Companies who focus on creating a product or service that embodies high value and quality are called value-driven companies.

Fig. 5.9 Determine cost structure.

The puzzle is complete once the cost structure is determined. Once everything has been determined, the business model is ready: it is clear for who you are working, what you offer, which relationships are important, and how the consumer will have access to the product and/ or service. The company has determined which element they want to organize themselves around, which are usually the elements that the company knows they are really good at in order to be successful and also which elements need to be outsourced; things they are not good at. With this accomplished, the company will have a clearer indication of what their revenue and costs will be and which part of the revenue will be the manufacturer's.

5.3 BUSINESS MODEL INNOVATION

The Business Model Canvas is not only used to create new business models, but is also used to innovate and renew existing business models. Osterwalder describes the following five building blocks for this process:

- **Consumer-driven innovation:** The main question here is 'How can we deliver our value proposition to another customer segment?' Dell did this by no longer supplying shops, but directly delivering their product and services to their consumers instead.
- **Resource-driven innovation:** The main question here is 'How can we apply available resources to achieve new value propositions?' The Efteling, which is a theme park in the Netherlands, is a perfect example. Its biggest talent is the telling and preservation of fairy tales, which they have been doing since the beginning of the 20th century. They are not only in a fun park, but they have applied their talents to the creation of TV programmes, online activities, musicals, a radio station, and even a bungalow park. The effective use of this talent has doubled the turnover and increased profits considerably for them.
- **Finance-driven innovation:** The main question here is 'How can we increase profits or how can we decrease cost?'

- **Offer-driven innovation:** The main question here is 'How can we improve our value proposition, expand, or renew it?' Amazon.com did this by not only selling books and CDs, but also toys and household items.
- **Multiple epicentre-driven innovation:** Innovations driven by multiple epicentres can have significant impact on several other building blocks. Apple does this continuously by adding new elements to their value proposition by simultaneously looking for new customer segments and exploiting their resources.

5.4 THE IMAGINEER'S ROLE IN INNOVATIVE BUSINESS MODELS

Imagineers invent and design from the perspective of their user groups, as this knowledge can be applied to innovating the business model. The Imagineer can play an important role in consumer-driven and resource-driven innovations. Consumer-driven innovation requires the Imagineer to look at things from the perspective of the consumer in order to create more meaning and meet the needs of the consumer, which is not necessarily obvious. With the available resources, he centralizes the story of the provider and imagines how this story, key activities and existing resources can be combined to bring in new user group(s) or chances.

Imagineers understand how customer segments function and the way a relationship between a brand and the user group can be established, by responding to individual motivations and key values that are required for follower groups to emerge. As a result, Imagineers can help companies to fine-tune their value proposition to the emotional needs of various customer segments. This has a positive influence on the choices of distribution, communication, interaction and involvement of user group(s), and additionally, the continuation of the relationship and loyalty of the consumers.

5.5 SUMMARY

The cost structure and revenue model of many business models have changed as a result of online and offline co-creation. It is because of this that many companies are looking for ways to innovate their business models. In this day and age, the consumer demands to be a co-producer and for companies to thrive in this Experience Economy, this demand must be fulfilled. This strong consumer need and the related expectation, in terms of customization of a product and service, forces companies to arrange more flexible processes, which at the same time give direction to consumers' desires, within a specified framework. Osterwalder's Business Model Canvas meets these needs. It specifically clarifies whom you work for, what you offer, which relationships are built, and how the consumer will have access to the product and service. It clarifies revenue, cost, and which part of revenue is allotted for the supplier. The Imagineer can make an important contribution to the establishment of a Business Model Canvas, as the new model explicitly includes co-creation from the consumer, which is the field of expertise of the Imagineer.

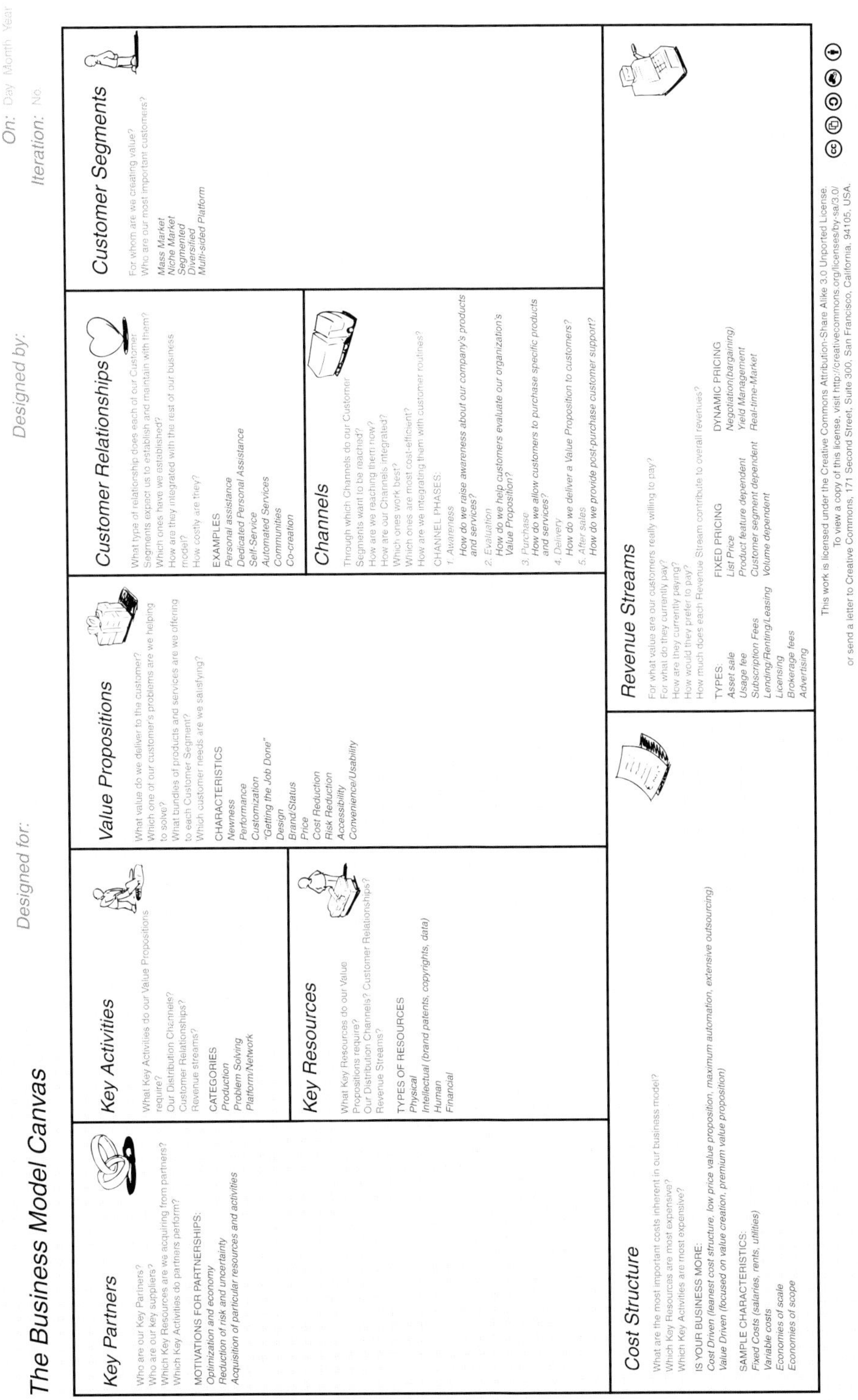

The Business Model Canvas
Designed for:
Designed by:
On: Day Month Year
Iteration: No.
Key Partners
Who are our Key Partners?
Who are our key suppliers?
Which Key Resources are we acquiring from partners?
Which Key Activities do partners perform?
MOTIVATIONS FOR PARTNERSHIPS:
Optimization and economy
Reduction of risk and uncertainty
Acquisition of particular resources and activities
Key Activities
What Key Activities do our Value Propositions require?
Our Distribution Channels?
Customer Relationships?
Revenue streams?
CATEGORIES
Production
Problem Solving
Platform/Network
Key Resources
What Key Resources do our Value Propositions require?
Our Distribution Channels? Customer Relationships?
Revenue Streams?
TYPES OF RESOURCES
Physical
Intellectual (brand patents, copyrights, data)
Human
Financial
Value Propositions
What value do we deliver to the customer?
Which one of our customer's problems are we helping to solve?
What bundles of products and services are we offering to each Customer Segment?
Which customer needs are we satisfying?
CHARACTERISTICS
Newness
Performance
Customization
"Getting the Job Done"
Design
Brand/Status
Price
Cost Reduction
Risk Reduction
Accessibility
Convenience/Usability
Customer Relationships
What type of relationship does each of our Customer Segments expect us to establish and maintain with them?
Which ones have we established?
How are they integrated with the rest of our business model?
How costly are they?
EXAMPLES
Personal assistance
Dedicated Personal Assistance
Self-Service
Automated Services
Communities
Co-creation
Channels
Through which Channels do our Customer Segments want to be reached?
How are we reaching them now?
How are our Channels integrated?
Which ones work best?
Which ones are most cost-efficient?
How are we integrating them with customer routines?
CHANNEL PHASES:
1. Awareness
How do we raise awareness about our company's products and services?
2. Evaluation
How do we help customers evaluate our organization's Value Proposition?
3. Purchase
How do we allow customers to purchase specific products and services?
4. Delivery
How do we deliver a Value Proposition to customers?
5. After sales
How do we provide post-purchase customer support?
Customer Segments
For whom are we creating value?
Who are our most important customers?
Mass Market
Niche Market
Segmented
Diversified
Multi-sided Platform
Cost Structure
What are the most important costs inherent in our business model?
Which Key Resources are most expensive?
Which Key Activities are most expensive?
IS YOUR BUSINESS MORE:
Cost Driven (leanest cost structure, low price value proposition, maximum automation, extensive outsourcing)
Value Driven (focused on value creation, premium value proposition)
SAMPLE CHARACTERISTICS:
Fixed Costs (salaries, rents, utilities)
Variable costs
Economies of scale
Economies of scope
Revenue Streams
For what value are our customers really willing to pay?
For what do they currently pay?
How are they currently paying?
How would they prefer to pay?
How much does each Revenue Stream contribute to overall revenues?
TYPES:
Asset sale
Usage fee
Subscription Fees
Lending/Renting/Leasing
Licensing
Brokerage fees
Advertising
FIXED PRICING
List Price
Product feature dependent
Customer segment dependent
Volume dependent
DYNAMIC PRICING
Negotiation(bargaining)
Yield Management
Real-time-Market
This work is licensed under the Creative Commons Attribution-Share Alike 3.0 Unported License.
To view a copy of this license, visit http://creativecommons.org/licenses/by-sa/3.0/
or send a letter to Creative Commons, 171 Second Street, Suite 300, San Francisco, California, 94105, USA.

Fig. 5.10 The Business Model Canvas. (Courtesy of businessmodelgeneration.com)

5.6   ASSIGNMENTS

Assignment 1

1. Choose a well-known brand, research the brand and make a Business Model Canvas for this company. Use Fig. 5.10 to quickly create your own canvas.
2. What chances for resource-driven innovation do you see for this company?

5.7   RECOMMENDED READING

One of the challenges faced in innovation is the status quo that forms an obstruction to imagination. Asking questions such as 'What if…' can be of help when thinking outside of the box:

- Osterwalder, A. and Pigneur, Y. (2010) *Business Model Generation: A Handbook for Visionaries, Game Changers, and Challengers*. Wiley, Hoboken, New Jersey.

By adapting a more open business model, economic value arises as a result of innovation, without fearing loss of intellectual property:

- Chesbrough, H. (2006) *Open Business Models*. Harvard Business Press, Boston, Massachusetts.

Part II

Imagineering – Who, What and How

In the first part of this book we addressed the question of how companies function in an increasingly complex economy, and which management issues are a result of this. We further explained that the way to ensure survival in this complex economy in the long term is the creation of meaning via the emotional experiences of users. The Imagineer is a professional who can design and direct meaning and experience.

In this part of the book we will explain the theory behind the profession of Imagineering. We describe how he works, and which design methodology he uses in order to achieve meaningful transformation when addressing management issues. The three chapters in this part are:

6. How Do You Become an Imagineer?
7. The Imagineer's Work Process
8. The Imagineer's Design Methodology

chapter 6

How Do You Become an Imagineer?

Gabriëlle Kuiper

When we get close to the circus we can already hear the music getting louder. The circus band is playing. We see the red carpet bordered by little white fences, a candy floss vendor and polished brass ornaments, while bellboys dressed in red suits with gold ribbons, are welcoming the guests. We see German cakes, popcorn, decorative lights, ladies wearing make-up, circus artists and a marching band playing catchy tunes. The transition has started as 'home' slowly disappears into the background, or sometimes even is forgotten. The show starts; even the introductory part of the show provides us with different experiences that are all related to, and part of, the whole show. Step by step, as if they are building blocks, the experience takes shape. We immediately identify ourselves with, and even emotionally connect to, the underdog, the floor sweeper in the limelight of the circus floor. The stage sweeper, who is at the bottom of the so-called circus hierarchy, the person who is able to shine in the limelight once, simply because of the fact that the actual performer didn't show up. The dramatic character of the stage sweeper becomes the red line throughout tonight's show. The show is fast-paced, each and every performance transitions into the next performance, none of which lasts longer than 10 minutes. Each performance contains a short story about love, hope, passion and strength. Enchantment, awe, impressions, enjoyment, laughs and being on the edge of your chair are all part of the experience.

Circus Roncalli is a phenomenon that I should never have missed out on in my search for Imagineering. During an interview with the gurus of experience creation, Arjan van

(Continued)

> **Continued.**
>
> Dijk and Constant Geerling, I was privileged enough that one of them made me aware of the fact that this renowned, well-established circus was visiting our country. It is renowned because of the fact that it is a real circus. I was quite negative in my thinking beforehand. I believed it wouldn't be as good as people said it was. Just the same way when you get disappointed when you watch a movie based on a book you've read. However, Circus Roncalli was really different: as a matter of fact, THE place to get inspiration as an Imagineer. Circus Director Berhard Paul is the passionate owner of the largest collection of circus posters, costumes and travels all over the world, meanwhile using numerous eye-catching train carriages. He clearly understands how to create the dream circus experience.

In this chapter we will have a closer look at who the Imagineer is. First we will explain the position of the Imagineer in relation to his colleagues and his team. We will also take a look at his role and his tasks in the execution of his assignment. After that we will explore his artistic qualities and his vocabulary. We elaborate on which skills he needs to have or develop in order to fulfil his mission and to create his added value.

There are different kinds of Imagineers, each possessing their own set of specific characteristics, skills and talents. It is these specific characteristics, skills and talents that, when combined, form the specific artistic signature of an Imagineer.

By the end of this chapter you will have a better understanding of:

- the added value of an Imagineer;
- the position of an Imagineer;
- the role and tasks of an Imagineer; and
- Imagineering-related vocabulary and the signature of an Imagineer.

6.1 WORKING ENVIRONMENT

In this book, we focus on reframing and solving management issues by focusing on the experience perspective. This approach is relevant as it enables the Imagineer to create economic and social value in the form of loyalty, raised selling prices, user value, etc. Most of the time, management issues for which the input of an Imagineer is required relate to the fields of branding, marketing, human resources management (HRM) or sales.

In order to solve such management issues, the Imagineer will need to encounter the stakeholders involved. As the output of Imagineers is focused on the experience of involved stakeholders he will need to understand their perspective on the issue at hand. The Imagineer designs:

- the format or shape of a service and/or product;
- the introductory processes; and
- development of follower groups.

In relation to HRM and strategies, an Imagineer is able to orchestrate the internal and external experience world and culture of an organization, meanwhile striving for the following goals:

- to reach a higher level of efficiency and productivity;
- to create better loyalty, which should result in a lower turnover of staff; and
- to attract new potential employees.

These three goals lead to lower HRM costs, which represents their economic value.

6.1.1 Relevance of an Imagineer in Relation to Management Issues

Many management issues require a thorough understanding of human behaviour. Some issues are related to individuals (consumers, employees), some are related to groups of people (departments within a company, competition between companies). They can be related to interaction between people (cooperation, conflict and communication) or relations between groups of people. As Imagineers specialize in connecting people to concepts (brands) or through concepts (e.g. events), the management issues Imagineers focus on can be found at any strategic, tactical or operational level within an organization. Examples of such management issues, for which the Imagineer could be useful, are:

- strategy development;
- human resources management;
- branding, marketing and communication;
- research & development; and
- process management.

Let's have a closer look at each example separately in order to get a better understanding of these issues:

Strategy development

- **Branding and organization:**
  - Leadership style
  - Developing a vision, identity and core values
  - Organization and management style (level of self-steering)
  - Trend watching and market development, e.g. sustainability, transparency, responsible, socially sustainable entrepreneurship
- **Organizational competency development**, namely:
  - Expansion of portfolio and organizational development
  - Managing core competences
  - Developing new business models

HRM and people management

- **Internal branding** (anchoring identity, vision and core values in the organization), for example:
  - Culture change (for instance with a merger/takeover)
  - Recruitment and selection of new employees

- ○ Motivation of workforce (commitment to the mission and vision of the company)
- ○ Team building and teamwork processes
- **Competency management**, namely:
  - ○ Diversity in human resources
  - ○ Retention of staff (employee loyalty)
  - ○ Development of knowledge within the organization (knowledge and skills exchange)

Branding, marketing and communication

- **Brand management**, for instance:
  - ○ Brand identity construction
  - ○ Brand development
  - ○ Loyalty programmes
  - ○ Implementation of co-branding
  - ○ Service design: presentation in shops, workplace concepts, online services, etc.
- **Marketing and communication**, for example:
  - ○ Communication of brand identity and brand values
  - ○ Implementation of experience as part of customer satisfaction, improvement management and quality management
  - ○ Product launches
  - ○ Implementation of experiences as a sales tool
  - ○ Developing follow groups and tribes

Research & development, namely:

- Development of experiences connected to new and/or already existing products and services
- Applying different forms of co-creation to research new business models, crowd sourcing, crowd funding and/or prosuming

Process management, for instance:

- Synchronizing business processes with vision and brand values
- Synchronizing operational processes with vision and brand values

6.1.2   General Task of the Imagineer

The Imagineer's mission is to create meaningful concepts with the goal of emerging groups of (positively) motivated followers. These groups are connected and committed to each other and/or the concept, for a longer period of time. Obviously the chosen concept should be related to the management issue at hand. These could be concepts related to organizational change, a brand or a (new) service.

Imagineers try to create an emotional connection between individuals and the concept or through the concept which leads these individuals to involve other relevant people from their social network. The concept and the physical environment it is created in can be designed in such a way that it steers the behaviour of individuals and groups, which enables achievement of predefined goals and strategies.

This design and the execution of the design by the Imagineer generates economic value, because it leads individuals to involve more and more or their social network, spreading it like wildfire (e.g. viral movie clips that are shared online), at the same time the behaviour of the people involved is subconsciously steered in a certain direction. As a result the (groups of) individuals involved are connected to each other and the concept for longer.

6.2 POSITION

An Imagineer can hold different positions that enable him to create added value. It is possible for him to be a member of the organization, which enables him to continuously be occupied with the design of a concept over a longer period of time, as is the case with Disney Imagineers, for example. In other cases he will be employed externally for a limited period of time (as a consultant) with the purpose of designing solutions for predetermined management issues that have been identified and named by the client organization. In such a case it is possible for an Imagineer to, for instance, specifically consult a marketing or HRM department.

6.2.1 Visionary Entrepreneur

As an entrepreneur the Imagineer himself is responsible for identifying his goals and the obstacles he needs to take care of – this allows him to be in charge of the overall and final decisions. To illustrate this, one could think of the Imagineer as the owner or founder of the organization he designs for. In such cases he manifests himself as a visionary entrepreneur. Some famous examples spring to mind, such as Steve Jobs at Apple, or Ben Cohen and Jerry Greenfeld of Ben & Jerry's. They knew how to tie a group of different experts together, which led to the creation of successful, innovative and meaningful products or experience worlds.

When the Imagineer himself functions as the core of the organization, he will continuously influence and motivate others by having them look through his lens in terms of his vision and imagination. This way the organization will be inspired to further think, design and develop through this lens. Imagineering becomes an effective and consistent tool. It is most effective when the desired imagination seeps through all layers, and expression of the organization through this lens.

6.2.2 Internal Imagineers

The Imagineer can also be part of an Imagineering team or department. He then contributes his expertise to a team of other experts. The team could, for instance, consist of a marketer, an engineer and a graphic designer, who as a team will start the Imagineering process. By combining expertise, views and perspectives, synergy and space for innovation are created.

Fig. 6.1 Tributes to Steve Jobs after he passed away. (Courtesy of Mr Muddy Suitman.)

Disney's Imagineering Team

Disney is in need of a special department, responsible for the creation of experience worlds. In Disney's case, it is possible that an Imagineering team would consist of more than 20 Imagineers:

Research & development
Concept designer
Creative development
Animator
Show animation and programming systems
Show writer
Scope writer
Graphic design
Special effects designer
Concept integration
Landscape design/architecture
Creative systems analyst

(Continued)

> **Continued.**
>
> Show lighting
> Imaging and effects
> Architecture and engineering
> Construction manager
> Theatrical design and production
> Ride mechanical engineering

An Imagineering team works internally within an organization for which they design and develop. They could be in a separate department, which is necessary in some cases, as for example in the Disney Company. On the other hand, the team members can also be part of the marketing or strategy department. In this case, different issues are addressed by different people from within the organization. In some cases external expertise can be added to the team.

Examples of situations in which a team is composed to address specific issues are:

- Co-creation with the purpose of designing new business models.
- The communication department, in close cooperation with different representatives from the company, designs a concept for a staff party.

Such constructions require a central visionary person with leadership qualities, who can steer the process, translate the goals, and who is capable of decision making. Moreover, this visionary person is also responsible for decisions in terms of who will participate in the design process and why. In this case the Imagineer functions more or less as an art director.

6.2.3 External Imagineers

An Imagineer can also be an external advisor or coach. In such cases, the Imagineer receives an assignment from an organization that is struggling with a certain problem or goal.

The client can be an entire organization, but can also be a department within an organization, depending on the type and importance of the management issue. Often, the Imagineer is hired by a marketing, strategy or HRM department. The external Imagineer investigates and evaluates existing products or processes. In his role as an external coach, he will further implement this information in an advisory report. Below are some examples of assignments by external clients:

- an event organizer has to develop an event that has to contribute to culture change in an organization;
- to design an exhibition for a museum;

- to design a shopping experience;
- to design and develop contact moments and meetings between staff and visiting customers from a service-design perspective.

Naturally, an Imagineer can be used strategically as the driving force behind the innovation process of designing a new business model. It becomes easier to bring the application of experience to a strategic level when an Imagineer is connected to a specific client for a number of years.

To demonstrate, it enables the Imagineer to develop sequenced experience moments for his target audience (subjects) that will cause and perpetuate behavioural change in the target group.

An external Imagineer quite often works within and as part of the Imagineering team himself. One could think of a department for concept development of an advertising agency, a design company such as IDEO or an engineering company. In certain strategic phases Imagineering teams are completed by members of the intended audience and/or members of the leadership team of the commissioning company.

The Imagineer could hold the following positions:

- visionary entrepreneur (intern);
- member of an Imagineering team (internal); or
- advisor and coach (external).

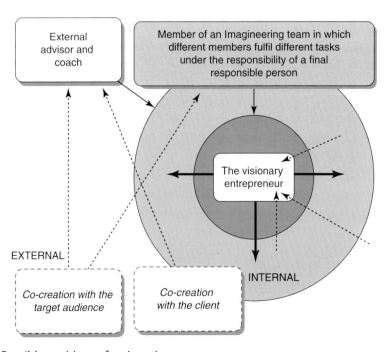

Fig. 6.2 Possible positions of an Imagineer.

6.3   ROLE AND TASKS

One role

Six tasks

The Imagineer is the instigator of the creative process. He composes an experience in which the design and the concrete execution of the design match the predetermined goals and user enjoyment. He studies the expected effect of the design on the target audience, both on a micro and a macro level. On a micro level he steers individual stimuli such as colours, images, scents, etc. On a macro level he distils both what kind of effect a detail might have on the created experience as a whole, and on the emotional experience of the individual, but above all, the meaning the individual attributes to the experience in the long run.

As a result, six specific tasks can be distinguished, namely:

1. Leader and final decision maker.
2. Translator and connector.
3. Motivator.
4. Researcher.
5. Designer.
6. Director.

We will further elaborate on these tasks in the next sections.

6.3.1   Leader and Final Decision Maker

The Imagineer leads the creative process in terms of content of the assignment. He steers where necessary, to make sure that the deadlines for the final design are met, while at same time keeping an eye on the predetermined specifications and goals. At certain important stages of the process he will make the necessary decisions in terms of content. Examples of such decisions are:

*   What is the goal of the creation process?
*   Which research methods will be used?
*   What final conclusion can we draw from the analyses of the collected data?
*   Which design will be presented to the client?
*   Which details of the design will generate a successful effect on the participants, and therefore have a priority?

The Imagineer is the final decision maker; however, during the Imagineering process, the Imagineering team will give suggestions and advice. It depends on the leadership style of the Imagineer as to how he will include the team in making decisions. In the end the team will have to agree to the decisions that have been made. This is important to keep up motivation to continue the project.

Leading a team requires specific knowledge and experience. A good leader possesses certain skills. Stephen Covey (2004) concludes that there are seven essential qualities for effective leadership:

1. Proactivity: A good leader soul searches and keeps in touch with his environment and is therefore well informed about what goes on around him and can anticipate accordingly.

2. Clear goals: When a leader has a clear vision about the goal that needs to be achieved, this will enable the team to follow this vision.

3. Set priorities: He tries to achieve the goal by effectively and efficiently using time, people and resources in the correct proportions.

4. Create win–win situations: When there is a common goal, the leader should enable participants to feel that their participation is valuable, while at the same time it adds something valuable.

5. Seek first to understand, then to be understood: Positive relations develop when there is good communication between all stakeholders. Communication, specifically between the team and the client, is a critical success factor in guaranteeing the final result through engagement (the wish that something will be successful) and support for the development of a concept.

6. Synergy: In order to be innovative and successful, synergy is necessary between people and materials, as well as synergy amongst all participants.

7. Reflection and development: The leader carefully considers the experiences and learning processes of this team, and this enables him to stimulate the learning process of the team and provides an opportunity for team members to further develop professionally.

Leadership styles

Quinn and Rohrbaugh developed the so-called 'organizational cultural assessment instrument' in 1983, by describing different leadership styles. Quinn states that an effective leader can play more than one role, and even that opposing styles can be integrated. This is what Quinn refers to as **behavioural complexity** (Quinn, 1997). Also an Imagineer needs to apply different leadership styles. An Imagineering process consists of different aspects and parts. One could think of creation and design, which requires different expertise from different team members within the Imagineering team. However when, for example, during the construction and execution phase things do not go according to plan, this might require a different style of leadership to get everything back on track.

The focus of the innovator and entrepreneurial styles is primarily on adaptation and responsiveness of the team. This leadership style is quite important during the first phase of the Imagineering process.

- **Innovator:** Focus is on innovation and creation.
- **Entrepreneur:** Focus is on external relations and effective negotiations with the client.

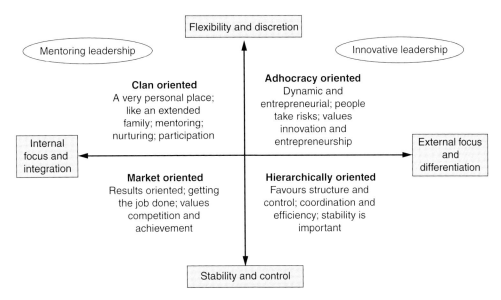

Fig. 6.3 OCAI model (adapted from Quinn and Rohrbaugh, 1983).

The top left quadrant in Figure 6.3 shows the roles of mentor and facilitator. This leadership style requires engagement and motivation of the team in order to create a successful design. This particular leadership style will be applied during the second phase of the process.

- **Mentor:** Focus on people development, looking after people and preparedness to help.
- **Facilitator:** Focus is primarily on improvement of cooperation and teamwork; solving possible conflicts.

The remaining leadership styles are mainly applied by the producer or project manager, who further shapes the design. The Imagineer will take on a leadership position in terms of content and makes decisions accordingly. The producer needs to meet the expectations of the Imagineer, with regard to content and artistic vision, whenever possible within the predefined conditions in terms of budget, manpower and time.

6.3.2 Translator and Connector

The Imagineer starts by translating the management issue of the client. In some cases he is faced with a problem for which he wants to seek a solution, without a formal assignment of a client.

He translates content goals to working principles. He then continues by connecting all the different views, ideas, perceptions and desires of the team members and the client to his own overall vision.

Sustainable relationship with the problem and the client

A critical success factor in a successful design for a client is the sustainable relationship of the Imagineer with the problem. The Imagineer needs to understand the language, desires,

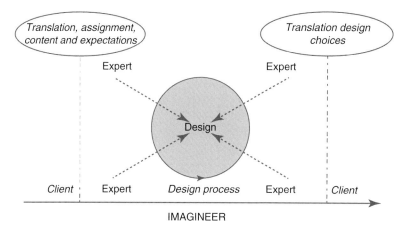

Fig. 6.4 Translator and connector.

expectations, perceptions and assumptions of the client. This enables him to translate the expectations correctly and adjust the design accordingly. This sustainable relationship works two ways, because the client who is engaged in such a sustainable relationship gains more insights into how and in what way the expectations can be realized.

6.3.3 Motivator

During the process of the team of experts, the Imagineer is the driving force in keeping everybody engaged and connected to the design. The team can vary, and sometimes certain experts will only temporarily join the team, but each team member has to be 100% committed. This is only possible when all participants believe in a positive end result, as well as the purpose of their own contributions. The task of the Imagineer is to monitor motivation. It is his goal to continuously keep motivation at the highest possible level. The higher the motivation, the higher the chances of an excellent end product.

Keeping up motivation

The Imagineer starts by generating a clear vision about the process and the end product in order to prevent any obstacles and insecurities within the team. The leadership style he adopts to do this is the role of 'mentor' and 'stimulator'. He creates a safe environment, in which people aren't afraid to share knowledge, cooperate and share feedback. A creative team needs a safe environment in order to excel.

The Imagineer maintains contact between the internal and external client, and keeps track of the client's desires, conditions and expectations. This is necessary because the client also needs to stay motivated. The Imagineer keeps the client motivated by keeping him engaged from the first moment in the design process. This could be done by engaging the client in co-creation (strong engagement), or by just telling him about a future design and starting a dialogue (less engagement). Client feedback is an essential part of research in order to further improve the design.

6.3.4 Researcher

Research is an important part of Imagineering. The Imagineer is very much aware of this. An important task of the Imagineer is to conduct research and experiments and to analyse the results of the data collection. He will come up with innovative research to gain both irrelevant and relevant knowledge to gain a better insight into consumer behaviour. He stimulates research by the team, and uses the outcome of this research to support his choices when in dialogue with the client.

> Thomas Edison, the designer of the electric lamp, experimented. In his opinion, user enjoyment was key, and with this in mind he developed and designed his inventions together with a team of talented thinkers, improvisers and experimenters – a process of many trials and errors. The same way we should understand Edison's famous quote; 'Genius is 1 per cent inspiration and 99 per cent perspiration' (Brown, 2008, p. 1).

6.3.5 Designer

The Imagineer is the ultimate designer. The first elements of the overall design (of an event for example) might be a team effort, but he will have the final say in the end design, and, when necessary, will adapt elements. This is part of quality control: he checks whether the final design still meets the predefined goals. In this way, the final product has his specific signature, namely, the way he perceives the world. Each and every Imagineer delivers a different kind of atmosphere in the experience worlds; they are an extension of his own experience world. Similar to, for instance, movie and theatre directors, Imagineers also try to leave their signature mark on the experiences they create.

6.3.6 Director and Producer

During production and execution of the design, the Imagineer works in his capacity of director. He steers the team and the process, he makes decisions and improves the design, possibly in consultation with the team.

Responsibility for adaptations and choices

When moving from abstract (the idea on paper) to the concrete execution of the project, adaptations are often necessary during the process. This is due to the fact that in reality, sometimes things don't turn out the way we had anticipated. Experienced event directors know that quite often they develop a concept that at execution can only be 80% realized. This is due to restrictions in terms of time, money, materials and manpower, etc. The design then has to be adapted, which means that choices have to be made. The task of the Imagineer is to keep the concept alive by sticking to the original core idea and goals.

Should the occasion arise that it is impossible to execute a certain part of the design, the Imagineer will contribute by finding solutions without making too many concessions, such that the effects will still be same.

Steering

When the Imagineer designs a live performance or a service, he will steer the performance continuously on location in the same way a theatre director directs a play. This is especially the case when the live performance is staged – for example a one-off event – when the Imagineer, in his role of director, needs to make many concessions due to time and budgetary restrictions. Sometimes during long-term productions or recurring events design, items can be evaluated and adapted without changing the backbone of the original design.

Arjan van Dijk (the renowned event organizer mentioned at the start of this chapter) decided at the last minute to have his staff buy horse blankets for an important management meeting, because the outdoor location he had arranged for the meeting turned out to be a lot colder than he had anticipated. The participants in the event thought that the (late) timing of handing out blankets was part of the event, and were pleasantly surprised. Because of the timing, the experience had a heightened emotional impact on the participants in comparison to an experience where the blankets would have been handed out in advance.

6.4   THE IMAGINEER'S VOCABULARY

The vocabulary concept is used in the art scene. It refers to the expressive means (song, dance, image, etc.) an artist has mastered, and determines to a large extent the signature of his art. In a similar way, the Imagineer also has his own vocabulary and signature, which he uses to create meaningful experiences. The vocabulary of the Imagineer is built on six traits or five trades. By applying his own talents, knowledge, experience, memories, skills, experiments, fantasy and imagination while preparing the concept and design, this unique combination of input will, in the end, generate a clearly recognizable signature of the Imagineer. Besides mastering a number of these trades, Imagineers also possess a particular combination of characteristics. We will refer to these as the 'six traits of an Imagineer'. Using the traits and trades, the Imagineer creates his own typical way of conveying his designs to others. These trades and traits will be discussed in the following sections.

6.4.1   Six Traits

Being an Imagineer requires a certain attitude towards the assignment and work that needs to be done. You can only be innovative while creating experiences if you are open-minded and a free thinker. We distinguish six traits any Imagineer should possess in order to enable him to execute his mission with high quality.

1. Entrepreneurship.
2. Ability to innovate.
3. Emotional intelligence.
4. Curiosity.
5. Creative urge.
6. Chemistry and synergy.

Entrepreneurship

Economist Joseph Schumpeter defined an entrepreneur (during the first half of the 20th century) as 'a person who is prepared and able to transform a new idea or invention into a successful innovation'. Entrepreneurship means that you are able to create value by applying creativity, vigour and being prepared to take risks.

Considering the fact that an Imagineer creates added value by creating innovations, Imagineers need to think and act like entrepreneurs. The entrepreneur within the Imagineer makes sure that he:

- focuses outwards and is interested in the world around him;
- recognizes opportunities and has an intuition for opportunities; and
- has the guts to walk on a path less travelled and is able to transform his ideas into concrete actions and products.

Entrepreneurship doesn't work without creativity, innovation and risk taking, but entrepreneurship also requires the ability to plan and manage projects. Entrepreneurship also entails realistic optimism: a strong belief in the design (and the execution) and the ability to anticipate possible risks and assess those in advance (Mulder and Ten Cate, 2006).

Relevant aspects of entrepreneurship for an Imagineer are:

- **Vision:** the Imagineer needs to be able to develop a vision on how to reach his goals.
- **Innovation and renewal:** Imagineers use their vision to innovate and renew concepts, products, markets, etc.
- **Value creation:** Imagineers understand what creates value for his clients and end-user.
- **Enterprising:** Taking risks by offering new perspectives and taking responsibility for them.
- **Decision making:** the Imagineer's vision and enterprising qualities make him a decision maker.
- **Perseverance:** Imagineers need dedication and perseverance.
- **Leadership:** For his team, the Imagineering process and himself as Imagineer.
- **Performance focused and decisive:** He needs to be able to reflect and improve on performance.
- **Independent:** Imagineers need autonomy and self-responsibility to execute Imagineering projects and to develop themselves.

Innovative ability

An invention is usually the result of a coincidence, which is at the same time the difference between invention and innovation. An innovation is a planned development or application of an existing idea and design (Pijnappels, 2009). The Imagineer should on the one hand be able to generate ideas using his creativity and on the other hand be able to create economic value by applying the ideas in those situations where they create a competitive advantage. Innovation is, therefore, a conscious executed renewal/innovation with a focus on a predefined advantage (Pijnappels, 2009). This means that the advantage has been predefined in terms of what kind of value it should add.

An Imagineer must believe in his own ability and be self-confident. If he lacks these, he won't be able to work autonomously, nor break existing conventions. As innovator he understands the value of unexpected events, and anticipates accordingly. He is someone who understands that irrationality sometimes has a bigger impact than rationality (Pijnappels, 2009). The Imagineer is creative in terms of innovating products, services, processes and organization. He looks after achievable innovation, which inspires and motivates, connects and adds value to groups of people, which might result in an emerging group of followers.

An innovator (De Jong and Harkema, 2007; Pijnappels, 2009):

- uses his left brain hemisphere (analytic) and right brain hemisphere (imagination);
- is persuasive and is confident in his beliefs;
- understands the business model, and recognizes the economic value of possible innovations;
- is confident about himself;
- is autonomous and headstrong;
- is an extrovert;
- has the capacity to interpret and analyse complex patterns and the connections between the elements the pattern is built on;
- has a problem-solving attitude;
- is able to apply creative techniques and generate original ideas;
- follows the latest developments and trends;
- recognizes innovation opportunities;
- has analytical abilities; and
- knows how to take advantage of opportunities.

Emotional intelligence

Emotion is a source of inspiration for the Imagineer. To tap from this source, a certain emotional intelligence (EQ) is required. People who have a high EQ, according to Howard Gardner (1999), usually possess 'both interpersonal and intrapersonal intelligence'. Interpersonal intelligence means they can read other people's intentions and moods, and work closely in groups. Intrapersonal means they understand their own feelings and use that insight to steer their behaviour.

People with a high EQ can be recognized by the following characteristics:

- **Know thyself:** You are aware of who you are, your feelings, strong and weak point, pitfalls, your impact on other people and so on.
- **Optimistic:** You think positively about your own abilities and don't get easily taken aback
- **Perseverance:** You stay intrinsically motivated to work on something that will only be realized in the long run.
- **Social abilities:** You naturally get along with people you are familiar with, as well as strangers.
- **Empathic abilities:** You have the ability to be empathetic to other peoples' feelings and certain events.

Empathic ability is important. This is the ability to feel empathy with other people and have an intuition for intentions. Empathy is founded in correctly 'reading' or understanding verbal and non-verbal communication (as in body language or symbols) of other people. This means that the Imagineer is sensitive to other people's moods, feelings and needs. We therefore refer to this as sensitivity and empathy. Empathy requires a high level of knowing thyself – an Imagineer needs to particularly recognize his own emotions, and understand what triggers these emotions in order to recognize them in other people. A lack of empathy does not necessarily mean that someone doesn't try to empathize with the other; it simply means that he or she doesn't exactly feel or understand the emotions of the other and consequently assumes that the other person experiences similar emotions as he does. This is what is usually referred to as **projection** rather than empathy.

In an interview to prepare this book concept developer Kile Ozier (who has previously organized the NFL Super Bowl, amongst other events) defined five critical success factors of an experience with high concept and high touch.

- **Exploration of assumption:** Explore your own assumptions about the design and target audience, as well as the expectations and assumptions of the target group itself. The Imagineer needs his empathic ability tool to investigate this.
- **Liberation of preconception:** Liberate the target audience from assumptions and expectations.
- **Comfortable disorientation:** Create a feeling of safe disorientation with the target audience.
- **Successive revelation:** Purposely reveal layers in a sequence, one by one and not all in one go.
- **Subliminal engagement:** Engage in a subliminal relationship with the target audience. Ozier means that the participants, for whom the experience is created, will feel subconsciously connected to the experience on an emotional level. The Imagineer can only achieve this by understanding the emotions of this target group.

The Imagineer tries to empathize with his target audience and by doing this, he really needs to take Kile Ozier's first two points to heart: he needs to investigate his own assumptions and prejudices about his subjects and compare this to his own emotions and the anticipated emotions of his subjects, for whom he will design the experience against his own emotions, the anticipated emotions and emotional needs of his subjects. He does not project his own emotions (in terms of what he would enjoy or find annoying) on his subjects, but actively empathizes with this group of subjects.

Curiosity

Curiosity is important in overcoming existing prejudices. However, it only works when sincere interest without expectations and assumptions is shown. As a consequence, you can become titillated, inspired or amazed by the world around you.

By actively observing the world around you, an Imagineer continuously collects data, images, symbols, stories and situations. This input in the brain of an ever growing collection of images, stories, situations and emotions that come with these, can be compared to filling a backpack. The backpack contains an ample supply of ideas and inspiration, which you can tap into for any amazing or inspiring design.

Most of his professional life, an Imagineer will consciously and subconsciously collect data to further complement, adapt and maintain his data collection in the brain. This is not only done through observations, but also by starting conversations with strangers or by consciously choosing to visit places he would normally not go. It is important to actually learn to see things, instead of just looking at things. This can be done by learning to see the details of a

Fig. 6.5 Backpack. (Courtesy of brainware3000.)

design (all the different parts of a bicycle, for example the broken seat, the rusty handlebars, the tyres, etc., instead of the bicycle as a whole), or by consciously studying the historic and/ or anthropological background of the item or event.

Another way to fill your backpack is by combing the streets, while giving everything you see your thorough attention: the bicycle stand, headlines, magazines, accessories people wear while sitting on a terrace, body language of people who are communicating with each other. You could contemplate what they might be thinking at any given moment. Another way of collecting data for your backpack is by participating in culture and art. A visit to a theatre or a museum usually supplies you with a lot of inspiration and visuals. Art uses symbols to convey ideas and present you with information. Some museums and theatres try to create an atmosphere around a piece of art or play that stimulates the emotions linked to these (see realms of experience, Chapter 4). In a museum you can see how experiences are created and how they can influence people's behaviour and the ways they experience the museum. During concerts you can observe how people react during a shared experience and how this sharing aspect is constructed by the act on stage (the fan on stage, the ballad with all the lighters being lit in the audience). Films and books tell stories and give insights into life in general. Pictures and images can be collected from magazines or television.

Additionally, the backpack can be filled by actively listening instead of merely hearing. This means that one should ask questions, start conversations with strangers and listen to what motivates them. Continue to ask questions when people start talking about a certain topic. Ask others for their input in terms of interesting places to visit and their most memorable experiences.

Playfulness

Play is an integral part of curiosity. It enables the Imagineer to enter the experience worlds of children. By reading a children's book, or by watching a movie, he can escape to, and enter, the fantasy world of children. Play can be seen as some kind of test situation: you can learn how to value emotion and discover what triggers emotion. According to IDEO owner Tim Brown, play requires a social script that is reality-based. This way, it serves as an inspiration for a designer, whereby possible effects of certain actions, which could manifest in reality, are tested.

The Imagineer is open to new information and experiences. He is sincerely interested in people and situations he encounters. He is non-judgemental and lets the experience take over. This experience will be added on to the ones already existing in the backpack.

New things require energy, and the formation of new neurological pathways in the brain requires energy, but by continuously filling the backpack, the brain will automatically start to create new pathways. Despite the fact that this is an exciting and amazing process, you are additionally rewarded with new exciting images as a result of unexpected combinations and connections, which are subconsciously made in the brain.

> **Street-combing**
>
> Many marketers remain locked up between the four walls of their offices, whereas most brilliant ideas can be found in the street. This way they miss out on great opportunities. Richard Stomp goes street-combing once a week. He takes snapshots of anything he finds interesting and publishes one of his findings on a daily basis, which serves as an inspiration for new ideas. (Source: www.straatjutten.nl)

Creation

The continuous urge to create, build, make, design, prototype and execute is what inspires the Imagineer in his work. He is curious and likes to investigate and is outward-focused. He is thorough in his designs and thoughts and follows this through to the final design. The whole process starts in his imagination and becomes clearer every step of the way in terms of how the final product should feel, and what it looks like. This provides him with new energy, the urge and enthusiasm to experiment and test the environment, to start a dialogue, and to continuously adapt and change the ideas in his mind.

The Imagineer creates continuously, even when there isn't a concrete assignment or goal that needs to be achieved. It is part of who he is: continuous research, experiment, test, play and scout new frontiers. He creates stories via storytelling and by starting dialogues, or by writing. He creates situations by saying certain things or by doing certain things to evoke a certain response. He is able to draw conclusions based on the response and learn from it. He creates images by drawing or making pictures. He creates images by daydreaming and fantasizing.

In case there is a specific assignment, slowly but surely the Imagineering process starts with the first steps of a design. These first stages are the search for the story behind the design, why this particular design and the emotional value of the design. The design should express a certain emotional value so as to attract people, the same way magpies are attracted to shiny objects. The Imagineer has to empathize how this design could meet people's emotional and social needs; how interaction and play can invoke people to be open to a new experience and take this new experience in. Additionally, how all these separate items and elements become one inspiring positive whole.

Chemistry and synergy

The Imagineer operates as a chemist, who combines separate elements and blends them into something new. This chemical reaction causes synergy and added value with meaning. These separate elements could be, for example:

- the people the design aims to reach or connect;
- the instruments he has at his disposal to create an experience such as visuals, sound, light, decor, story, location and staff; or
- the transformation that he wants to achieve with the created experiences.

The correct combination and order of these elements intensifies the effect in comparison to each individual element added on to each other. Kile Ozier calls it 'Successive Revelation', 'Subliminal Engagement' and 'Comfortable Disorientation' (Section 6.4.1, Emotional intelligence).

Each element is revealed to the participants of the experience in a strategic way, based on innate behavioural patterns at the right moment, in a thought-out chronological order, with the correct time to generate the maximum effect. Moment after moment, the audience will be captured. The audience is given the space to identify with the experience, make it their own experience and give meaning to it. To understand and steer this has to be one of the most powerful skills of an Imagineer.

6.4.2 Five Trades

The work of an Imagineer starts with ideas and intangible imagination. However, even at this stage, he should be able to convey these ideas and imagination to others. Even before the design has been produced, making it tangible, he must be able to convince others of the future success of his concept. His audience has to believe in the concept in order to further invest time and/or money to actually produce it. They must be able to imagine the product, react to it and give feedback, which enables the Imagineer to further improve the design. To convince others of the Imagineer's ideas requires different trades, each applied in different ways.

An Imagineer should master at least one of the following trades. He is a(n):

- orator (word);
- writer (letter);
- illustrator (image);
- conductor (sound and music);
- game designer (game/play).

The preacher: the power of charisma

Most Imagineers are **strong orators** by nature. They dare to stand up for themselves in terms of their vision and will convey this message, whereby they won't shun critical feedback or any other possible feedback which might follow. They understand that feedback will enable them to improve the design, and that specific critical feedback will lift the design to higher levels. The Imagineer-preacher is able to convey his imagination and visions via the power of speech. As a preacher he understands how to capture his audience. With his powerful and appropriate body language, he knows how to engage and capture the audience. His empathic abilities help him to find the correct intonation, format and register in order to engage the audience in the story.

Even though we believe that preachers possess a somehow innate skill of oration, this skill needs further development and one has to learn how to use this skill effectively. People who aren't that talented by nature will find that learning this skill is quite challenging – they will most probably keep finding it difficult to convey any concept convincingly by means of oration and appropriate body language that will capture the audience. However, this does not necessarily

Fig. 6.6 President Obama is known for his historic speeches. (Courtesy of Becky F./Flickr.)

mean that they aren't able to convey their imagination to others. As a matter of fact, there is a strong chance that they will be able to convey their ideas via one of the other trades.

Once the Imagineer starts talking about a future design, this usually results in a dialogue. The dialogue can be used to improve the design, a form of **co-creation** as Prahalad and Ramaswamy (2004) describe it. The Imagineer-preacher possesses the skill of capturing the audience and pulling them into the story, even in terms of main storylines and the smallest details. There is room for dialogue at the appropriate/right time. When all goes well, the audience will be convinced fairly quickly of the Imagineer's profound knowledge and the possible effects of his concepts. Additionally, the Imagineer will use the feedback of the audience for further research: How does the audience react? What does this tell the Imagineer in terms of his own expectations? Should it be adapted on nuances?

The preacher also takes his audience into consideration – who are his audience? Feedback from an investor is rather different from feedback by someone from the future target audience. The Imagineer-preacher is probably a charismatic leader, who motivates and keeps people engaged by speaking to them.

The writer: writing as a medium

Another way of conveying the Imagineer's thoughts, imagination and experience worlds in a convincing manner is by writing a story that captures the reader and enables him to create

Fig. 6.7 J.R.R. Tolkien was able to create the Lord of the Rings 'Middle Earth' in words, thus capturing the minds of millions of his readers.

his own vision of what the Imagineer intended. The advantage of this trade is the fact that the Imagineer does not necessarily have to be personally present in order to convey the images and convince people of a future successful design.

A reliable, tested technique is writing a scenario for the user's experience, or for the designed experience of the participant. Step by step, he captures the reader's attention by engaging the reader, while having him experience different situations and emotions that accompany these situations. Additionally, this gives the reader a clear picture of the intentions of the Imagineer. A description of the experience by the Imagineer also serves as a research method in order to predict the emotional effect of the created situation on the participant.

The trade of storytelling helps the Imagineer, while he is developing a concept, to add a story element in order to make his concepts stand out and be different. He not only works with objective information and facts (for example 'the king is dead, the queen is dead too'), but he knows how to use this information and facts to create a story that triggers people's imagination, while at the same time, it emotionally affects people: 'After a long and difficult time due to illness, the king passed away. The deeply saddened queen mourned the loss of her husband for more than a month, and sadly succumbed to a broken heart.' A story is usually easily remembered in comparison to individual facts. Participants will take the experience home, and share it with others. It is engraved in their memories, as it has affected them emotionally: they were engaged in the story and related to the grieving queen, and they were impressed by her love for her husband.

The illustrator – the impact of images and illustrations

'A picture is worth a thousand words' is a well-known idiom. Sometimes the best way for an Imagineer to convey the design of the created experience is via the impact of images.

One of the first people to be called an 'Imagineer' was the futuristic illustrator Arthur C. Radebaugh (1906–1974). It is no coincidence that the founder of this particular metier was an illustrator, as the experience an Imagineer envisions is best conveyed through images. Anyone will immediately understand what the end result will look like in terms of atmosphere,

Fig. 6.8 Futuristic illustrator Arthur Radebaugh.

images, sentiments, details, colours, emotional impact, etc.

In order to convey the concept through images, and to start a dialogue between the design team and/or client, the Imagineer could opt for a **mood board** or **storyboard** (see Fig. 6.9). A mood board somehow conveys the feeling of the experience in colours, atmosphere and other elements. A storyboard gives a step by step, logical storyline in the form of a comic; in this way it gives an impression of the entire experience. When an Imagineer is not as talented as illustrator Radebaugh, he could create a storyboard based on simple basic drawings. Another possibility for creating a storyboard could be a collage of pictures that represent the story or convey the idea.

The Imagineer-illustrator looks at all visual stimuli and assesses how far they match the emotional atmosphere he designed. He plays with light to create the correct atmosphere, or creates an interaction of sound and light. He considers whether to cover certain stage areas with black cloth or put spotlights on other parts of the stage, or he could even consider leaving parts of the stage in their original condition.

The composer: the sound-image maker

Music can take the listener to another world. Music has the ability to touch you on an emotional level.

Music determines the atmosphere

The bombastic 'O Fortuna' from *Carmina Burana* by Carl Orff immediately gives the audience a vivacious and dramatic feeling. The French chanson 'Je ne regrette rien' by Edith Piaf has something sad about it, but at the same time conveys a feeling of pride!

For a very long time, in fact since the silent movie era, film directors have used the possibility of combining music and sound to enhance the synergetic emotional effect of the experience. Film music composer Ennio Morricone made history by composing this music for the classic Western movie: 'Once Upon a Time in the West'.

Fig. 6.9 Example of a storyboard. (Courtesy of Andy Stips.)

The Imagineer-composer is a '**sound-image creator**'. He knows how to strike the right chords and to use the right music at the right moment to get the exact emotional reaction of the participants. This can be achieved in different ways. We have already shown that by using a certain type of music, a certain atmosphere can be created. Music can also be used as a symbol, representing something else. This could be a national anthem, for example. People will have associations when they hear the song. Music can also be archetypical for earthly feelings and urges.

The Imagineer has a sense for this, and knows how to use sound and music, or has a music piece composed in such a way that it reaches the audience and causes the desired effect.

He composes a symphony of images, sounds and light, people present at the scene, location and all other available elements he could possibly use. He makes sure that it becomes a holistic experience, in which the participant is taken by the maelstrom the experience creates.

'The right music at the right moment is the perfect medicine for inner peace and harmony of human beings.' This is what Pythagoras wrote in the 6th century BC. Music as medicine was taken very seriously in Antiquity, this can be derived from the fact that there were special music hospitals.

The Imagineer-composer needs to have a good **knowledge of music** in order to create a certain atmosphere. He needs to have an understanding of different genres and styles of music, because he will use these to create different emotional effects in a variety of different people. He has to listen to music and be swept away by it, feel it, understand which part of a piece of music is relevant to create an experience, and so on.

Music is often more effective than images, as it touches people immediately and directly. People can be inundated with music, while imagery needs to be given in smaller doses as people can only assimilate seven images simultaneously. Furthermore, music tones varying between 8 and 15 Hertz cannot be heard by the human ear, but are felt by the body. These very low tones cause alpha-waves in the brain, which brings people to a state of *flow*. A specific combination of light flashes and low tones even synchronizes people's heartbeats, which has an even bigger effect on how people undergo a certain experience. The Imagineer uses the knowledge of the effects of stimuli on the brain to further adjust the design.

The interaction designer

By applying theatrical techniques Imagineers play with their audience. They combine light, sounds and décor to set the stage for interaction. Choosing the right moment for interaction can help to keep the attention, and the same thing goes for breaks and pauses. This goes beyond the theatre as the setting in a shop or hotel can also be seen as stages, with the shop as décor and staff and even the guests as the actors.

Games and play are interactive. By having people play games, it enables them to enter a different world, in which existing conventions and relations of the real world can easily be forgotten for a while. In a game situation, people have agreed to have different sets of rules within that game setting. This enables the participants to be more open and to somehow lose themselves in the game. The impact of game and play elements are to deepen and strengthen the experience and emotional reactions of the participants in the event.

Game design has emerged as a profession in the last few years. When someone designs a game with a set of rules, this could be a suitable way to guide players (people) in a certain direction or move towards a certain goal. This is not only possible in the virtual world but in the real word, offline, where real physical players (people) can be found. In general, the purpose of most games is to most effectively and efficiently as possible beat the opponent. This is usually done by practical actions or proceedings that help the player to become a better player. The player who does this best receives the award or wins. A good game designer is able to come up with a set of different rules in order to stimulate or steer new or desired behaviour of people.

In **serious gaming** this is done by reaching transformation through the game. These particular games require predefined (learning) goals, which need to be translated to a suitable set of rules for these games. These sets of rules are often based on already existing and fixed social scripts, which the participants subconsciously follow. They encounter predefined situations in which they can further develop themselves through choices they have to make.

The game element can also be more **implicit**. The Imagineer can also apply his knowledge of game techniques and rule setting for the construction of a design. He can integrate certain choices the participants need to consciously or subconsciously make in the design, or even integrate implicit meetings with other participants or professionals. Gaming in this way can increase involvement of participants and allows for customization of the experience. By choosing when the audience can influence events the interaction designer still controls the experience, as all choice options are worked out in scenarios. However, the feeling of control the audience can get when they are allowed to influence the storyline dramatically raises their interest and involvement in the story or game.

6.5   TEAM OF EXPERTS

In this chapter, we discussed the Imagineer's position, his role, tasks, talents, skills and trades. These are all the requirements he needs in order to fulfil his mission. Of course it is not always possible for one person to possess all these talents, skills and trades. Even the team of Disney Imagineers consists of different people, who have different areas of expertise, which supplement each other. Together they create the ultimate experience, by adding each one's expertise in particular areas of knowledge. The composer gets together with the décor designer and the light technician to create a new, inspiring image that will have a bigger impact than if each one had worked on the project separately. The integration of different disciplines in one team is the critical success factor of innovation and creation of new, exciting, surprising and meaningful experience worlds.

The Imagineering team is composed based on different expertise that is required. The Imagineer plays the role of art director, who composes, motivates and directs the combination, structure and organization of the available trades. He has an eye for professionals with the right set of skills, knowledge, characteristics and expertise.

In many cases, this 'art director' steers and motivates the other specialist Imagineers of the team. He gives feedback to his team in relation to the designs and will be responsible for all decisions regarding the final design.

6.6 SUMMARY

The mission of an Imagineer is to create meaningful experience worlds with the goal of creating positively motivated groups of followers (subjects). These groups of followers should be committed to not only each other, but to the predefined strategically chosen object (the company organization, product, services and the object, which is a result of the management issue that needed to be addressed). The Imagineer's role is to make sure that the design meets the predefined goals. He needs to approach this from the perspective of the subjects' user satisfaction.

To achieve this, he has six tasks: leader and final decision maker; translator and connector; motivator; researcher; designer; and director. The Imagineer is someone who imagines. Due to this, his own experiences and vocabulary will have a big influence on the style of his designs.

The Imagineer should possess six universal skills: entrepreneurship; innovation; emotional intelligence; curiosity; the urge to create; and synergetic thinking.

In order to translate his imagination and designs to the outside world, the Imagineer has one or several trades at his disposal, for example, as a preacher, he is able to inspire and convince people. As a writer he can translate his ideas expressively. As a draftsman he is able to direct his ideas through drawings, while as a conductor he is able to compose through sound and atmosphere. In his role as a game designer he leads his subjects in a subtle and playful way in the desired direction.

6.7 ASSIGNMENTS

Assignment 1

Have a look at what you have accumulated in your backpack. Take a moment to stare outside. Unpack your backpack and see what is relevant to you as an Imagineer. Which films did you watch, what did you see during your nature trip, which play did you visit? How often do you speak to strangers? Have you noticed anything special in your street lately?

Assignment 2

Fill your backpack. For the coming week you should dedicate one hour for street-combing. Bring a notebook and a camera; moreover, don't forget to look at and observe things carefully. After street-combing, evaluate the contents of your backpack, and give a short presentation.

6.8 RECOMMENDED READING

Positivity and creativity are interrelated. Fredrickson describes how positivity can be developed and cultivated:

- Fredrickson, B. (2009) *Positivity. Groundbreaking Research Reveals How to Embrace the Hidden Strength of Positive Emotions, Overcome Negativity, and Thrive.* Crown Archetype, New York.

How does the power of persuasion work and which psychological processes are involved?

- Cialdini, R. (2007) *Influence, the Psychology of Persuasion.* Harper Business, London.

chapter 7

The Imagineer's Work Process

Gabriëlle Kuiper and Bert Smit

King Hieron of Syracuse wanted to offer a special gift to the Gods and assigned a gold smith to make a crown. When the crown was finished and handed to Hieron, he wondered whether the crown was actually made of pure gold. It could be a mixture of silver and gold, a trick many counterfeiters used in those days. The king asked Greek philosopher Archimedes if he could establish whether the crown was made of pure gold without having to melt it. Archimedes was different from other Greek philosophers at that time. He not only thought about all kinds of topics and problems, but also did experiments to

Fig. 7.1 Archimedes.

(Continued)

Continued.

actually test and research them. Archimedes couldn't come up with a solution that easily, and gave it careful consideration. Only later on, while having a bath in a local bath house, he unexpectedly came up with a solution. The moment he got into the bath he noticed that the bath water, which spilt over the edge, equalled the volume of his immersed body. He realized he could use this principle to find out whether the crown was made of pure gold. By putting it in water he could measure the volume of the crown. He was then able to compare the weight of the crown to the weight of an equal volume of gold. When Archimedes realized he had solved this problem he exclaimed: 'Eureka, eureka! I found it!'.

In this chapter we will discuss the Imagineering process and the position of the Imagineer in this process. Although the steps in the process are nearly always the same, the outcome of the process depends on the particular management issue the Imagineer faces.

Disney's way of working

Disney starts by designing a simple concept, which is then conceptualized in a storyboard and script. Furthermore, Disney tries to find out what a visitor sees, hears, feels and even thinks during the initial experience during the new theme park attraction/ride. Based on

Fig. 7.2 Prototype of the Imagineers.

(Continued)

> Continued.
>
> these findings, a model is made, which is also referred to as a prototype. Engineers will further design and develop this prototype and translate this to realistic, feasible technical solutions. These prototypes are tested in the parks, and the audience's reaction is observed.
>
> When a project seems feasible, they will start by designing the decors in terms of architecture, paint, upholstery, different materials, lighting and other details. The design phase is followed by actual construction. Imagineers work in multidisciplinary teams in which various characteristics, knowledge, skills and talents are represented. The team leader looks after integration of various knowledge, and as a consequence; necessary innovation can be achieved.

By the end of this chapter you will have a better understanding of the following:

- Imagineering is a team effort and is based on thorough analyses and research.
- The Imagineering process is an iterative process (steps are being repeated until everything is right) to enable application of newly obtained knowledge and understanding as a tool for improvement.
- The process consists of four phases and eight stages.

7.1   LONELY GENIUS OR LEADER OF A CREATIVE TEAM?

Creativity is often regarded as something intangible: a genius has inspiration and creates something new or unique, and is sometimes referred to as 'The Lonely Genius'. One can think of Albert Einstein's relativity theory, which he devised during a train trip, or Archimedes' famous eureka moment, two mythical examples of creative geniuses, who were solely responsible for world-changing ideas.

We are aware of the end results of these myths, however we often forget that even these geniuses have come a long way in terms of preparation and development. Albert Einstein had already been involved in research on time and space. He had deepened his knowledge by reading literature, did experiments and discussed the topics with other colleagues and experts of other fields. This is how he got his inspiration and discovered new perspectives. The train trip was 'just' that moment where knowledge and experience came together and answered the question. Strategies, visions and ideas also flow from a predetermined process, which is partially conscious and partially subconscious.

Hence, the creative Imagineer is not a lonely genius. He leads an expert team and facilitates necessary synergy between knowledge, skills and experience, which enable innovation. He uses research, observation and experiments to make people-focused designs that have to meet the consumer's need for enjoyment.

During the first phase of the Imagineering process, the Imagineer will form a strategic team and put in as many view points, knowledge, expertise and visions in the design process. The Imagineer functions as instigator, motivator and chairman, in doing so he creates ample

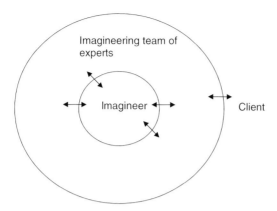

Phase 1 Flat model: collection of knowledge, research, ideas and vision

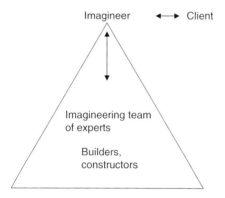

Phase 2 Hierarchical top-down model: decision making, final design and execution.

Fig. 7.3 Position of the Imagineer in phase 1 and 2.

opportunities for his team members' contributions. During the second phase a more hierarchical model is required as the Imagineer has the final responsibility and needs to make top-down decisions about the final decisions about the design and its execution.

7.2 THE IMAGINEERING PROCESS IS ITERATIVE

The Imagineering process is iterative (repetitive). This means that each step of the project is tested and when necessary, based on feedback, adapted immediately. The design method is cyclic. This means that the developed prototype is tested over and over again, analysed, improved and tested yet again. This is referred to as a **consumer-focused** way of designing, due to the fact that consumer groups actually test these prototypes.

By the end of the iterative design process, there won't be a revelation. During the process, several tests of small prototypes are conducted to measure quality performance and consumer delight. The results and findings of these tests will be used as input for the next iteration.

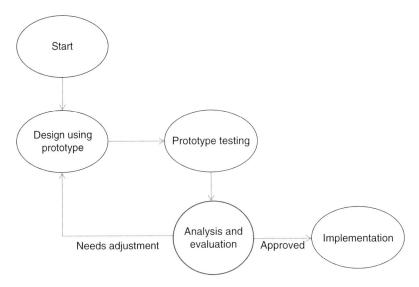

Fig. 7.4 Simple diagram of an iterative process using prototypes.

Interim analyses and evaluations are extremely important in the iterative process. As a consequence, more pressure is put on the team; however, this pressure is spread throughout the entire duration of the project, and is not only concentrated on the period just before the deadline of the final delivery.

7.3 FOUR PHASES, EIGHT STAGES

The Imagineering process consists of four phases. Each phase is repetitive until sufficient quality has been achieved before moving to the next phase. The Imagineer leads this process.

1. Information: The Imagineer collects information and tries to understand the background of the assignment. The outcome of this will determine composition of the team. The team needs to be composed in such way that it represents the right experts, who are capable of facing and solving possible challenges.

2. Inspiration: The Imagineer is not only inspired by expertise, perceptions and his team members' knowledge, but also adapts a proactive attitude, gathers, asks and researches possible questions.

3. Imagination: Imagination consists of development and design. Creative techniques are applied to encourage higher order thinking skills, build and test prototypes to achieve a more effective end result.

4. Implementation: After sufficient tests, outcome analyses and improvements, we enter the next phase, which is called the implementation phase. During this phase the final product is built and applied. The Imagineer directs this phase. The implementation is followed by a thorough reflection and evaluation as part of information collection for a follow-up.

The four Imagineering phases consist of eight stages:

1. Formulation.
2. Composition.
3. Research.
4. Development.
5. Prototyping.
6. Design.
7. Application.
8. Evaluation.

Each stage is iterative. This means that each stage results in something concrete, which can be evaluated and analysed for improvement. This process is repetitive until the Imagineer decides that it has produced enough information and quality to move on to the next stage. The stages research, development and prototyping will successively be repeated at a high pace. Due to the fact that each cycle provides more knowledge and understanding, more relevant questions can be asked in the research stage. This process repeats itself until sufficient knowledge and understanding have been generated to design a well-founded and tested design, which is of sufficient quality before starting the design and application stages. The Imagineer looks at each phase and decides which expertise is required within the team. As a consequence, the team might change during the process. All eight stages have certain criteria that need to be met before moving to the next stage. We will describe these conditions step by step. We will then summarize the individual stages and four phases in a model of the Imagineering process.

7.3.1 Stage 1: Formulation

Definition

The Imagineer designs solutions for **management issues**, or **problems**. The Imagineers gathers information during the first stage; based on this information it is important to understand the problem that needs to be solved. The Imagineer's design represents economic value for organizations and brands that want to use their management goals as a tool for growth, consolidation or assurance of long term survival of their organizations or brands. In terms of management issues, it is the client who faces management issues: the party that needs to achieve goals, for which the Imagineer's design can be used. A client facing these issues could also be the Imagineer; this could be the case when the Imagineer himself is a visionary entrepreneur (see Section 6.2.1). Throughout the remainder of the book we will refer to the party that faces management issues as **the client**.

Briefing

The client can implicitly and explicitly convey his expectations and set goals, by giving the Imagineer an assignment for solving certain management issues. **Implicitly**, when the client is not entirely aware of the fact that he has management issues, for which a possible solution could be designed by the Imagineer. This could be due to the fact that the client doesn't have enough experience or knowledge. In such cases, a conversation, meeting or observation of the

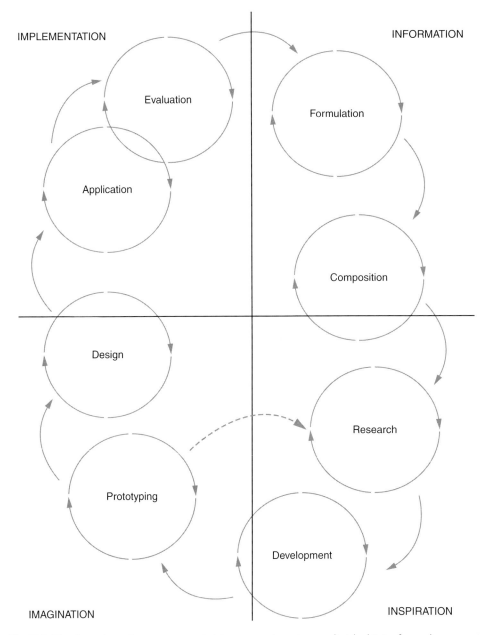

IMPLEMENTATION

INFORMATION

Evaluation

Formulation

Application

Composition

Design

Research

Prototyping

Development

IMAGINATION

INSPIRATION

Fig. 7.5 The Imagineering process: eight sequencing stages divided into four phases.

situation can help the Imagineer to recognize whether he will be able to be of added value, and to make the client aware of this. In current times, strategy and communication departments of organizations are more and more aware of the added value of an Imagineer. Moreover, organizations become aware of the added value of working with external bureaus, for example commercial agencies, or event organizers, which also start their work with a clear formulation of the assignment, goal(s) and preconditions.

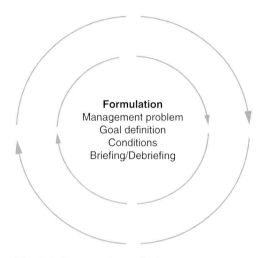

Formulation
Management problem
Goal definition
Conditions
Briefing/Debriefing

Fig. 7.6 Stage 1: Formulation.

When the client is aware of the issues and goals, he can explicitly share these with the Imagineer by means of a briefing. This briefing by the client to the Imagineer, who is the future supplier, generally consists of (Reynaert and Dijkerman, 2009) ten parts:

1. Strategy: Current position and identity of the (organization or brand) of the client, i.e. the one facing management issues.

2. Problem: Issues and assignment of the client, i.e. the one facing management issues.

3. Proposition: The intended promise to the target group and justification of this.

4. Description: A detailed description of the user group(s).

5. Expectations: What are the expectations, the starting position/motivation of user group(s).

6. Current contact moments: Contact moments with the user group(s).

7. Tone of voice: Guidelines for communication (register).

8. Possible ways of communication and other **Goals**.

9. Conditions and limitations for what concerns budget, time, manpower, conditions, rules and regulations, etc.

10. Relevant background information on **previous projects**, designs, expressions and degree of success.

To ensure delivery of the highest quality, the Imagineer will most likely discuss the briefing document in a personal one on one moment with the client. Preferably, various other representatives from the client's organization will be present as well. This way the Imagineer will be exposed to various views on the formulated issues. During the meeting, the Imagineer will ask as many questions as possible, to reach the so-called question behind the question.

The question behind the question

This is the deeper essential question of the client, as well, the core of the Imagineer's research and design. The Imagineer is able to find out the question behind the question by conducting **Socratic Dialogue**. This means that he will continuously ask for reasons behind the assignment, until he completely and clearly understands the issues and essential questions. A good base for such a dialogue is: When will the sponsor consider the outcome of the Imagineer's assignment to be successful? After further questioning, the issue is formulated to a question with a maximum of seven words (Kessels *et al.*, 2002). This way, the client is forced to name his real expectations or needs.

Research and debriefing

The moment the question behind the question is known and reformulated, the Imagineer will start his independent research. Firstly, he collects data about the topic or issue, evaluates his already existing knowledge, and the requirements in terms of knowledge and expertise. He continues to have a thorough understanding of what kind of added economic value needs to be created, and which business model is used for the design. A first brainstorm enables him to think freely on how to approach the assignment. He then makes a selection based on priorities. The focus of this is the question of what needs to be done to deliver a minimum desired quality to the client. This is included in the debriefing with the client. During the debriefing all items from the client's previous briefing will be repeated and supplemented with a reformulated question, the outcome of the first inventory inquiry and how the project can and will be designed.

The debriefing has several purposes:

- to inform the client;
- to start an in-depth dialogue; and
- to develop a first draft of a prototype, which the Imagineer assesses to see whether he has clearly understood the vision, expectations and vision of the client.

Debriefing also consists of a written document and a dialogue, as well as visuals such as mood boards, for example. This gives the client the opportunity to react and give feedback. The debriefing results in a final question and a mutually agreed approach to the project. This step not only requires the analytical, left side of the brain but also requires right-brain thinking, as imagination is needed to meet the vision of the problem holder, the client.

To repeat or finalize?

The client and Imagineer hold dialogues, reformulate research questions, and in some cases it is possible that the client discovers that his priorities or vision for what concerns the design have changed. In such cases they can both opt for redoing stage one. This stage is finalized when there is sufficient, balanced and approved information from the client in terms of:

- definition of the exact assignment;
- expectations of the client with regard to outcome;
- preconditions that need to be taken into consideration during and after execution;
- critical success factors to solve the issues;
- when the issues are solved (what are the minimum requirements); and
- which social, cultural or economic value will solve the issues.

When the Imagineer himself is the client, this phase will be less elaborate. He understands the problem for which he wants to create an experience for a group of people and knows how to solve possible issues by himself. There is no need for dialogue with an external client to understand his vision and expectations. However, in some cases when the Imagineer is the client, he will need to convince and persuade a financial investor of his goals and added economic, cultural and social value of his future creation.

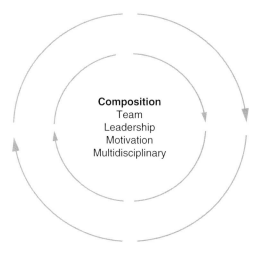

Fig. 7.7 Stage 2: Composition.

7.3.2 Stage 2: Composition

Once the assignment has been clearly formulated, the next stage within this phase is the composition of a team, which will take on the assignment. In general, a starting team, which will mainly focus on preparation and content of the project, is put together. During the implementation phase, extra team members will be added. The starting point of composing a team is to use a **combination of expertise**, in order to encourage an exchange of knowledge and know-how. Design bureau IDEO only works with people who have a double professional background, for example someone who is a psychologist and an architect at the same time (Brown, 2008). Should it occur that there is only one Imagineer working on a small project, a multidisciplinary background is desirable for achieving a better result.

Understanding your own assumptions

This step in the process is about understanding your own assumptions. Which assumptions and preconceived ideas do the Imagineer, the client and the expected target group have? What does he know and where is this knowledge based on? Which sources does he use, and are these sources reliable? Does he understand whether he has preconceived ideas, or if his ideas are founded and substantiated? Does he think in terms of his own preferences or does think from the perspective of his target group or client? In case the Imagineer doesn't understand his own assumptions, this could be an obstacle in starting the project and briefing the team, as he could influence his team by briefing them based on his own assumptions. It could prevent an exchange of different perspectives.

Priority list

The Imagineer will then try to formulate what is needed in terms of knowledge and know-how in relation to the assignment and his own assumptions and preconceived ideas. He objectively makes a list of priorities: what is important and what is possible within the set preconditions (budget or time). Prioritizing determines the selection of future team members. Once the team members have been selected, a briefing of the assignment will be a priority. This briefing has the goal of enthusing the team, as only a **positive approach** will lead to a successful design.

Briefing and feedback

After reading and understanding the assignment, and once the team is composed, it will provide **feedback** on the management issue and the main question. Each team member will also investigate his own assumptions and preconceptions in relation to the design, the problem, the client and even each other. During the process this second stage might be done again, when, for example, during evaluation of the team's own assumptions there is reason to believe that the team lacks perspective or discipline.

Bringing user groups into action

Co-creation requires user groups. The team and the user groups can connect via virtual platforms and join forces in terms of knowledge, desires and needs. **Crowd sourcing** is used to tap into these user groups. The Imagineer can actively respond to the needs of the users by creating a platform for communication and development via an intense exchange of communication.

7.3.3   Stage 3: Research

Csikszentmihalyi says it is only possible for creativity to lead to innovation when the person who participates in the developing process has sufficient knowledge and experience in the related area of creativity (Csikszentmihalyi, 1996). It is virtually impossible to be innovative in any area without a minimum work experience of 10,000 hours. In other words: creativity is only productive when it is based on sufficient experience and knowledge of the team, in order to get an in-depth understanding of the ideas. Simultaneously, this gives an indication of the importance of this stage, namely, a thorough preparation for the next stage: development.

What kind of knowledge do we need?

Each team member brings knowledge and ideas to the table. All these Imagineers are curious, investigative and have inspiring ideas, which serve as a starting point for further investigation or a new approach to the design or topic. As the team investigates its own assumptions and preconceptions, they come to an understanding through which lens they will approach the project. This is the starting point of the next stage, which will land them in the inspiration phase: doing research. From the main question, which was formulated in cooperation with the client, other questions that relate to other areas of knowledge are derived and further investigation is required.

These questions can relate to future **users**:

- What is the exact target group?
- Have they previously been in touch with the client?
- Which needs and expectations does the target group have?
- How are they connected amongst themselves, which media do they use to connect?
- What is the common language and codes of the user group? What is acceptable and what isn't?
- Why does this group spend time on something and what motivates them?

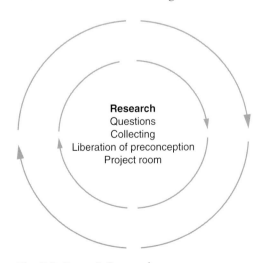

Research
Questions
Collecting
Liberation of preconception
Project room

Fig. 7.8 Stage 3: Research.

Or questions about a **product**:

- What are the technical preconditions?
- What are the latest technical developments or trends?
- Why does this product exist and what is its added value?
- Who wants to profile the product or be involved with it and why?

Or questions about the **environment**:

- Which changes were observed in the past and what are the expectations for the future?
- Who is the competition and what do they offer?
- What are possible limitations or chances of the physical or virtual environment?

Or questions about **current events**:

- What is currently happening?
- Are there any new developments?
- What is outdated?

Or questions about **trends**:

- What are the latest technological developments?
- What is trending in major themes such as 'sustainability'?

Depending on the content of the assignment, more areas of research can be formulated by the team. In the sample questions above, we mainly use the so-called 'wh' questions such as who, what, which and when. However, there are also some 'why' questions; when 'why' questions are used, we really want to understand motivation, preferences, predilection, needs and desires. This information is vital as the final design is focused on this. The more the end design meets the needs, the more successful it will be.

Human focused design

Much data from formulated areas is collected from various sources, without drawing any conclusions in this stage. In a so-called **project room**, the epicentre of the team, all data are collected and organized in a visual manner: visuals are put up on walls and are spread amongst the team, in order to actively inspire the team members with new knowledge, understanding, visuals, ideas, statements, etc. Information is mainly gathered by looking at the future users' context, to get to know them as human beings. The Imagineer's design is focused on the human being.

In this stage, research can be defined as **observing and asking questions** (Brown, 2008).

The Imagineer needs to study and observe future users' behaviour, he will look at what they do in their leisure time, what kind of behaviour they show, when do they show it, what are their social relationships and dependencies, but also understand, through for example Google Analytics, their Internet behaviour and usage. One gets to know the users individually by asking questions. During a dialogue or in-depth interview, questions can be asked about motivation, preferences and why, what are their expectations about the topic and through which lens do they look at things. Another method is **becoming a participant of the group you are designing for** and spend some time with them.

> In case you are approached to design an experience for elderly people, it is advisable to spend a few days in an elderly home and participate in all activities with the elderly. You need to understand your own assumptions and preconceptions beforehand. You then will undergo the experience. What are these people facing on a daily basis? What are their routines? What kind of conversations are they having? What is important to them?

After this research period, old preconceptions can be compared to the actual experience, which in general will shed new light on the starting points for the design.

> Imagine that you need to redesign the service department of a large hamburger chain. To get a clear and correct real-life picture and employee experience, you decide to work as an employee in the restaurant in different positions. One of the critical success factors for redesigning the service department is the employee who needs to provide a service. It is only possible to actually make a design for the employee when you know how he thinks, what he finds important, as well, what needs to be done in order for the employee to be prepared to change or render services differently. In some cases it can be related to details such as an extra break, or a door that opens to the left instead of to the right. Besides, you will need to experience the current service as a customer yourself, moreover, speak to customers and ask why they come and what makes them satisfied customers.
>
> **What can we learn from this new information?**
>
> In the last part of this third stage, the team will 'learn' how to do an analysis of the collected data, which will be evaluated in a dialogue. The team could opt for a SWOT analysis (strengths and weaknesses, chances and threats), or assess the competition based on a competition analysis, or determine the target group through target group analysis. Possible video material of the Imagineer's experience as an employee can be watched and assessed.
>
> Do you remember design bureau IDEO from Chapter 4? IDEO got an assignment to make a better service design for the hospital's first aid department.
>
> One of the designers posed as a patient and spent the day in the first aid department. He recorded his experiences on camera. After the experience the team watched the video and noticed that there was mainly footage of the ceiling. This is what patients see. How does this affect a patient? How does this influence his sense of safety? The footage gave an important insight of the user experience.

Persona

After data analyses, the first prototype of a persona is created: a quite reliable possible representation of the user group. The persona is constructed based on all available data. This persona will be the leading factor within the design's decision-making process. In this phase the following questions will be asked: how will the persona react to the design? What kind of mental process will the persona experience? What kind of behaviour does the persona show during the experience? The persona becomes an individual instead of a thing and this is helpful to the Imagineer. The persona becomes tangible in terms of how the individual will undergo the experience, how tall he is, what kind of clothing he wears, whether it is a male or a female, the expectations, needs, and so on.

Basic rules of experience

Another simple prototype, which flows from the research stage, is a simplified construction of basic rules of an experience. *Urban Game* is played outdoors, on the street. In this phase a simple board game is made to see what will be the future players' rules for this particular game. During the research stage, the exact mental and behavioural process of the persona is worked out in detail, in order to reach the desired goal: from his starting point (knowledge and expectations) until the end situation. However, interaction between the Imagineer's offered elements and the experience's participant (the subject), creates a certain **dynamic**, which is partly unpredictable as it originates from mental and behavioural processes (Hunicke *et al.*, 2004).

This is one of the reasons that this stage requires iterations too, in order to test which dynamics emerge, and how they can be improved. Co-dependency between these lose elements on the one hand, and the mental and behavioural processes of the subject on the other hand, requires careful consideration. Behaviour, which is caused by the experience, is followed by the mental process. Together they represent the (social) **artefact**, that the experience produces. In other words: not the event or its related elements form content of the experience, but the elicited behaviour and opinion it produces after participation.

The **simplified version of experience**, which elicits behaviour and mental processes via certain dynamics, is mapped out. In a game, the setup of a set of rules will elicit behaviour of a player that creates a sense of 'fun' for the players (Hunicke *et al.*, 2004). Think for instance of going bankrupt in Monopoly or breaking a non-aggression treaty in Risk.

During the development and design stages, the Imagineer also takes into consideration the relationship between mechanics, dynamics and aesthetics, as they influence each other: by adding certain mechanics (such as light, location and layout), dynamics are created (the way group member interact with each other and the environment), which as a result influence the (aesthetic) experience of each of the group members (Hunicke et al., 2004). In the game example, Monopoly money, for instance, leads to exchanges and trades.

Fig. 7.9 Eliciting behaviour through a game.

Fig. 7.10 Cause and effect in experiences.

Repeat or wrap up?

Data are analysed during the research stage. The outcome of these analyses are possibly helpful in putting aside certain preconceptions and assumptions of the team. When new assumptions or preconceptions have appeared, or when current data and analysis don't necessarily solve all assumptions, then this stage could be repeated as well. It is possible that data collection was done through a blurred lens, which requires, yet again, data collection in search of new, different and additional sources. Even in later stages, for example after the development and design steps, it is possible to repeat the research stage. This is most certainly the case when in later stages, certain challenges have come up, which lead to another kind of knowledge scope. In case the Imagineer hasn't got much information at the beginning of the design, it is highly likely that the research, development and design stages will be done and possibly repeated at a high pace.

The research stage of the Imagineering process is finalized when sufficient information and understanding is reached in terms of:

- the social context (including language and codes) of the future user group, based on the group's assumptions and preconceptions, but also of the user group in relation to the design (co-creation);
- the physical context;
- the personal contexts, in terms of existing expectation and assumed knowledge;
- possible stimuli and the anticipated effects of this (perception, anticipated attitude towards certain stimuli);
- understanding the client, the goal of the assignment, previous meetings with user group and client;
- understanding human behaviour, communication and group processes users will undergo during the experience;
- knowledge and experience concerning different disciplines, and possibilities within these disciplines;
- knowledge of new technologies and trends.

7.3.4   Stage 4: Development

Stage four is development. During this phase the Imagineer is able to work and think explicitly in terms of creativity, as neither a decision, nor direction have to be taken. In the beginning of this stage the team can think freely, as direction will be decided on

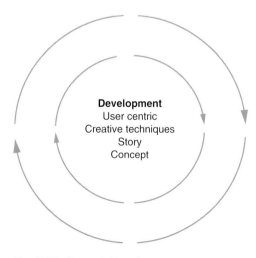

Development
User centric
Creative techniques
Story
Concept

Fig. 7.11 Stage 4: Development.

only later in the process. This stage therefore starts with an analysis of what was learned in the research step. What was the outcome that is relevant for development? How does this relate to preconditions or starting points? How does this information affect the original main question? Which persona has been used as point of departure? (It is very well possible that this analysis leads to reformulation of the persona). Consequently, the creative phase is formulated.

The goal of the development stage is to **think integrally from the user's perspective**. Integrally, in this context, means that design is people focused, whereby various disciplines are combined and something new arises. During this phase the designer thinks in terms of suitability, applicability, desirability and user satisfaction. For example, a technological feature of an urban game is added to iPads, to show your current position through a GPS system. New developments of different areas can lead to surprising and unexpected elements. Data from the research phase serve as input for this.

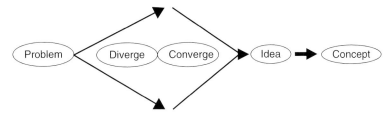

Fig. 7.12 The process of Stage 4 (development).

Diverge

During the research stage, the team has put together a **project room** where all collected information and visuals are collected. In this space, the team is surrounded by inspiration, visuals, input and content. In this phase, all input is used to diverge and generate new ideas. To generate ideas and invent new applications, the team can use **creative techniques**.

The persona needs to pass through certain mental and behavioural processes. During the development stage, there is a lot of reflection on how to start mental and behavioural process of the persona: **mechanics, dynamics and aesthetics** are further filled in/addressed.

From the Imagineer's perspective, mechanics cause certain dynamics that result in an aesthetic experience. From the user's perspective this is the other way around: aesthetics set a certain tone from which observable dynamics and governed mechanics arise (Hunicke *et al.*, 2004). A comparison to a car can clarify this: the mechanics are all the separate elements of a car: the tyres, the motor, the steering wheel, etc. The dynamics are the drivers who drive the car. Aesthetics are for example in the driving experience, the feeling driving evokes when driving (dynamics) a car (mechanics).

Fig. 7.13 Mechanics, dynamics and aesthetics of a car.

The designer designs a car that can be experienced by driving it. The driver experiences the car by being in the car (observable) and by driving it (operational).

The **aesthetic goals of an experience** can be broad, and, depending on the formulated goal of the first step of the Imagineering process, be referred to as the formulation stage. You could think of feelings in terms of sensation, fantasy, friendship, discovery, story, challenge, self-discovery, etc. During the development stage, specific vocabulary (active verbs) is developed by the team. If the goal is safety of employees, than it is important for all employees to go through a process in which they become aware of employee safety, why it is important and how to achieve it. The active verbs that are linked to this are 'search' (looking for information), or 'explore' (look around you), and 'analyse' or 'hold a dialogue' (with colleagues) or 'networking'.

The team evaluates each verb in terms of importance and logical sequence and how it can be applied in the process.

Tools to generate new ideas: divergence

When the starting formula is clarified to each team member, it could be useful to apply creative techniques to generate new ideas. There are numerous creative techniques, as a matter of fact too many to discuss them all in one book. We will only discuss a few of these techniques we (the authors) believe are most suitable and practical. All three techniques have some common features, particularly, the facts that they encourage dialogue between team members, and make use of creative skills of team members.

Provocation is adding an extra limitation/restriction to a problem, which activates critical thinking skills (Galjaard *et al.*, 2007) to understand and clarify the core of the problem by looking at different viewpoints and to decide which direction to take in terms of finding solutions. Finding bad or bizarre solutions for the added limitation or restriction, immediately gives inspiration for new ideas. At the same time, you will have a better understanding of the core of the problem by exploring different dimensions behind the problem such as the physical, social and interactive components.

> Think of a random problem for which you seek a (creative) solution. Try using the following provocations for what concerns the problem:
>
> - Make it bigger.
> - Make it smaller.
> - Make it digestible.
> - What happens when there is no gravity?
> - What is the worst solution?
> - How would the queen solve this problem?
> - How would the Chinese solve this problem?
> - Romanticize the problem.
> - How does it look in a photograph?
> - How would it sound if it were music?
>
> *(Continued)*

Continued.

- Which famous person would it be?
- Make it bearable.
- Make it heavier.
- Make it cheaper.
- Make it more expensive.

You must have noticed that provocation generates numerous useless ideas, but at the same time, an opportunity for finding a solution in different directions, which otherwise might not have emerged. By using different provocations, various trades are triggered (vision, sound, words, story, etc.). Provocation is often used as some sort of warming up exercise for creative session, as it stimulates active participation and involvement of the participants, which should give them a better understanding of the problem.

Mind mapping works in a similar manner as our brain. It combines textual and visual thinking. Both sides of the brain are activated as you zoom in and zoom out on the problem. Mind mapping can be used during the research stage, to understand the context of, and associations with the problem. It helps team members to structure their thoughts and get a better overview. Mind mapping, in combination with free association, can also be used to map solutions during

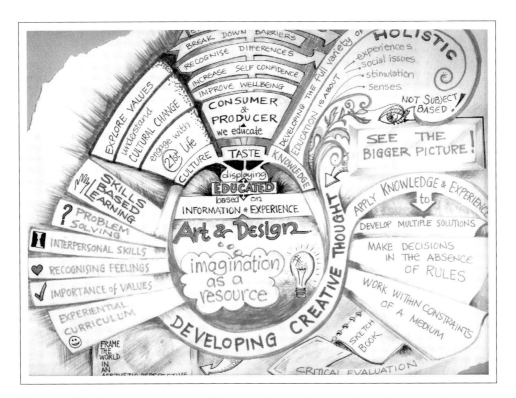

Fig. 7.14 Mind mapping example. (Courtesy of www.freemappingsoftware.net)

the development stage. A mind map can consist of words or images, moreover, an insight in different connections between various elements. Different team members of different trades can contribute to the full picture through the mind map. A mind mapping session usually starts by writing a word in the middle of a whiteboard or large piece of paper. Associations with the words are noted around the word; one can think of names, terms, definitions and images. All associations are placed around the word. Lastly, clusters of associations and connections are made between different elements of the mind map by using different shapes and colours.

Brainstorming is probably the most well-known term for what concerns generating new ideas. A successful brainstorm session generates numerous new ideas in a relatively short period of time; however, eight basic rules are required and need to be taken into consideration. The brainstorm session should be done at a relatively high pace, as lower order thinking skills are addressed instead of higher order critical thinking skills. The basic rules are:

1. Quantity leads to quality: The essence of a brainstorm session is to generate many ideas.
2. Associate: A creative session becomes a 'brainstorm' when one idea leads to the next and when you are able to freely say anything you like and associate this with (combinations of) previous ideas; that is what creates a brainstorm.
3. No negative feedback: During a brainstorm session, no idea should be rejected, no matter how ridiculous or impossible it seems. Negative feedback blocks the free flow of ideas.
4. Note everything down: Only by noting down each and every idea can you produce a full picture of possibilities and school of thought. In a later phase, various ideas can be clustered to form a solution.

For many people it is quite challenging to think freely, which is a requirement for a brainstorm session. A warm up at the beginning of the session will help the participants to become less inhibited, and more free and energetic. These so-called energizers are often physical activities in combination with language: for example throwing a ball to someone at high speed and each time you throw the ball you need to say the name of the receiver.

A **mood board** is helpful to literally visualize a concept, idea or feeling. Mood boards are also referred to as collages. They give a visual and contextual impression of the experience you create. Mood boards are also valuable in terms of the style or feeling that you want to project. Sometimes pictures and photos can convey more than just words, therefore, mood boards are very effective in terms of communication within the team and with the client. By visualizing a concept through a mood board, the concept emerges from the brain of the designer, and has become visible to other people. Visualizing the concept makes the concept somewhat more concrete. It limits the chances of misunderstandings and miscommunication; a conversation, story or dialogue always allow for the receiver to have his own interpretation. This can be pre-vented by offering a visible concept. Typical elements of a mood board are pictures that tell something about:

- physical environment (a forest or a historical city, for example);
- brands that match the experience (Harrods or AllStars);

Fig. 7.15 Mood board for waterfront hotel in Vancouver. (Courtesy of VFS Digital Design.)

- the feeling the experience needs to elicit (romantic feeling or aesthetics);
- lifestyle (hip-hop or classical music);
- materials (concrete, wood, steel, silk); or
- texture (rough, soft, hard, smooth).

Convergence

Once the team has generated various ideas, the convergence phase will start. During this phase, various ideas will be selected, worked out and refined. Different techniques have been developed for convergence. One of these techniques is the so-called COCD box, which was developed by Mark Raison. Ideas resulting from the creative session are put in a grid. There are two rows, 'feasible' and 'unfeasible', and two columns, 'ordinary' and 'new'. This generates new types of ideas, the so-called:

- **NOW ideas,** feasible ideas with low risk, high acceptability, earlier examples available;
- **HOW ideas,** future ideas, not (yet) feasible, challenging and inspiring; and
- **WOW ideas,** innovative ideas, energetic and feasible.

From idea to concept

Once the WOW ideas have been selected, they need to be prioritized. The WOW ideas seem to be the most beneficial in terms of finding a solution to the central question that will be put on top. One (or some) idea will be further worked out in a concept.

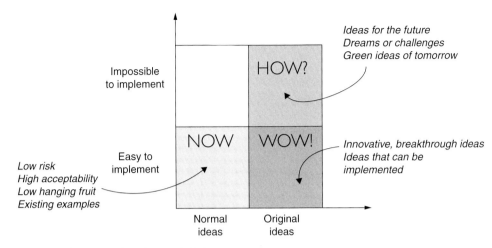

Fig. 7.16 The COCD box by Mark Raison.

At first, the concept consists of aesthetics and the chosen verbs as was discussed during the divergence phase. Additionally, the dynamics that result from the aesthetic experience, this is caused by the story that is to be conveyed (story), the interactive element of play (play) and the level of empathy of the persona (empathy).

Symphony provides for a logical unity of lose elements into a mechanical whole, while design in the shaping stage makes it attractive to the users.

Going through the whole experience generates meaning. The goal is that all subjects feel personally engaged during the whole experience.

Describing the experience of a persona requires a scenario technique. In the scenario each stage is worked out from the user's perspective. Additionally, more drafts are made to represent the user's experience. In this first concept, the 3Cs of Imagineering are taken into consideration; furthermore, time slots are assigned/worked out for each precondition of the experience.

Table 7.1 3C Framework

Concept	Connection	Consistency
Values	Communication platform	Integrated communication
Design	Interpersonal relations	Symphony
Vision	Empathy	Tuning
Story	Involvement	Synergy
Play	Meaning	Brand personality
Autonomy	Co-creation	Business model

An idea that is the basis for a concept needs to meet the following criteria of the SUCCESS formula (Section 4.2):

- **Simple** is the necessary balance between challenge and own competencies, and a symphony of different elements, which blend into a unity that is comprehensible for the user.
- **Unique** stands for authenticity, which is meaningful in social context and in terms of offering transformation.
- **Credible** refers to the fact that authenticity makes something credible and gives meaning by offering transformation.
- **Concrete** means that there has to be a clear goal.
- **Emotional** feeling of being in control of the situation by responding to the expectations and needs of the user (empathy); touch the person on an emotional level by using all senses and offer a desirable design.
- **Story** stands for the story and positive interactivity with the user (a form of co-creation) by adding an element of ' play'.
- **Subliminal** stands for a changed perception of time through concentration and focus.

Consequently, the first concept is assessed on its merits. If it meets the requirements it is now time to start stage 5 (prototyping); if not, this stage is repeated to fine-tune the concept.

Wrap up or repeat?

The first concept and feedback system form the point of departure for the design stage. When the concept is ready, an analysis is made in terms of whether the first concept meets the research outcome and the main question. After a positive evaluation, this first concept will serve as input for the Imagineer's design phase. After a negative outcome, the decision could be taken to go through the development phase again, in order to generate new ideas based on newly acquired knowledge. The outcomes of the development stage are:

- creative interpretation of the team's knowledge and skills, with the addition of newly acquired knowledge from the research stage;
- a high-quality concept that meets the requirements of the SUCCESS formula and the 3Cs;
- some prototypes such as a scenario, a mood board or a simple feedback model, which induce aesthetics.

7.3.5   Stage 5: Prototyping

The concept of the development stage is the point of departure for the prototyping stage. This stage falls under the imagination phase. Within the concept, the Imagineer makes choices that are based on rational as well as emotional considerations: left and right brain. He rationally looks at economic value and whether the concept meets the requirements of the predetermined goals. He looks at the emotional reactions of the users, as well, how it adds to beliefs, inspiration, connection and positive energy of the concept users (social and cultural value).

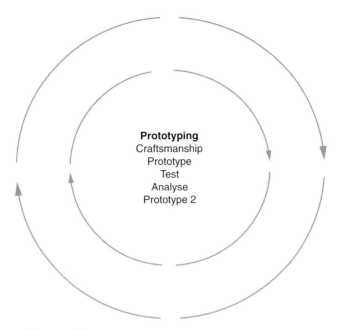

Prototyping
Craftsmanship
Prototype
Test
Analyse
Prototype 2

Fig. 7.17 Stage 5: Prototyping.

Processing outcome

The outcome is processed in a combination of **different elements that create the mechanics**. Mechanics are all activities, behaviours and control mechanisms the participant is offered in context of the experience (Hunicke *et al.*, 2004). It is comparable to entering a gate, meeting a fairy-tale character, watching a movie, moving an object, etc. The combination of all elements creates the experience in the mind of the participant, which will eventually lead to a memory of and satisfaction with the experience. Adapting mechanics directly affects dynamics. For example, when an experience lasts longer, or when participants are offered more elements during an experience, it will have consequences for the attention span and level of involvement of the participants.

With help of the **transformation design model**, the experience of the individual user can be mapped. This model enables construction of the experience via the precise combination of building blocks (mechanics) to create the desired dynamics, which result in a meaningful experience with memorable aesthetics. (This model will be further discussed in Chapter 8.)

The prototype

During the prototyping stage, the Imagineers apply several trades to move from concept to design. Despite the fact that the design doesn't exist as yet – it still needs to be constructed – a prototype is made through dialogue between users and non-designers about the design and its success factors. The prototype is made by using different trades, sometimes with co-creation, sometimes without co-creation of the client and/or some of the future users (subjects). When the design is done by co-creation, it allows for investigation how to fine-tune to the user's enjoyment or how to meet the expectations of the client.

A prototype is a way to effectively test and research the design's effect in terms of emotions, experience and user friendliness. It enables designers to directly connect to the users and clients and discuss what works, what doesn't and whether it 'feels' right. It can also be used for testing what effects the future design has while using it (this is referred to as **play test** in the gaming industry).

The first prototype doesn't have to be in perfect working order as yet. At this stage it is important to have an impression and understanding of the user experience, as this is of importance to the Imagineer in terms of understanding the design's requirements. To find out more about additional requirements, it is possible to go through the research and development stages again. The purpose of the research is to uncover assumptions and expectations of the subjects, the prototype gives valuable feedback on this. For this reason, users are being filmed using the prototype, this way, designers can analyse and evaluate what kind of implication it has for what concerns the final design.

Alternatives for the prototype

Building a tangible prototype is impossible for intangible products, such as a service or an experience. Role play could be used to experiment with the design. During role play, people automatically follow social scripts that are normal in terms of human communication. You immediately realize when something is right or wrong. Role plays are a suitable tool for assessing emotional effects of a service, experience or idea on people (Brown, 2009).

> IDEO designed a sleeping experience for passengers of an airline company. They put six chairs in a row, in the exact same configuration of an aeroplane. They then sat on the chairs to get a good feel of the situation and how it felt sleeping in a confined space.

Analysis

The Imagineer and his team will discuss the effects and outcome of the role play. They will jointly decide which critical success factors were responsible for the effects and how it could be reproduced in the final design. In order for the subjects to put aside their assumptions and expectations, a thorough analysis of feedback on the prototype is desirable.

> **When cooking dinner is a priority**
>
> Remarks made by participants or consensus about certain topics can serve as a starting point of design. These could be very simple remarks, such as 'Red gives a warm, cosy feeling' or 'It has to be ready on time, as I have to cook dinner tonight'. These particular remarks give an indication of their occupations and priorities. The design will be based on these. For someone who values family and family life, you shouldn't create an experience on a Sunday that is not a family event. In case you do decided to organize such an event, you can be sure of the fact that the person won't attend, unless he can't get away with it (when it is mandatory and work related). The problem is then the fact that he will come unmotivated, when people attend with no or little motivation, the effect of the experience will not have the intended effect.

During the prototyping stage it is possible to test several prototypes on different types of groups. This can be done internally within the team itself, or for example by a panel of users, even with the client or even by creating a mini experience in real life. As we previously discussed at the beginning of this chapter, Disney Imagineers do this in the Disney theme parks. They are continuously experimenting, assessing and evaluating their work to come up with innovations based on new solutions and designs.

Final design and outcome

The meaningful, high-quality concept's preconditions are translated to a meaningful transformation process. This can be achieved by using other instruments such as scenario techniques or a mood board. The outcomes of the prototyping stage are:

- composition of an individual or common experience by means of a complete design model;
- the exact and detailed story that is to be conveyed to the participants;
- a thoroughly tested prototype with possible additions for the final design;
- a complete scenario or storyboard; and
- a creative briefing for the designers and engineers based on the Imagineer's design.

7.3.6 Stage 6: Design

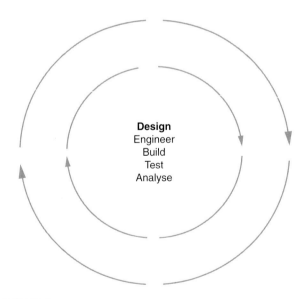

Design
Engineer
Build
Test
Analyse

Fig. 7.18 Stage 6: Design.

Once the concept of the development stage is translated to a detailed design and a working prototype in the prototype stage, it is time for the final design. In this stage, the prototype is rebuilt and becomes a working model. This is referred to as the 'engineering component' of the Imagineering process: moving from imagination to building something abstract or tangible.

This stage could require additional team members with specific skills and expertise. The Imagineer supervises and directs the entire construction and execution processes.

The team starts with an analysis of the design, after the analysis the design will be built based on the materials and technical expertise represented within the team, or based on what was generated during the research stage. Certain team members will do more work as they possess knowledge and skills for building the design. In case the design had been an event for example, the decor builder would have been part of the team from the beginning in order to give his input, set preconditions and work independently on shaping the décor.

The Imagineer is responsible for the overarching vision: he makes sure that all separate elements are combined in one fine-tuned overall design. This stage is a transition between imagination and implementation, the core of Imagineering. Outcomes of this stage are:

- prototyping and design of decors and costumes;
- lighting plan;
- video materials;
- sound materials and specifically composed music arrangements;
- logistics in terms of location, crowd control;
- transcripts for employees or people who will be in direct contact with the visitors; and
- training for employees or people who will be in direct contact with the visitors, etc.

7.3.7 Stage 7: Application

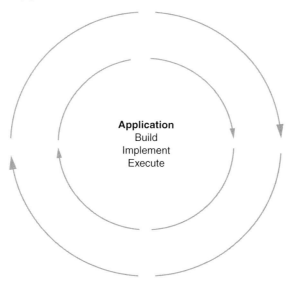

Application
Build
Implement
Execute

Fig. 7.19 Stage 7: Application.

Stage seven – application and execution of the design – is part of the implementation phase. During execution there is still room for spontaneity and experimentation. As it concerns new designs that are being trialled physically, it is possible that during these trials special things happen that could add value to the design. The Imagineer pays particular attention to these possibilities and continuously analyses the effects during construction. This process is iterative as well: when an analysis shows that parts of the design are dysfunctional or not up to standard or could achieve a higher success rate, parts of the design will be rebuilt.

7.3.8   Stage 8: Evaluation

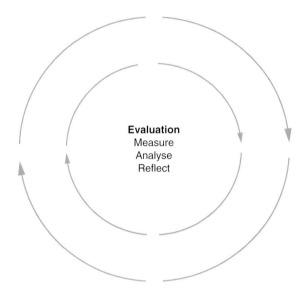

Evaluation
Measure
Analyse
Reflect

Fig. 7.20 Stage 8: Evaluation.

During the execution stage, the team collects research data as well. The subjects' reactions are registered on video or observed by the team members at all possible times. Google Analytics is studied to look for online effects: how do follower groups emerge and what kind of comments are given?

Subsequently, the Imagineer and his team will reflect on the outcome of collected data and the effects it has on the subjects. When do we have people's full attention during an experience? How many people were invited and how many actually turned up? What were the comments of people when they entered and when they left? What were the online comments? Do people still remember the experience after one week, and what do they remember of the experience? To what extent does it solve the client's problem? In other words, to what extent has the management issue been solved?

Answers to these and other questions provide an understanding of how the design can be changed and improved and what can be learned in terms of future designs. It could also result in an adaptation of the current design, which means that the whole Imagineering process can be repeated again. The whole Imagineering process is iterative until all results are positive.

Eight stages in Disney's World of Experience

Any new attraction or experience in a Disney theme park goes through eight stages of the Imagineering process.

- **Stage 1 Formulation of management issues with preconditions:** A new section in the park, which needs to generate new visitors or repeat visits. The new attraction should fit the existing vision and identity.
- **Stage 2 Construction of a team:** A team consists of people from different disciplines, who will design the new attraction in an innovative way, for example: a decor builder, a technical engineer, an architect, an opera director, a circus connoisseur, an animal tamer, an illustrator and a project manager.
- **Stage 3 Research:** Understand already existing knowledge within the team. At the same time, it is important to make an inventory of what new knowledge is required. What are the trends and future technological developments? What is the competition doing? What are the visitor's expectations. Try to fill the shoes of the visitor and look at the experience from his perspective and try to understand his fantasy world so to speak.
- **Stage 4 Development:** Imagine without any limitations, think and discuss it within the team. What is the basic story (vision) of the new section in the park? For example, a small, sweet little animal (underdog), which is going to save the world (idealism) and makes many friends on the way who will help him (social interaction).
- **Stage 5 Prototyping:** To design a story that will be introduced to the target group, step by step. One can think of technical tricks that can be applied to surprise the audience. These so-called test versions are vital in order to see the audience's reaction to the experience and to understand whether design needs adaptation.
- **Stage 6 Design:** The design is executed in different parts: the decor builder builds the decor, props, reception, etc. The architects design the physical surroundings, the costume designer makes costumes for the staff, the lighting professional makes a light show, the video editor uses necessary audio visual equipment to register for example, singers practice their part.
- **Stage 7 Application:** In his capacity as a director, the Imagineer combines all separate elements, before it is shown to the audience for the first time. Each time it is shown, the execution will be fine-tuned and improved. This is also an iterative process, which means that sometimes a revisit of the research stage is required to redesign certain parts, in order to have a bigger impact.
- **Stage 8 Evaluation:** Disney evaluates whether the new section was received well by the audience? How does the audience react to the experience? How do they convey their experience to other people? Are people specifically attracted to this section of the park (this is particularly the case with Space Mountain)? Based on this information, Disney decides whether the predetermined goals have been reached.

(Continued)

Continued.

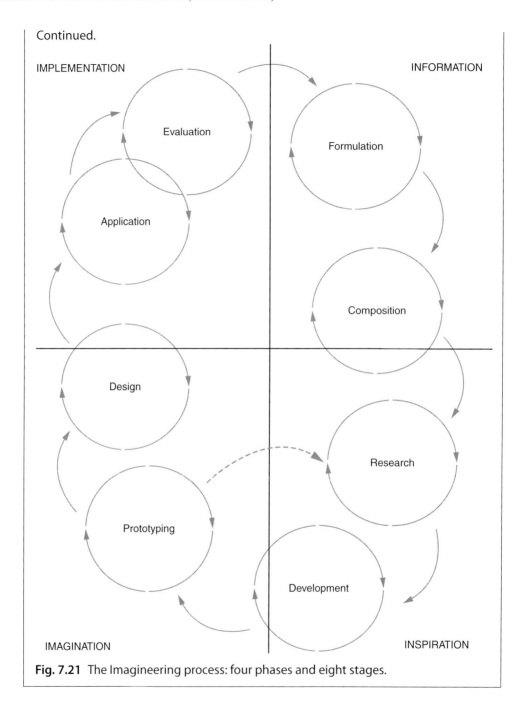

Fig. 7.21 The Imagineering process: four phases and eight stages.

7.4 SUMMARY

The Imagineering process consists of four phases; information, inspiration, imagination and implementation. These phases consist of eight stages; formulation, construction, development, prototyping, design, application and evaluation. The user is always the main focus during this process (through observation, asking questions and careful listening). Experimentation is an important tool for research on how to improve user satisfaction. The Imagineer learns from prototyping and testing prototypes. The Imagineer participates in the Imagineering process by supplying the team with his knowledge, stories and provides a certain perspective. A multi-disciplinary team adds several other perspectives, in a way that maximum innovation is guaranteed. Creative techniques help the team to use their critical, higher order thinking skills, which should result in innovative ideas that can be translated to realistic concepts. To achieve a meaningful transformation process, the Imagineer can use the design model to test whether the concept meets the experience criteria. Trades are used to make a first prototype for experimentation. This generates co-creation with the client's user group.

7.5   ASSIGNMENTS

Assignment 1

Go online and search for prototypes of existing car models. Which differences do you notice while comparing the prototype and end product of the car model that was produced in the end? What does it tell us about prototypes?

Assignment 2

Do a role play of buying bread in a shop. What do you notice in the process? What can you say about the shopping experience afterwards?

7.6   RECOMMENDED READING

The interdisciplinary design process in the creative industry:

- Best, K. (2010) *The Fundamentals of Design Management*. AVA Publishing, Singapore.

How to build a story around a brand:

- Fog, K., Budtz, C., Munch, P. and Blanchette, S. (2010) *Storytelling: Branding in Practice*. Springer, Berlin, Heidelberg.

chapter 8

The Imagineer's Design Methodology

Gabriëlle Kuiper

Just a typical summer day, almost at the end of summer, there are huge white clouds in a clear blue sky. A familiar scent of summer, peace and quiet, not a soul in the streets as the school holidays near an end. We are on a boat tour through the backwaters of Amsterdam in a place called Waterland. Just five minutes away from this metropolis and world city, in a place where silence prevails, sailing through the backwaters, surrounded by high reeds and green pastures. I am in wonder and proud of the fact that this is part of the Netherlands and that we have access to it. Singing winds, playing birds and occasionally a splashing fish. Sailing and enjoying our surroundings while taking it all in. Sometimes I feel the water streaming through my fingers. No obligations, just peace and quiet. A field, the grain is harvested manually. Three sun-tanned, silent famers in white trousers and bare chests using large scythes. Sensuality, masculinity. Just behind them the recently cut grains light up.

The smell of fire, smoke and small flames on the ground, popping sounds. Authenticity. The large white clouds slowly drifting by. The sun just behind the clouds, yet low enough to give it a surrealistic feel. Slowly we continue to float, in silence and in wonder. These unexpected moments present us with images that will remain engraved in our memory. Is it possible to actually compose and direct an experience like this in advance?

In Chapter 7, we described the Imagineering process in four phases (information, inspiration, imagination and implementation) and eight stages (formulation, composition, research, development, prototyping, design, application, evaluation). The imagination process was described in big lines, and is further discussed in more detail in this chapter. We will elaborate on which tools the Imagineer can apply, and moreover, in which ways he can step by step built a meaningful experience.

After this chapter you will have a better understanding of:

- designing behaviour;
- the critical success factors of designing behaviour;
- how the participants digest information of the design;
- how concentration span works and how to take this into consideration while designing transformation; and
- how to test the imagined transformation of the design and to communicate this to the team members and clients.

8.1 DESIGN

Based on the outcome during the research stage, and the ideas that were generated during this stage, the design is made in the design stage. The design is focused on the individual participant within a group. Step by step, the individual will go through a predefined emotional and intellectual development, creating a transformational experience.

The Imagineer needs to keep in mind that the design is focused on solving a management issue and not primarily on finalizing a tangible design. In other words, the designs are the means to reaching a predefined goal (e.g. loyalty, learning, team-building, etc.).

> 'By designing all of the touch points between people and organizations we create meaningful and genuine experiences.' Craig LaRosa – Continuum; www.continuuminnovation.com

8.1.1 The Holistic View

The Imagineer has a holistic view on design. This means the following:

- He uses several disciplines to reach the end goal (for example film, theatre, decor, technology, game, physical location, sound).
- He uses his own sources (backpack collection) in terms of inspiration, experience and knowledge.
- He transforms his knowledge of human behaviour and motivation and learning processes into designs for meaningful experiences. A learning curve of a human being means that s/he automatically attaches meaning to the experience at an individual level. The higher the relevancy for the participant, the more he will learn or remember making it more meaningful. To reach its full potential it is crucial that participants are highly motivated and in a positive mood.

8.1.2　Design is an Iterative Process

Designing something means more than just creating something beautiful or fun. It is a process in which you, step by step, improve your concept, while this should lead to an end result with a 100% satisfaction rate. The design process is therefore often iterative: it is repeated over and over again. Each step generates specific information which results in adaptation and improvement of the design.

Imagine you are having people over for dinner, and you really want to prepare a wonderful meal. First of all, you will do some research: what shall I make, what are the best recipes, how do I combine these to a well-balanced, yet exciting meal?

The actual cooking requires preparation of the right ingredients, in the correct order, with the correct measurements at the right temperature. When you try out a new recipe, you are only able to fully understand the recipe after trying it two or three times. If you want to be sure of a perfect dinner party, it is advisable to try out new recipes beforehand. This way, you will discover that a quiche requires a longer time in the oven, or that less sugar is required in the dessert. In other words, you make prototypes.

On the evening of the dinner, you taste the dinner to see whether the sauce is tasty enough, or whether it needs more spices.

The Imagineer uses prototypes to test how the end result can be improved.

8.1.3　Design Behaviour

Designing a meaningful experience to solve a management issue literally means designing behaviour of an individual (subject). Meaningful experiences are the means to accomplish this, as we have seen previously. Figure 8.1 represents how individual experiences come into existence.

In his design, the Imagineer orchestrates the combination of different elements of the design to achieve the desired individual experience. He uses stimuli framed in time and space in the physical and social context to trigger behaviour (e.g. dancing, laughing) of the participant.

Orchestrating stimuli in such a way that not only the individual behaves a certain way, but also the group of people they are part of, enhances and deepens the experience for the individual. Sharing the moment and the memory with group members creates bonds and connections.

Figure 8.1 can be filled in with the introductory case of the beginning of this chapter. The result can be seen in Fig. 8.2.

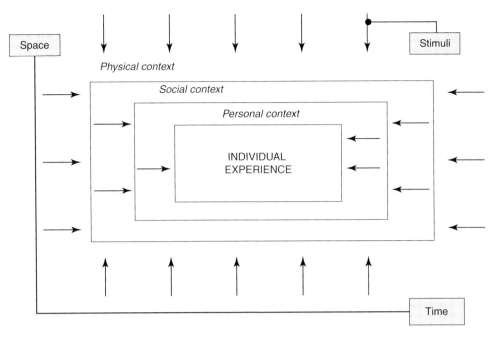

Fig. 8.1 Space, time, social context and individual perception.

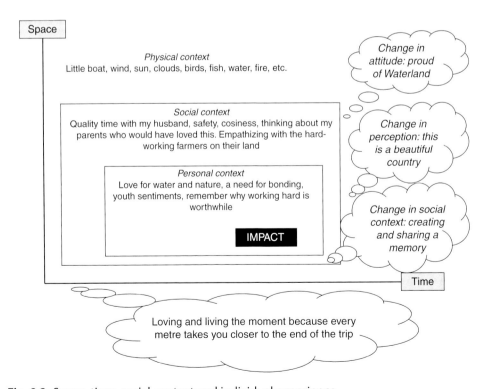

Fig. 8.2 Space, time, social context and individual experience.

8.2 ATTENTION AND RETENTION

The management issue will be solved, to some extent, through the change in behaviour or attitude. The behaviour and/or attitude change represents the economic value of the design. The Imagineer therefore directs the transformation process of the subject, with the help of the experience. When the subject subconsciously recognizes the experience, it is stored in his memory, whereby the memory is responsible for the attitude or behaviour change.

Remembering this experience, and it being stored in the memory of the subject, is called **retention**. The aim of the design is to achieve maximum retention.

McGuire's model shows which steps precede retention. The model clearly shows that an experience not only requires designing certain stimuli, but also needs to take into consideration the behaviour of the subjects in such a way that the subjects actually notice the stimuli, understand the stimuli and accept it. Critical success factors are therefore:

- selective attention and awareness;
- comprehension and understanding; and
- acceptance.

In the next section we will further elaborate on certain aspects of McGuire's model.

8.2.1 Stimuli

The subject uses several senses to absorb the combination of stimuli during the transformation process. This is what is called the presentation of information to the subject. The strength of

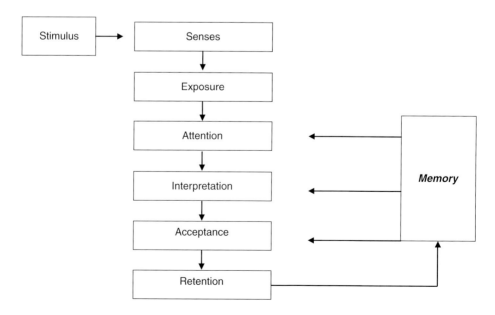

Fig. 8.3 Retention process (adapted from McGuire, 1976).

stimuli and the moment of presentation are the deciding factors of how the subject is going to accept the information. Depending on the moment, the stimuli are adjusted (sometimes stronger, sometimes less strong). In the initial state of catching the attention, the stimuli have to be stronger in comparison to the state of flow of a subject. When a subject is in flow, only minimal stimuli are accepted and retained. We will elaborate on this in the following sections.

8.2.2   Selective Attention and Awareness

> When you are having a dialogue with someone during a party, you most probably won't hear the music. The same happens when you have a dialogue while driving a car; in some cases you don't even remember how you got to your destination.

Attention is a cognitive process in an individual. Full attention covers all parts of the brain. Fully concentrated, conscious focus, is what Csikszentmihalyi refers to as *flow* (Section 4.5.2).

Living organisms use attention skills to react effectively to certain stimuli (fight or flight). The brain should not be distracted by other stimuli that are less important, and can be neglected. The above examples show that even without threatening situations our brain can neglect unimportant stimuli. For this to happen, the entire focus of the brain needs to be on something entirely different. This is referred to as **selective attention**.

> It is highly possible that a plane flew over when we were sailing through the river in our little boat; however, we completely missed it, as our entire focus was on the beautiful images we experienced. The same happens during Santa's visit: children believe in Santa and are so focused on him that they don't realize it is an ordinary man, dressed in a red suit, wearing a fake beard.

Motivation

To establish selective motivation in a subject is only possible when he is motivated. This requires a predefined understanding of his assumptions and prejudices. What is his attitude in relation to the design? What kind of expectations does he have before participation in the experience? What are his/her starting points/point of departure? What is the point of departure in terms of his knowledge and experience? The Imagineer has already researched and analysed these questions in the research stage.

In Section 4.5.6 we discussed that motivation in subjects depends on:

- level of challenge;
- self-confidence in this area;
- verifiable outcome;
- the expectation that a good achievement leads to the desired outcome; and
- value-attachment based on someone's primary needs.

Furthermore, the Imagineer needs to be aware and take into account the fact that positive emotions are more motivating than cognitive knowledge (Franzen, 2004). People primarily strive for pleasure and happiness (Sigmund Freud called this the 'pleasure principle').

Attention span

A good attention span is not only necessary to get the attention but also to keep it for a longer period of time. The attention span can be specifically designed to make sure that the experience has a bigger impact, and as such increases retention. This is further explained in Section 8.3.

8.2.3   Interpretation

The interpretation of offered stimuli depends on different factors:

- **The starting situation of the subject,** particularly on how the offer meets existing know-ledge, experience and attitude. When the offered stimuli and information don't comply with the experience world of the subject, chances are slim in terms of interpreting the design in the desired/anticipated way.
- **Social and cultural aspects.** When language and codes differ from the subject's, this will interfere with the interpretation.
- **Suppositions and assumptions about a design.** These should have emerged during the research stage in order to meet the subject's experience needs in the right way.

The Elaboration Likelihood Model (Section 2.5) shows how the offered information can be assimilated.

8.2.4   Acceptance

After acceptance of the received and interpreted information, the subject assesses whether he agrees with the information. His assessment is based on knowledge, opinions but also the social context, which is quite influential. When a group accepts an experience, the individual is more likely to do this too.

8.2.5   Design with the Purpose of Increasing Retention

The design is focused on retention: a thorough build-up of type, and number of stimuli combined, which stands out, and gives sufficient exposure to the subjects.

Reception and assimilation of stimuli

Sensory stimuli are offered from the physical context. Retention is only possible when these stimuli are offered at the right moment, in the right place. This principally means that at that specific moment the correct quantity of motivation is available to recognize the offered stimuli.

Whether this is actually true, depends largely on the personal context. When motivation is sufficiently present, in such a way, that it enables selective attention for the specific offered

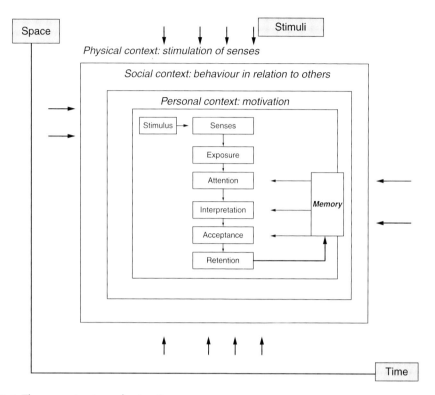

Fig. 8.4 Three contexts and retention.

stimuli, reception and assimilation are possible within the receiver. Assimilation starts with a personal interpretation of stimuli, based on the individual emotional reaction, expectations, personal interests, present knowledge, memories and culture; however, whether this actually happens depends on how safe someone feels, and whether or not the person gets distracted by physiological needs or challenges (thirst, an environment that is too cold or too hot).

Personal factors determine whether interaction takes place in the first place, and if stimuli are received. Received stimuli is mirrored on social context. This not only influences the behaviour of the receiver but also on the interpretation of the received stimuli: when everybody rejects it or thinks it is silly, then the receiver will most probably experience it in a similar way.

8.3 THE ATTENTION SPAN

During the design stage, all details of the experience are completed. Each second is composed and directed, all layers are filled in in detail and become concrete, all based on a predefined attention span. This attention span ensures fully engaged subjects during the experience. The subjects' attention is continuously held during the experience. This results in a state of 'flow', which means that they forget time and are fully engaged in the experience (they won't leave halfway, for example).

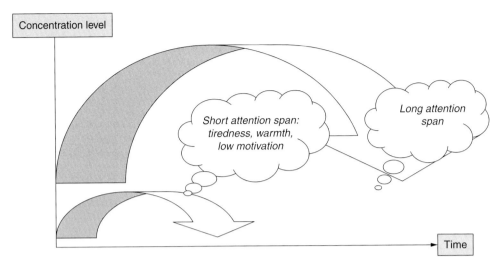

Fig. 8.5 Short and long attention span.

An attention span gives an indication how long someone can be focused and concentrated on something. The attention span starts, when something or someone catches an individual's attention. The moment the individual starts losing focus, and starts thinking of other things, the attention span is over and concentration is lost. People in groups reinforce each other: when everybody is concentrated, as an individual, you put in more effort to stay concentrated in case your thoughts wander off. The social context is therefore influential in terms of the attention span of an individual. On the other hand, a number of people who are disengaged, might start talking to each other, or even distract other people, whereby continuously the whole group suddenly loses focus.

8.3.1 Factors That Have an Influence on Attention Span

Ancient Greek philosopher Aristotle was a theatre scientist *avant la lettre*, he made an inventory of different factors that influence attention span:

1. **Plot.** The actual story with all the events and the sequence of events.
2. **Theme.** Meaning: What kind of impact will it have?
3. **Character.** The human factor, empathy and the personality of the persona.
4. **Diction and Language.** Appearance, design, language and codes that are used.
5. **Music and Rhythm.** The symphony of sound, melody of the play.
6. **Spectacle.** The play, interaction and visual elements.

There are other secondary factors that influence the level of concentration.

- **What kind of concentration is required?** With an alternation of visual, auditory and tactile concentration, it will be easier to stay focused.
- **What kind of activity is it?** While watching an exciting movie, one usually has a longer attention span in comparison to listening to a lecture of a not so gifted orator.

- **Motivation.** When people voluntarily participate, they usually have a higher motivation than when participation is mandatory.
- **Age.** Children up to 6 years old have an attention span of 10 minutes (mandatory activity), while adolescents and adults have an attention span of maximum 30 minutes.
- **The level of which primary needs are met.** People can only allow for meaningful experiences when their primary needs are met. For example, people are unable to concentrate for a longer period of time in an environment which is too hot. The optimal situation is an environment with fresh oxygen-filled air at a temperature of 20°C. Furthermore, people shouldn't be hungry, thirsty, sleepy or distracted by physical discomfort or pain (a sore back as a result of sitting on bad chairs).
- **The space.** The safer the place, the higher the concentration. In general, people don't like to stand or sit down in the middle of an empty space and prefer walls, as it provides some cover. Therefore, most tables in a restaurant that are near the window, wall or in a corner have the guests' first preference in comparison to the tables that are in the middle of the restaurant.
- **Stay focused.** By varying and alternating different kinds of concentration (visual, auditory, tactile), people can stay focused for a longer period of time, which increases the attention span.

Another way to keep the receiver engaged is by keeping him in suspense. TV series apply this in the so-called **cliffhangers**.

When an episode has an open ending right at the moment-supreme, your viewers will want to see the continuation and are therefore focused, and look forward to the next episode. This trick extrinsically motivates people to watch. Soap operas use this trick to their advantage.

The attention span needs to be taken into consideration in music, literature, movie and theatre experiences. In the remainder of this section we will further investigate how we can work with these within artistic disciplines.

8.3.2 Attention Span in Music

In music compositions, alternation between tension and relaxation keeps the attention of the auditory focused listener. A commonly accepted principle is that the more tension, the more the listener longs for relaxation. In music, relaxation can be offered by changing a dissonant to a consonant.

In a longer composition, different attention spans can be found. In Figure 8.6, a large, over-arching attention span can be seen. It covers three smaller attention spans, which on their part consist of smaller attention spans. The attention span of a music composition can be steered in different manners. A composer can build it in while composing, whereas a conductor can steer it during the execution of the composition by building tension and releasing it with:

- varying rhythm and dynamics (loud and soft);
- different tones or riddles in the melody;

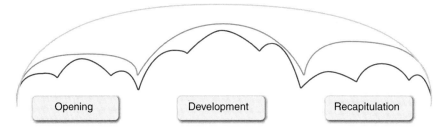

Fig. 8.6 Attention span in a classical sonata.

- repetitive melody lines that are recognizable;
- a Q & A game between instruments and singers;
- a logic or illogic line in harmony;
- silence; or
- a musical cliffhanger (via suspense of an expected chord).

8.3.3 Attention Span in Literature

A writer needs to make sure that his readers stay visually focused. Curiosity needs to be triggered continuously, so that the reader will finish the book in one go. This is referred to as a **page turner**: the reader wants to keep reading, and continues to do so by turning page after page.

Each chapter could have a small attention span and falls under an overarching attention span of the whole book, as we have seen previously in music. The story in itself also needs to have its own attention span, which basically covers the whole book and each part of the book adds to the build-up of this attention span. Most authors think of this in advance.

An author can use different 'instruments' to build up tension.

- **Leaving out specific information on purpose,** this way the reader's mind is activated: he wants to know what is going to happen, or what happened and starts having his own presumptions.
- **A shock effect,** unexpected events, often in an uneventful part of the book.
- **Variations in time.** When we talk about 'story time' we mean the time covered in the story. The story could cover five centuries or five minutes. The story time varies from the time it takes the reader to actually read the story. The general rule of 'story time' is the more exciting the story, the slower the pace of storytelling. In an exciting part of a story, each detail can be described. This increases tension. Less exciting parts in a story will require a higher pace and the story will then be told in big lines instead of detail.
- **Hope** is a very powerful way to build up tension. The reader will wonder whether the main character will be saved or not: 'I hope all turns out well!' The author needs to find a balance between sufficient hope for a good ending, but not too much in the sense that the outcome is clear and predictable.

8.3.4   Attention Span in Movies and Theatre

Movies and theatre require a combination of visual and auditory concentration. Alternation of these two results in a higher attention span.

A play has a fixed structure, which is based on the understanding of how to keep the audience focused.

- A performance usually starts uneventful.
- As the story develops, more and more tension is incorporated into the story.
- Before the ending of the performance, the tension is at its highest level, and tension is released towards the end.

Similarly to music and books, each and every scene of a performance also requires a new tension span. The progress of the story will look like a wave motion.

A scenario always consists of:

- a beginning;
- a body (confrontation and crisis); and
- an ending (denouement).

Beginning

The beginning consists of:

- an opening scene (exposition, attention grabber);
- an introduction scene (identification);
- an exposition scene (start of the plot); and
- a moment of change (mistake, transition to body of the play).

The **exposition** is the introduction of the story, it serves the purpose of explaining the context of the story, the main characters and how they relate to each other. The characters are presented in such a way that the audience **identifies** itself with certain characters, and feels engaged in certain events. To instantly engage and get the focus and attention of the viewers, modern movies usually start with a so-called **teaser** or **hook**, a spectacular starting scene, which ideally (however not necessarily) refers to the plot, for example 'Rambo's narrow escape from the police station', followed by some wild chase scenes. The first transition in a narrative structure is mostly the **harmatia**, Aristotle and Torok, a tragic flaw of the main character, which sets the story in motion, and simultaneously is the transition to the body of the story.

Body

The body consists of:

- a crisis; and
- obstacles (mini attention span).

The body always contains a **crisis**. The action begins and is explained. The main character has to overcome certain **obstacles** to reach his goal.

Denouement

The third part consists of:

- a confrontation;
- a climax;
- a denouement; and
- a resolution.

An important event occurs (**confrontation**), which leads to a dramatic development (**climax**). At that particular moment, the character is forced to choose from different options, choices, and ways to deal with the situation. Due to this choice, there is a twist and the story line changes unexpectedly (**denouement**). The story and events have done 'something' to the main character and have led to evolving to a higher level.

8.3.5 Building Tension

The Imagineer will build up his design in such a dramatic way that the maximum tension span is reached. This build-up looks as follows:

- a pre-experience moment prior to grab the attention;
- a transition moment to start believing;
- an identification moment;
- the continuation of the plot and the build-up to change;
- possible obstacles to postpone the denouement; and
- finally the climax.

The above leads to a solution that transforms the believer, the subject. The subject not only observes the movie-hero's transformation, but engages in the transformation, and therefore gets transformed in some way.

The model in Fig. 8.7 will be further developed, step by step in the remainder of this chapter.

Tension arc stage	Pre-experience	Transition	Introduction and change	Obstacles and crisis	Confrontation	Climax	Resolution	Continuation
	Symphony							
	Time →							

Fig. 8.7 Dramatic build-up of an experience: Design Model of Imagineered Transformation.

The Imagineer takes the following conditions into consideration while working on the construction of the tension span.

- The theme of the story has meaning for the user group (social context) and the individual user (personal context).
- Language and diction of the users – all the staff the user is exposed to – are target group specific, this means that they meet the expectations and experience of the target group.
- The design consists of a well-balanced alternation of shock effects (wake up the participant) and quiet moments (time to digest the experience), interaction, incomplete information, tactile, auditory and visual concentration.
- The physical context not only triggers the senses, but also meets the primary needs (such as ventilation, temperature, spatial awareness and so on).

8.4 DESIGN MODEL OF IMAGINEERED TRANSFORMATION

In the Design Model of Imagineered Transformation the physical, social and personal context are explicitly described. This is further worked out in a scenario and a 'storyboard'. Besides a description of the scenes, it also specifies how the scenes will be executed.

After step 1, the Imagineer and his team know which management issue they need to solve. After step 2, they know each other's strengths and weaknesses. In step 3 they have gained knowledge and experience in order to start a multi-layered concept during the Development stage (see Section 4.3). This concept should actually solve the problem. This is done in the design stage. Below we will illustrate how concept and completion relate to each other in two examples.

Sesame Street

The concept of Sesame Street is a TV programme in which animal-like dolls and people experience all kinds of adventures, and follows social interaction, which follows real-life conventions. The essence of the Sesame Street concept is the stimulation of fantasy, mutual understanding and honesty in a specific age group. The essence of the concept for each episode is completed during the design stage.

Harry Potter

The concept of the Harry Potter books and movies is an ordinary boy with exceptional magical powers, who experiences many exciting adventures together with two friends, as a result of a wicked sorcerer who wants him dead.

This concept is worked out in detail and completed in different adventures that he encounters, which are developed over several years. Harry slowly transforms in to a strong magician. Each story has a tension build-up, the attention span with alternation between action scenes and silence to reveal the story layer by layer.

The aim of an experience designed by an Imagineer is to transform the participant (subject), by offering him something (knowledge, experience), which will change this behaviour or attitude. The Imagineer works according to the different steps which are described in Section 7.3.

In the following sections we will step by step complete the different components of an experience, namely:

- time;
- participants;
- emotional experience; and
- possible tools.

8.4.1 Time

The experience happens within a certain predefined time frame. Within this time frame, participants encounter different elements of the experience, which are appropriately spread within this time frame.

This time frame can be relatively short (for example an episode of Sesame Street), or extremely long (some months or even years). In order to achieve behavioural changes, longer periods of time are required. It takes time and repetition to develop new habits. This doesn't mean that an experience of just a few seconds can't have a big impact, for example when something is funny or touches you emotionally.

A flash mob is a good example of a high impact within a short time frame.

Symphony

The Imagineer creates symphony between all the elements of the experience, even when the experience covers a time span of 4 years.

The effect of symphony is the fact that all elements become one logic, holistic entity, with a synergetic effect. To maintain symphony the concept is used as checking tool.

The tool checks whether an element fits the concept. The concept can be compared to an umbrella under which all the elements fit logically.

Gut feeling

This necessity for symphony entails that the Imagineer keeps the overview at any given time. Later on, when his team needs to start completion of the details during the design stage, he still needs to steer and test whether all fits and matches the overall vision. He consciously does this while using the design model, however he intuitively feels whether a combination of elements works or not. This gut feeling warns you when something doesn't feel right, the same way when you find a bump on a smooth surface which doesn't belong there. In order to formulate what it is that isn't exactly right, you need experience.

Even as a starting Imagineer, by being open-minded and when you dare to use your intuition instead of your mind, you are able to understand when something isn't entirely right and doesn't run smoothly.

Division of different phases over time

The different phases are divided over time, as can be seen in the model of Figure 8.8. The first phase can cover quite a lot of time. For events this is a period of minimum 6 weeks; however, a teaser campaign could start a year in advance.

A longer phase in advance will be divided in several mini tension spans. The transition phase is a short ritual. The introduction phase requires some more time; however, the focus in the experience is in phase four (obstacles) and phase five (crisis). The climax is dealt with in a reasonably fast manner, equally the resolution.

8.4.2   Participants

The design is focused on steering emotion and behaviour of the participants. The Imagineer is aware of the subjects for whom he designs: what are their expectations and how will this group give meaning to the experience? He will design in such way that the participants will reach a state of flow, to reach a guaranteed maximum focus/attention of the participants.

The fact that the subjects are able to focus during the experience and actually start 'believing' it, the predominant goal. We will illustrate with the following examples.

> A serious game, which can be played for a longer period of time, needs to engage the players. Additionally the players need to appreciate the game and lose track of time while playing.
>
> When people enter a ghost house, the focus of the house should be on ghosts. You don't want them to focus on technique or how the decor has been built.
>
> In a Disney Park, people should be able to recognize the real Mickey Mouse, instead of a man in a plush (Mickey Mouse) suit.

Participants must dare to engage in the offered immersive experience.

Tension arc stage	Pre-experience	Transition	Introduction and change	Obstacles and crisis	Confrontation	Climax	Resolution	Continuation

Symphony

Time →

Fig. 8.8 Time division of dramatic stages.

8.4.3   Emotional Experience

The Imagineer plays with the emotional experience of the subjects. He anticipates how the participants feel because of the experience, what kind of atmosphere should be created and why this should be created.

Emotional experience results in meaning and transformation, therefore it needs to be constructed carefully. An alternation of different kinds of concentration is necessary for the participants to get into, and remain in a state of increasing flow.

8.4.4   Tools

The Imagineer has different tools to build the tension span and to steer the subjects' behaviour and emotions. In essence, all these tools are used to offer sensory stimuli.

> An entering elephant has a tremendous visual impact; more so when you hear or smell him. An elephant touches people on an emotional level, it affects them. In general people have respect for elephants; they are huge and strong, and at the same time 'cuddly', people want to protect elephants. This makes an elephant into a suitable 'tool'. The Imagineer considers in which way stimuli should be offered and wonders how he will use the elephant as a tool: Will he have ten elephants entering the scene in order to create a spectacle? Or, should he use a construction of a giant elephant, like the one in the Take That concert?

8.4.5   Tension Span

The Imagineer strives to keep the participants focused, keep their attention, moreover get and keep them in a state of flow.

During the entire period, the tension span needs to vary by alternating action and relaxation. Excitement and relaxation alternate. The tension is created and directed with the use of elements of time, participants, the emotional experience of the participants, and the tools that are used to achieve this. Each part of the experience has a different level of excitement and relaxation.

8.5   THE DESIGN MODEL

The different phases of the Design Model of Imagineered Transformation are completed step by step.

8.5.1   Phase 1: Pre-experience

During the first phase the subject is not yet a participant in the experience. The first phase mainly focuses on giving every future participant the same **starting motivation** as point of departure. The Imagineer works on the added value of the experience and initial knowledge.

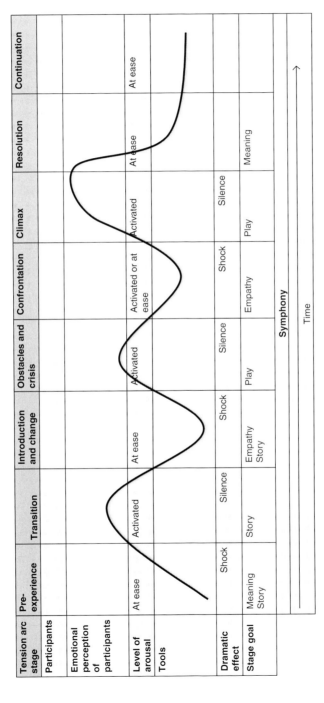

Tension arc stage	Pre-experience	Transition	Introduction and change	Obstacles and crisis	Confrontation	Climax	Resolution	Continuation
Participants								
Emotional perception of participants								
Level of arousal	At ease	Activated	At ease	Activated	Activated or at ease	Activated	At ease	At ease
Tools								
Dramatic effect	Shock	Silence	Shock	Silence	Shock	Silence		
Stage goal	Meaning Story	Story	Empathy Story	Play	Empathy	Play	Meaning	
	Symphony							
	Time →							

Fig. 8.9 Design Model of Imagineered Transformation with tension span.

Tension arc stage	Pre-experience
Participants	(Self-) Selection Expectations Context clear Give meaning
Emotional perception of participants	Anticipation Hope Curiosity Motivation
Level of arousal	At ease
Tools	Map
Dramatic effect	Shock
Stage goal	Meaning Story

Fig. 8.10 Pre-experience phase.

To get all participants on the same page

The experience focuses on a group of individuals, who all come from different backgrounds and have a different **point of departure**. The point of departure is determined by experiences of the past and existing knowledge. Based on these, the participant has certain assumptions, suppositions, preferences for colours, smell, other people, locations, etc.

The first phase has the aim of getting all participants on the same page and to make sure that everybody starts the experience with the same expectations and motivation, this way the social context deepens the experience.

The phase also serves as an **entrance policy.** Everyone is well informed about what is to be expected, and why they would be able to participate in the experience. This gives people who are unmotivated a chance to opt out.

People who visit Disney World can decide for themselves whether they want to participate in an experience or not. Anyone who doesn't want to participate simply doesn't.

When people need to participate in a **mandatory event,** for example a staff meeting or a hospital visit, it is still possible to, despite the fact that it is a mandatory event, motivate participants by giving correct information, and having a nice approach and manner. Trust is gained this way, which leads to a more positive expectation of the participants, while they become aware of the added value of participation in the event.

Additionally there are **imposed events,** this kind of event is usually a surprise to spectators and participant. Special ambush-marketing events like flash mobs or the Bavaria Brewery dresses during the World Cup in 2010 serve as a good example of this.

Arouse interest

During this phase the Imagineer tries to arouse interest of the future participants for an event/experience:

- to arouse **curiosity**;
- to create a sense of **anticipation** ('something is about to happen and I want to be part of it');
- to give the participants **hope** of added value, whatever this may be, it doesn't have to be explicit (it might even arouse curiosity, however, it can be necessary to indicate what kind of direction; is it something immaterial such as friendship or a beautiful memory, or even knowledge you gain, something tangible, etc.

All these items should induce participation of the future participant.

The future participant decides whether to participate or not, based on desirability, feasibility and the added economic, cultural or social value. Furthermore, he will be more open to the experience when he has the sense that he is in control of the outcome of the experience.

Balance between transparency and challenge

It isn't that difficult to provoke expectations and attract participants; however, for an experience to be successful, the invoked expectations need to be met. Luring people with false expectations is counterproductive.

People need to know in advance (approximately):

- What is the context of the experience?
- Is it in leisure or work time?
- What is the code of conduct, what are the rules? This serves as a safety net for the participants, which should give them the courage to participate in the experience.

At the same time, there should be the prospect of sufficient challenge. This means that the Imagineer needs to find a balance during the first phase between transparency and challenge.

When students choose a study in the humanities based on a study guide with course specifications and expected study load, they know what to expect during this course (transparency) and what is expected of the them (challenge). The motivation of these students will be higher than students who chose the same course based on a vague description such as 'fun study, which is beneficial if you are interested in working with people'. Students who choose this study because they like to go out with friends and therefore believe that they are people's people, won't be that motivated when studying for sociology for example.

Translating meaning to a personal context

During the first phase, the Imagineer completes the following elements:

- meaning; and
- story.

During the research and development phases, the Imagineer has tried to imagine how he will offer meaning to the future participants. This is where the personal context is translated to a story.

Meaning in the Harry Potter story is the fantasy people have that they are able to do more than others. For example, someone at your front door, who tells you that you have magic powers.

The audience that identifies itself with Harry might feel endowed with these powers as well. Meaning has been translated to a story of Harry Potter, a poor, maltreated orphan, who, one day, appeared to be a grand magician. This is a wonderful story for a certain age group.

Similar meaning can be seen in fairy tales (for example the story of Snow White, who despite her nasty stepmother, becomes the queen), or in ancient myths (Hercules, who discovers that he is the son of a deity).

Meaning in all these stories is quite similar; however, the completion of the final story focuses on people who will be completely engaged in the meaningful adventure.

Map

Step by step, the story unfolds during the next phases. During the first phase, only a tiny bit will be revealed to arouse curiosity and to create a sense of 'longing for more'.

The future participants are provided with a 'map' of the future experience. This map will not only provide him with the time, place, location and code of conduct.

This map can be the explicit invitation or a card, some information on the website prior to the event. It can also be implicit, as in the following example of the Amsterdam Hans Brinker Budget Hotel.

Guerrilla marketing with dog poop

Fig. 8.11 First guerrilla marketing campaign in the Netherlands by the Amsterdam Brinker Budget Hotel (1996). (Courtesy of Kesselskramer.)

(Continued)

Continued.

The Amsterdam Hans Brinker Budget Hotel had stuck little flags in piles of dog poop in front of the hotel. The flags had the following text; 'Now even more of this at our main entrance', with an arrow pointing in the direction of the entrance of the hotel. This is an invitation in the language and codes of the hotel, which leads to a selection of who fits and who doesn't fit this experience.

Tension span in the first phase

- Selective attention by arousing curiosity; and
- tension span starts through induced anticipation.

A museum experience

Your decision to visit a museum is made in the first phase. You already know why you want to visit the museum. You already have an image in your mind about the museum. You most probably gained some information from the website or people you know. Because of this you have certain expectations and hopes, as to what is to be expected. For example, a nice day with friends, or seeing the work of a famous artist for the first time, and as a result, enjoy the experience, get inspired and talk to your own network about this experience.

8.5.2   Phase 2: Transition

Tension arc stage	Pre-experience	Transition
Participants	(Self-) Selection Expectations Context clear Give meaning	Shared or individual experience? Transition
Emotional perception of participants	Anticipation Hope Curiosity Motivation	Anticipation Hope Curiosity Motivation
Level of arousal	At ease	Activated
Tools	Map	Spectacle Comfortable disorientation Physiological and safety needs
Dramatic effect	Shock	Silence
Stage goal	Meaning Story	Story

Fig. 8.12 Phase transition.

The transition phase is relatively short in comparison to the other phases; however, it represents an important moment of ritual. People 'enter the gate': people leave their ordinary lives behind and can fully engage in the upcoming experience, in other words, from now on, new rules apply.

> At Disney World in Orlando Florida people are transferred by boat to the other side. The participants are aware that they are transferred to a different world.

The physical context is the main focus during the transition phase

A transition can be accomplished in many different ways, however it is always a physical ritual. Changing clothes, getting into a boat as in Disney World, a handshake at the entrance, or a fairy-tale gate of The Efteling. In any case, during the transition phase the main focus is on the physical context.

Fig. 8.13 The fairy tale gate of The Efteling. (Courtesy of Moisturizing Tranquilizers.)

People venture in a ritual transition

A starting moment needs to be built into the experience, to indicate the start. This is called the **transition**: moving to another level. People have accepted to become a participant in a future experience. For entering the gate, and accepting the transition, a sense of safety is required. People need to venture into the experience without having to fear shame, loss of face, sense of guilt, or danger in any way.

> People shouldn't fear being made fun of in hindsight, merely because of the fact that they are in a picture with a man in a plush suit. Everybody needs to understand that it is Mickey Mouse and therefore the picture should be framed and put up on the wall.

Strengthen anticipation via shock moments

By going through the ritual transition, people feel more anticipation: the story starts to unfold from that moment onwards, whereby the atmosphere of the opening moment will determine the atmosphere for the remainder of the experience.

People are getting in the mood and form ideas about what is to come. The Imagineer strengthens this by adding some form of spectacle in the design; a short shock-moment in order to wake up the audience, and to make them forget daily chores and routines.

(This spectacle can also be the transition rite itself, just because of the spectacular boat trip or entrance gate.) 'First impressions last' is therefore a very true idiom. During this emotional experience, emotions need to be invoked that fit the purpose of the whole experience. Once can think of solidarity, joy, sorrow, awe, etc.

The shock moment, which can be relatively short, is followed by peace and quiet, tranquillity. It enables people to catch their breath. They were woken up and sucked into the experience. Emotions can calm down. The physiological and safety needs were met, now the focus can be solely on the social context and meaning.

Tension span

- Many sensory stimuli increase and strengthen selective attention.
- Tension increases due to the spectacle, which in its turn increases anticipation.

A museum experience

The transition phase of a museum visit already starts at home while you prepare for the visit. What are you going to bring with you? How will you dress? How do you travel? The actual transition happens the moment you enter the museum doors. Many museums anticipate by investing in impressive architecture that radiates a certain status and grandeur. This reflects the social norms that need to be taken into consideration inside the building. You might start speaking in a softer tone of voice, respect for and awareness of your surroundings in a different way.

8.5.3 Phase 3: Introduction and Moment of Change

Tension arc stage	Pre-experience	Transition	Introduction and change
Participants	(Self-) Selection Expectations Context clear Give meaning	Shared or individual experience? Transition	Common language Clear goals Structure Clear set of rules
Emotional perception of participants	Anticipation Hope Curiosity Motivation	Anticipation Hope Curiosity Motivation	Aspirations with regards to transformation Observed challenge
Level of arousal	At ease	Activated	At ease
Tools	Map	Spectacle Comfortable disorientation Physiological and safety needs	Subliminal engagement Mechanics, dynamics and aesthetics
Dramatic effect	Shock	Silence	Shock
Stage goal	Meaning Story	Story	Empathy Story

Fig. 8.14 Introduction phase and moment of change.

IMAGINEERING: Innovation in the Experience Economy

The introduction phase starts in a tranquil manner. This phase lasts longer than the transition phase; however, it is still relatively short. All characters are introduced and the social context becomes clear. Participants identify themselves with the characters, and with each other, whenever possible.

Drive-through meals

Transition during the experience of eating a 'drive thru' meal at McDonald's starts by driving through the gate. The introduction is at the order point, when a McDonald's employee addresses you via the intercom.

The language and codes that are used become clear. Which language do they speak? Is the setting formal or informal? It also becomes clear who is who and what is the role of the participant during the experience: who does he get in touch with, what is his relation with these people?

The underdog appears to be the main character

During the introduction of a Circus Roncalli show, the audience is introduced to the main character, the underdog clown, whose story serves as a red thread throughout the show.

Structure, rules of the game and purpose emerge

During this phase the general structure, as well as the rules of the game become clear. At the same time social norms of behaviour are linked to the game rules. This is the social script from which the language and codes are derived. Is it a shop, or are we a doctor and his patient? Maybe a teacher and a student? A boss and his employee? Are we idealistic or lazy? Are we attending a congress to learn what is the correct way for some reason? Are we here to relax or eat together? Are we here to give the children a place to play? The common purpose becomes clear and the participants start to feel connected (social context). They emotionally identify with the story that starts to unfold in front of them.

Personal aspirations

At the same time an individual connects his own personal aspirations to the desired outcome of the future experience. For example:

- wanting to be the best;
- wanting to relax;
- being part of an adventure that can be conveyed through a story;
- doing something impressive and boasting about it;
- learning something and using it to profile yourself;
- being inspired.

(Continued)

Continued.

My personal aspiration during my visit to Circus Roncalli was to be emotionally captured by the event and to be in awe of what circus artists can accomplish, and at the same time dream about what I could do; besides that, learn how they create experiences, so that later on – like now for instance in this book – I could talk about the experience.

When people have aspirations and can express these aspirations, the more committed and focused they will become. The Imagineer needs to help them to express these aspiration during this phase. This happens implicitly, this way the participants will be subconsciously engaged. Kile Ozier calls it **subliminal engagement**.

The observed challenge

During this phase it is important that the participants are aware and capable of facing the observed challenge. Participants wonder whether they are able to face the challenge in terms of investing sufficient time, energy, risk investment or not. Whether they decide to face this challenge depends on whether they feel confident enough, or whether the outcome is a realization of their aspirations. It is important that the Imagineer offers this confidence.

Moment of change

A shock is used to move from the introduction to the moment of change. The attention and focus of the participants is heightened, whereby sufficient interest is aroused to keep the attention and focus during the entire experience.

From the moment of change onwards, the search for a solution has started and the search for meaning is a fact. Step by step, the rules of the game are clear, aspirations are formulated and completed within the predefined conditions.

The visitors of Disney have oriented themselves. They have decided which park they will visit (introduction), meet Mickey Mouse and shake hands, they even take a picture together with Mickey Mouse. The travel through the park; the so-called fantasy world has officially started.

Of course there are different rides, which all have their own story and designed tension span.

Tension span

- The tension has somewhat decreased due to the silence at the end of transition phase.
- The quiet time enables participants to digest the offered information.

- Via shock we move from the introduction to the moment of change.
- After the moment of change the search for meaning begins.

A museum experience

After entering the museum we get introduced to the people who work in the museum such as the guards, the people in the wardrobe, the museum guide and the language of that guide. How playful is it and how playful can I be? (A Science Centre requires a different kind of language compared to the Museum of Modern Art).

The moment of change starts as soon as we have taken off our coats and put our bags in the lockers. We all got our aspirations from the guide or maps. What shall we do, what are we doing? Together we decide which floor we will visit first. The doors open into the first floor that we visit. Our voyage has started.

8.5.4 Phase 4: Obstacles and Crisis Phase

Tension arc stage	Pre-experience	Transition	Introduction and change	Obstacles and crisis
Participants	(Self-) Selection Expectations Context clear Give meaning	Shared or individual experience? Transition	Common language Clear goals Structure Clear set of rules	Obtain information Feel autonomy Mastery
Emotional perception of participants	Anticipation Hope Curiosity Motivation	Anticipation Hope Curiosity Motivation	Aspirations with regards to transformation Observed challenge	Participation Applying own capacities Flow
Level of arousal	At ease	Activated	At ease	Activated
Tools	Map	Spectacle Comfortable disorientation Physiological and safety needs	Subliminal engagement Mechanics, dynamics and aesthetics	Q & A Layered Successive revelation Mechanics, dynamics and aesthetics
Dramatic effect	Shock	Silence	Shock	Silence
Stage goal	Meaning Story	Story	Empathy Story	Play

Fig. 8.15 Obstacles and crisis phase.

During this voyage we encounter small obstacles, dramatic changes that require us to stay focused. This phase consists of several smaller tension spans. Part of an experience should last between 8 and 30 minutes to achieve an optimal tension span.

When one part of an experience last for an hour, the design will be divided in smaller tension spans. A one hour workshop could be divided into half an hour of auditory concentration, half an hour of participation or interaction through dialogue or a physical activity.

> Circus Roncalli designs its shows by alternating smaller 8-minute acts. In between the acts, the central character shows up with the overarching story (his dream of becoming a circus director himself once upon a time). This way, all the loose elements and small dramatic moments are connected and melt into one big symphony.

The social context

The social context has a large influence on the experience. The participants mirror each other and mirror the general response to the experience. A standing ovation has a big impact, the audience becomes more enthusiastic. On the other hand, when people are yawning or looking the other way, eyes will meet, and people will be easily distracted. The more participants are engaged in the experience, the more they are stimulated to enter deeper in the experience.

Participation

This phase requires active participation of the participants in order to actively involve them in the experience. An Imagineer can give his participants the feeling that they use their own capabilities to steer the experience.

> Circus Roncalli engages the audience in the experience by bringing them into the arena. They are allowed to participate in the act, throw things to the audience, whereby the audience is expected to catch these items. There is a sense of: 'That could have been me in the in the arena', or, 'pay attention, they might throw something to me'. It gives the participant a sense of autonomy: I need to do my best for something. This makes them part of the experience. The element of play promotes focus of attention and engagement. The visitors enter a state of flow.

Successive revelation

Short tension spans in which new obstacles are overcome result in what Kile Ozier calls **successive revelation**. Layer by layer the story is revealed, which makes people curious and wanting for more, the goal of the joint voyage.

Disney offers in his parks a variety of rides that people can visit. It is one big discovery in which all kinds of small stories tell the Disney story. The stories contain different layers. The purpose of these layers is to slowly unfold the story. The participants don't have the answer at the beginning of the experience. The top layer contains the mini stories, followed by the overarching story and in conclusion the meaning behind the whole story.

Small obstacles and crisis

During this phase small obstacles are overcome right up to the moment of crisis. During an event the obstacles could be the morning speeches of inspiring speakers. The question that arises for the participants explicitly or implicitly is: what will you do with this information in your own specific situation? You have heard, seen and felt everything, but what will you do with this experience? The crisis moment is short, followed by peace and quiet in the experience. Time is allocated for reflection. These are often the right moments for short breaks, depending on the time frame of the experience

The issue of breaks is less relevant in an experience which is spread over a longer period of time.

Tension span

The tension span is higher compared to the previous phase. People are focused, and this focus is further developed. Information, knowledge and sensory stimuli are gathered and digested.

- This phase consists of a variety of smaller tension spans; each small story befits the bigger story.
- This phase ends with a moment of reflection: 'what does this mean to me'?

A museum experience

The small obstacles and mini stories in the museum are the different rooms one enters. An exhibition is usually divided into separate parts, each with its own story and tension span. In a museum like Nemo in Amsterdam, each floor has its own theme.

8.5.5 Phase 5: Confrontation

The fifth phase is short, but it is important as it contains the learning moment (conscious learning). The Imagineer preferably applies this element in a playful manner, as play activates people and brings them in a positive mood, which leads to open-minded people and increases the chance of learning considerably.

Tension arc stage	Pre-experience	Transition	Introduction and change	Obstacles and crisis	Confrontation
Participants	(Self-) Selection Expectations Context clear Give meaning	Shared or Individual experience? Transition	Common language Clear goals Structure Clear set of rules	Obtain information Feel autonomy Mastery	Clear feedback Autonomy Mastery
Emotional perception of participants	Anticipation Hope Curiosity Motivation	Anticipation Hope Curiosity Motivation	Aspirations with regards to transformation Observed challenge	Participation Applying own capacities Flow	Participation Anticipation Flow
Level of arousal	At ease	Activated	At ease	Activated	Activated or at ease
Tools	Map	Spectacle Comfortable disorientation Physiological and safety needs	Subliminal engagement Mechanics, dynamics and aesthetics	Q & A Layered Successive revelation Mechanics, dynamics and aesthetics	Postponement Mechanics, dynamics and aesthetics
Dramatic effect	Shock	Silence	Shock	Silence	Shock
Stage goal	Meaning Story	Story	Empathy Story	Play	Empathy

Fig. 8.16 Confrontation phase.

Feedback

The Imagineer gives room for feedback, either from the participants or via the Imagineer, who composed the experience. Feedback promotes a sense of craftsmanship within the participants: they start to have a better understanding of the overarching story, physically master the experience, or have acquired knowledge.

Postponed final answers

In the design, the final answer is postponed. Participants are put on edge, while anticipating an answer. After a game this could be the moment the jury withdraws for deliberation and the participants wonder how well they performed. The Imagineer tries to postpone the climax as much as he can. Every time he gives the audience the feeling that the answer is nearly there, but will still postpone it. This way, the tension heightens.

Tension span

- Tension increases. A new sense of anticipation and hope arises.
- People are still in a state of flow, completely engaged in the experience.
- The tension increases by postponing the transition to the climax.

A museum experience

In a museum this is the moment when you have visited the last room. You suddenly realize what the purpose is: how the museum offers knowledge and imagery to its visitors. You are just about to visit the last room of the guided tour. You enter the room with certain expectations, which are based on the previous rooms. You anticipate one more incredible experience before your visit has come to an end.

8.5.6 Phase 6: Climax Phase

Tension arc stage	Pre-experience	Transition	Introduction and change	Obstacles and crisis	Confrontation	Climax
Participants	(Self-) Selection Expectations Context clear Give meaning	Shared or individual experience? Transition	Common language Clear goals Structure Clear set of rules	Obtain information Feel autonomy Mastery	Clear feedback Autonomy Mastery	Achieve goal Acceptance
Emotional perception of participants	Anticipation Hope Curiosity Motivation	Anticipation Hope Curiosity Motivation	Aspirations with regards to transformation Observed challenge	Participation Applying own capacities Flow	Participation Anticipation Flow	Hope Anticipation Flow
Level of arousal	At ease	Activated	At ease	Activated	Activated or at ease	Activated
Tools	Map	Spectacle Comfortable disorientation Physiological and safety needs	Subliminal engagement Mechanics, dynamics and aesthetics	Q & A Layered Successive revelation Mechanics, dynamics and aesthetics	Postponement Mechanics, dynamics and aesthetics	Spectacle Feedback
Dramatic effect	Shock	Silence	Shock	Silence	Shock	Silence
Stage goal	Meaning story	Story	Empathy story	Play	Empathy	Play

Fig. 8.17 Climax phase.

The climax phase is the phase prior to the final resolution and the revelation of the story to the participants.

Extra stimuli

During the climax, participants take in extra sensory stimuli. As in the transition phase, spectacle is allowed, it could even be the biggest spectacle ever. On the other hand the Imagineer could opt to go against everyone's expectations and surprise the audience.

> The audience expects a huge display of fireworks; however the Imagineer planned for a quiet confrontation, starting with a soft instrument, an oboe. The music swells to a crescendo followed by a gradual diminuendo, followed by silence. A moment of dead silence, then, unexpectedly, a beautiful firework fountain covers the skies, beautiful fire-stars whirl down.

There wasn't a spectacle, against all expectations. People were touched on an emotional level. The climax does not have to be bombastic by definition. Actually, the opposite could have generated the desired effect.

> Drumrolls can also be used for the climax, while the jury member slowly opens the envelope announcing the magic words; '… and the winner is'.

Tension span

- During this phase, the audience wants to be surprised, the moment this actually happens the tension rises to incredible heights (or tension increases tremendously).
- The audience anticipates the resolution and hope for a satisfactory solution. This is the moment when the final goal of the experience is reached and is felt by all participants simultaneously.

> **A museum experience**
>
> The climax in the museum is the final, large artefact, which is placed on your way out. It is the museum's show piece or the majestic architecture of the hall towards the exit.

8.5.7   Phase 7: Resolution

The resolution is the moment all puzzle pieces fall into place. The story is revealed, whereby all participants clearly understand the voyage of the experience: the story and its outcome. The outcome adds meaning to the whole experience.

Added value creation

This is when the Imagineer decides what kind of feelings the participants will experience and will take with them: relief, happiness, pride or quiet. Whatever he decides, it has to satisfy the participants. The participants need to feel contented after having undergone the experience, as well, that it added more value than they had anticipated prior to the experience. This added value is the transformation they have experienced. They have learned something, and gone through an experience that they would like to share with others (convey the story). They have stored something in their memory, which they can use at a later stage; this could be for example

Tension arc stage	Pre-experience	Transition	Introduction and change	Obstacles and crisis	Confrontation	Climax	Resolution
Participants	(Self-) Selection Expecta-tions Context clear Give meaning	Shared or individual experience? Transition	Common language Clear goals Structure Clear set of rules	Obtain information Feel autonomy Mastery	Clear feedback Autonomy Mastery	Achieve goal Acceptance	Meaning Retention
Emotional perception of participants	Anticipation Hope Curiosity Motivation	Anticipation Hope Curiosity Motivation	Aspirations with regards to transformation Observed challenge	Participation Applying own capacities Flow	Participation Anticipation Flow	Hope Anticipation Flow	Satisfaction Transforma-tion
Level of arousal	At ease	Activated	At ease	Activated	Activated or at ease	Activated	At ease
Tools	Map	Spectacle Comfortable disorienta-tion Physiologic al and safety needs	Subliminal engagement Mechanics, dynamics and aesthetics	Q & A Layered Successive revelation Mechanics, dynamics and aesthetics	Postpone-ment Mechanics, dynamics and aesthetics	Spectacle Feedback	Souvenir Feedback
Dramatic effect	Shock	Silence	Shock	Silence	Shock	Silence	
Stage goal	Meaning Story	Story	Empathy Story	Play	Empathy	Play	Meaning

Fig. 8.18 Resolution phase.

conveying the story (a fun story), think about it and recall the event (a nice memory), contemplate and reflect (you have learned something valuable which has changed your world perspective).

The resolution will provide the participants with a predefined end result, which will remain engraved in the memory of the participants. During an election this is the moment when the winner comes on stage and is honoured; in an adventure story, it is the moment of the hero's coronation; during a meeting about content, it is the moment the end conclusion is drawn. In all above cases it is the moment of relief and relaxation.

What are the participants taking home?

In this part of the design, participants are offered something, this could be material or immaterial. A souvenir could serve the purpose of supporting meaning, at the same time it can be shown to other people. Additionally, it keeps the participant connected even after the experience, connected to the experience as the souvenir reminds them of the event, and connected to the other participants that have the same souvenir.

During Lowlands Music Festival all people receive a bracelet at the entrance. It so happens that people still wear the bracelet even after the event. By wearing the bracelet with great pride, participants show that they attended the festival whereby it serves as a symbol of their attendance. A clear intangible bond emerges between these people, without any words spoken. Other examples are the furry animals you buy in Disney, or a glass snow globe with a landscape that you buy after your skiing holidays.

Tension span

- Relaxation, all pieces of the puzzle fit together.
- Satisfaction, people understand the meaning of the experience (subconsciously).

A museum experience

In a museum the relaxation moment takes place in the museum shop. You are confronted again with all the items you have seen in the museum. When you have a good feeling about the experience, you are likely to buy a souvenir, something tangible to remember the wonderful exhibition, or maybe even something you like to decorate your house with, to show others that you visited the museum, or even to show others your sense of taste. These expressions that are related to the experience become part of the individual participant's image.

8.5.8   Phase 8: Continuation

Hold on to positive energy

After the experience, the participants are connected with the design or the other participants through positive energy. The Imagineer likes to hold on to this positive energy as it ensures people to come back. Additionally, these people will bring along new people and become loyal guests. This is done by positively reminding people of the experience.

Facilitate connectivity

You can hold on by facilitating connectivity in the emerged group of followers. First, by offering a platform to the participants where they can keep meeting each other (reunion or a website). In order to be successful, the story of the experience needs to be continued and should be valuable for the participants.

Tension arc stage	Pre-experience	Transition	Introduction and change	Obstacles and crisis	Confrontation	Climax	Resolution	Continuation
Participants	(Self-) Selection Expectations Context clear Give meaning	Shared or individual experience? Transition	Common language Clear goals Structure Clear set of rules	Obtain information Feel autonomy Mastery	Clear feedback Autonomy Mastery	Achieve goal Acceptance	Meaning Retention	Autonomy Mastery
Emotional perception of participants	Anticipation Hope Curiosity Motivation	Anticipation Hope Curiosity Motivation	Aspirations with regards to transformation Observed challenge	Participation Applying own capacities Flow	Participation Anticipation Flow	Hope Anticipation Flow	Satisfaction Transformation	Connection
Level of arousal	At ease	Activated	At ease	Activated	Activated or at ease	Activated	At ease	At ease
Tools	Map	Spectacle Comfortable disorientation Physiological and safety needs	Subliminal engagement Mechanics, dynamics and aesthetics	Q & A Layered Successive revelation Mechanics, dynamics and aesthetics	Postponement Mechanics, dynamics and aesthetics	Spectacle Feedback	Souvenir Feedback	Souvenir Platform Mini-communication moments
Dramatic effect	Shock	Silence	Shock	Silence	Shock	Silence		
Stage goal	Meaning Story	Story	Empathy Story	Play	Empathy	Play	Meaning	

Symphony

Time

Fig 8.19 Final phase: continuation.

> Star Trek does this with Star Trek conventions; participants can become a character and create their own story. Disney stays in touch with participants using different platforms. They have platforms for visitors of the physical theme parks, the gamers, children who play with the Disney toys, etc.

Consistency

To hold on to the final image consistency in all moments of communication is of vital importance. This means that all the communication moments are connected within the same story, atmosphere and concept. This way the expressions of communication strengthen each other, and strengthen the experience. The Imagineer can arouse the attention of participants for a future event, this way the continuation phase transitions into the first phase.

Tension span

- People are reminded of the experience and its outcome via small pin pricks (stimuli) divided over a longer period of time.
- Give participants partial autonomy to further develop the story.
- Offer participants chances to develop mastery related to the topic.

8.5.9   Example: Filled Out and Completed Design Model

The entire Design Model of Imagineered Transformation process is shown below. An entire experience is used in order to, step by step, clarify the model.

A thousand employees of a large police organization work in different locations. The management issue is **formulated**: How can we create a sense of belonging, connection of these employees with the police organization, its mission, but above all, each other. The **goal** is to overcome geographical borders and to stimulate information exchange, which should automatically result in a higher efficiency of the organization. Participants are expected to attend the meeting, it is a mandatory meeting, whereby forced concentration is required. It is therefore of vital importance that the Imagineer needs to **investigate**, prior to the event, what inspires these participants, their pride and their ideals. For this group of police employees this means the outcome and the quality of their work.

The police organization is spread over different geographical locations with different tasks. Different nations as a matter of fact, but even though one is Welsh and another English, they all have the same pride in terms of their work output. This pride of doing their best is what connects them to each other. Their drive is the ultimate goal in relation to work. This needs to be strongly incorporated in the experience, expecting that people will be open to meeting each other, and to practising information exchange between people who work for the same organization, but have never met before.

This concept is made in the **development** stage, it is the story that is going to be told. In the **prototyping** stage, the concept is further completed based on the design model. Prototyping the concept and assimilation of feedback are followed by the next step, namely the **design** stage, which is done by different engineers: sound and light company, the décor builders, performers and game makers. The design stage is followed by the **application** stage.

The application stage

During the first phase, the participants are invited by the employer. This is done by invitation via mail and reaches your own home, to show that each employee is valuable. The rules of the game are clear: you must come, it is mandatory and work related, it lasts the whole day, this is the date and location. By sending an appealing picture on the invitation, a sense of anticipation is invoked.

The moment participants arrive, the **transition phase** starts. Easy and ample parking, location is easily reachable by public transportation, which already gets people in a better mood to start with. Twenty beautiful hostesses receive the guests and every participant receives a badge with the group division, which is not entirely clear to the participants. *Tension* starts to build up, participants *hope* that it is going to be *fun,* however there is a *slight fear* that it might not be the case. Good coffee is served with some nice accompaniments: the *primary needs* are immediately met.

Nothing much goes against the standard conventions, people can *calmly* start the day and accept that the tone is set, apparently with a nice edge, being received by twenty beautiful ladies.

People enter the hall where the **introduction** starts. The interior is different: a round stage in the middle (target), surrounded by chairs. Video screens facing all angles of the hall. A pounding heart in the background. This is not what they had anticipated and tension increases because of this. What can we anticipate about today? Is it fun or informative? What do they expect of me?

People sit down, admire the décor and wait in anticipation and **excitement** of what is to come.

The **moment of change** starts with a short light show and a *flashy* movie, a compilation of all kinds of actions and successes of their own work supported by *exciting* music. Important moments of resolution and moments that were exposed in the press are shown. Some people identify and recognize their achievements and feel *a sense of pride*. Others feel proud because these are the success stories of their own service, the police organization they are connected to. People become more and more open to what is coming their way. **Obstacles** are built up step by step. *Emotion* is added in specific dosage to further engage the participants. It starts formally with a serious speech by the Minister of Justice who solemnly addresses the participants. He refers to the important tasks he has bestowed on them, the level of quality he expects of them and why. Furthermore, he refers to the future challenges they face. This is *why* the organization exists.

This so-called first obstacle is followed by a colleague of another service. His work is quite dangerous and in order to do his work as safe as possible he depends on this service. For example, preliminary work needs to be done thoroughly before he can actually arrest someone. In somewhat *less than ten minutes* he tells the story of the Atheunis Street in The Hague, the one and so-far only arrest during which a grenade was thrown at the police. Without the thorough preliminary work of his colleagues, who are represented in the room here today, this arrest could have ended in a much more dramatic way. He appeals to their professionalism, the *common ideal*.

This obstacle is followed by a citizen, a lady who was specially flown in from the UK. She sits down on a stool in the middle of the stage. A girl, all by herself in the middle of the hall, she has a letter in her hand. She is physically challenged and therefore sits on the stool. Who is this girl?

She starts reading her letter a loud to the audience. It is the call of a citizen to the people of the audience. During the London Attacks in 2005, she stood right next to the bomb-maker in the underground. She saw him carrying his backpack. She was there when the bomb exploded and the carriage was blown away. She lost her leg and was dead for about five minutes. She was miraculously resuscitated and taken out of the wreckage. She wishes that no one ever has to encounter something like this. As a citizen and from the bottom of her heart, she appeals to the people in the audience to continue doing their work well. She is appreciative of them and grateful that there are people like them.

People realize now that their work is *serious* business. Their job is not just any ordinary job, it *isn't anything abstract*; it is the lady who sits before them, alive, however with a horrific experience and a lost leg.

These obstacles lead as some kind of funnel to the fourth speaker, who enters the stage all by himself. He is the head of the service; he talks about the direction for the future what he wants to achieve together with the people in the audience and how to achieve this. Everybody is now *open* to the story. They all feel responsible for a positive outcome. The *final message* is that cooperation and sharing information are of vital importance.

The hall doors open and people move on to the next space. It is time for the moment of **confrontation**, the main reason why they are all gathered here. There are long tables. All employees are randomly divided over these tables. They have lunch together. In their own newly established groups they work on a fictitious assignment: a case that needs to be solved within a set time frame.

The groups consist of different disciplines that also work in the same work-related field. The processes are the same, however they are more playful. People have to go outside, look for clues, find pieces of the puzzle, moreover approach other groups and obtain information. The goal is to obtain and share information in a *playful* and informal way.

The time pressure increases, and we head in the direction of the **climax**. Each group hands in its solutions and move back to the first hall. On stage the *tension* increases. A short show with drum rolls further increases the sensation. The jury explains the criteria for winning: correct answers, moreover the process of obtaining and sharing information. And the winner is…

The **resolution**: the winners climb the stage. They all receive a statue of The Thinker of Rodin, as this is the final image/idea that the head of the organization wants to give them; think more, cooperate and share knowledge. It is a souvenir /reminder that can be shown with pride, not only at home but also on the work floor, accompanied by the story of information sharing.

Continuation, in this case, the photos that were taken during this special day, as well as a follow-up meeting during the New Year's reception gathering. Dialogue about the event can be continued via all available communication platforms. The participants get more **autonomy** to further develop in terms of exchanging information and building networks. This case was executed by an external Imagineer and because of this, the Imagineer had less influence in terms of the continuation, on the other hand, the event, even after five years, is still engraved in each and every participant's memory.

The Design Model of Imagineered Transformation can be used and completed with meaningful experiences to solve all management issues of a user group. This means that time frames (time necessary for the user to go through the entire model) per issue can vary considerably, sometimes a few months, sometimes an hour, depending on the issue for which the design is made.

The design for co-creation

Co-creation requires a longer period of time. The user is motivated to start thinking in **the first phase**, right up to the moment that he is persuaded to really start putting time and effort in the process (**transition**). From that moment onwards, a platform is offered to give him the opportunity to co-create (**introduction** and **change**). The user can give input, discover, invent, communicate with others and go through a development himself, until the moment of **confrontation**, the outcome of the joint effort. The user group that has cooperated in this process is proud of the outcome and the problem holder rewards them with gratitude, communication about their share in the process and the final product (**climax**). The solution, which is a joint effort, is shown to the world, which can lead to a tangible **continuation**.

8.6 PROTOTYPING AND COMMUNICATION

8.6.1 Prototyping

Once the design model has been completed by the Imagineer, a first prototype can be made and tested. Based on the feedback of this prototype, the design can be adapted to become more effective and to heighten the tension span. The first prototype is tested internally and therefore won't have that much exposure. At this stage there is still the option of an official *go/no go* and consequently the design can be changed completely. It is a pity to invest heavily in technology or decor, when the whole structure of a design needs to changed.

Tension arc stage	Pre-experience	Transition	Introduction and change	Obstacles and crisis	Confrontation	Climax	Resolution	Continuation
Participants	(Self-) Selection Expectations Context clear Give meaning	Shared or individual experience? Transition	Common language Clear goals Structure Clear set of rules	Obtain information Feel autonomy Mastery	Clear feedback Autonomy Mastery	Achieve goal Acceptance	Meaning Retention	Autonomy Mastery
Emotional perception of participants	Anticipation Hope Curiosity Motivation	Anticipation Hope Curiosity Motivation	Aspirations with regards to transformation Observed challenge	Participation Applying own capacities Flow	Participation Anticipation Flow	Hope Anticipation Flow	Satisfaction Transformation	Connection
Level of arousal	At ease	Activated	At ease	Activated	Activated or at ease	Activated	At ease	At ease
Tools	Map	Spectacle Comfortable disorientation Physiological and safety needs	Subliminal engagement Mechanics, dynamics and aesthetics	Q & A Layered Successive revelation Mechanics, dynamics and aesthetics	Postponement Mechanics, dynamics and aesthetics	Spectacle Feedback	Souvenir Feedback	Souvenir Platform Mini-communication moments
Dramatic effect	Shock	Silence	Shock	Silence	Shock	Silence		
Stage goal	Meaning Story	Story	Empathy Story	Play	Empathy	Play	Meaning	

Symphony

Time

Fig. 8.20 Design Model of Imagineered Transformation.

Therefore the first prototype could be a written scenario with completed visuals through a storyboard. This storyboard can be discussed in a dialogue between the Imagineer and his client or focus group. Depending on the size of the project, during the first prototype phase, different numbers of people (fewer or more) are engaged in the thought processes or feedback. In relation to co-creation this could be the entire future user group. Once the Imagineer and his team have used the feedback from the internal prototyping to adapt and improve the design, they can make a model that can be prototyped externally.

- **Service design:** The first try-out could be observing the response of real guests by filming the response and evaluate and analyse the outcome with the team later on.
- **Play:** When play is an element of the experience, a *play test* can be done, to determine if play works, whether people understand it and how it will fit within the tension span.
- **Theatre:** It is possible to rehearse and to practise the sequence of events in the design and in how this can be achieved, followed by actual try-outs.
- **Event:** a *mock-up* model of the event can be built. A mini version of the experience, a try-out in front of a pre-selected group of people whose meaning is relevant. Their spontaneous remarks will be used to improve the design (see example of Disney's prototype at the beginning of Chapter 7).

8.6.2   Written or Represented Rendition

The completed design model of a meaningful transformation process scan be described in a scenario or a storyboard. These means can be used at a creative briefing to engineers and designers during the design stage.

Scenario building

A scenario is a written story. When you use a scenario to develop an experience, you always write the story from the guest's or client's perspective. This story renders the feelings, thoughts and behaviour of the guest during the experience.

The Imagineer writes a scenario from the perspective of the persona for whom he designs. This enables him to investigate in detail, the emotional impact of each and every detail of the design, additionally, which details need to be added or removed. The Imagineer describes this to the gatekeeper (*who*) in detail, whereby he lets go of all his own assumptions and suppositions. Subsequently, the experience is described in terms of *what, how long, when* and *where* it will take place and the available means. This is the articulation of the Design Model of Imagineered Transformation.

> When you write a scenario for a Lowlands visitor and start the moment she considers buying an entrance ticket, you are actually looking over her shoulder. What is she doing? What is she thinking? What does she feel? Once she has bought the tickets, continue
>
> *(Continued)*

Continued.

watching over her shoulder the day before she leaves for Lowlands. Describe what she puts in her bags, which means of transport she uses to get to the venue, what happens at the entrance, do her tickets get checked, etc. By looking and writing the experience down in detail, you understand what a Lowlands visitor actually does, what he feels, thinks, furthermore, you have a much better understanding of when to give stimuli, offer help or provide information.

Scenario building can also be used to:

- clarify the idea to all team members (for example by writing it together with all team members);
- evaluate an existing experience, for example the check-in procedure at an airport; and
- get an idea about the future – when you use it for this purpose, you need to use an already existing scenario and change one of the main variables, due to an emerging trend for example.

What happens when 'Lowlands Festival' (a three day music and cultural festival) becomes completely CO_2 neutral, or the average age of the visitors rises by 15 years as a result of an ageing population.

Storyboard

Using a storyboard is a technique that finds its origin in the movie industry. It is a combination of scenario building and mood boards. Storyboards show you the visual experience you try to create from the director's perspective. What is a guest supposed to see, at which moment and what does that look like? Moreover, what is a guest *not* supposed to see?

As a figure of speech, you put a camera on your guest's shoulder and you look over his shoulder, scene by scene, step by step, as you visualize what your guest sees and experiences. A storyboard looks like a series of drawings that are sequenced in time, just like in a comic. Storyboards help to complete the physical context and the role of the employees in that context.

Imagine yourself being the girl visiting Lowlands Festival; you carry a camera on your shoulder. Based on the information of your scenario and the mood board, you are able to see where the best location is for an information desk, a stage, or even sign posts and what they should look like.

A storyboard is based on the scenario of what a guest does (you miss certain items, for example the way a guest thinks and feels), and the mood board, which contains the core elements of the physical environment.

8.7   DESIGN AND APPLICATION OF THE MODEL

In the end, concept, scenario, storyboard and the completed Design Model of Imagineered Transformation, combined with a possible prototype will form the point of departure of the design stage. During the design stage, all the team members together with the Imagineer focus on 'engineering' and how the design can be executed in real life, serving its purpose within the predefined conditions in terms of available time, budget, technique and so on.

The team still experiments by trying to find unforeseen solutions within the limited conditions, through for example small tests with lighting, decor, an extra sentence or sound effect to get the maximum effects within the experience. The engineers and designers give proposals to the Imagineer in terms of the realization of the experience. This is then adapted based on the original vision the concept offers and the desired tension span that has been incorporated in the design.

8.8   SUMMARY

Designing an experience means designing a conveyance of information and stimuli in a continuing attention span, which leads to meaningfulness (something becoming meaningful). The physical, social and personal context are fitted within the design to achieve this meaningfulness. The design model is a tool used to build up the attention span of an experience. An experienced Imagineer does this intuitively and will only look back in hindsight how he subconsciously built in the different steps of the design model. The design model is therefore a tool for the future Imagineer to add quality to and steer the design. For an experienced Imagineer this could serve as a reminder of the importance of keeping the audience's attention span during the entire time of the experience.

8.9   ASSIGNMENTS

Assignment 1
Watch a movie and investigate how it was built up in terms of action and quiet moments, how do they alternate? How does it work? How does this alternation affect you as a viewer?

Assignment 2
Visit a theatre play or event and only observe the audience's behaviour. When do they really pay attention? What happened on stage at that moment? Have you noticed people losing their interest? How would you have prevented this if you had made the show?

Assignment 3
Visit a show (music, theatre, circus, cinema, museum, etc.) fill out a design model. What do you notice at which moment during the experience?

Assignment 4

Think of a memorable moment that is engraved in your memory. Describe your personal, social and physical context at that moment? What kept you engaged during the experience?

8.10   RECOMMENDED READING

The psychology behind games and video games (the process is comparable to board games):

- Schell, J. (2008) *The Art of Game Design. A Book of Lenses*. Morgan Kaufmann, San Francisco, California.

Real innovation flows from a thorough process of experiment and research – as a result the best ideas are selected and developed:

- Brown, T. (2009) *Change by Design. How Design Thinking Transforms Organisations and Inspires Innovation*. Harper Business, New York.

Arjan van Dijk, Imagineer in the Netherlands

'The urge to create runs like a red line through my life. The urge to create, finding and testing boundaries, change and overstep them. I think and work in images and visuals, I visualize and in my fantasy, all is possible. Only in the second phase I consider whether it is possible to execute the ideas. The world is my inexhaustible source of inspiration' (Arjan van Dijk, 2010).

Core Characteristics:

decisiveness • authenticity • creativity • passion • fairness • honesty • vision • zeal • courage • sustainability • beauty • adventure • non-conformism • empathy • space • sincerity • passion • goal-oriented • determination • love

To give guests the feeling that they are lifted into another world was Arjan van Dijk's mission when he started his company in the late 1970s. To inspire and enthusiast employees, as well as having fun at work and give them wings to take off.

> Imagination is more important than knowledge,
> as anything you can imagine is real.

He was a pioneer in a relatively new unknown area of expertise. Meanwhile his event organization has become an official study. As a pioneer, he received the Golden Giraffe Personal Event Award for his work within the event branch.

> Translating imagination into concrete concepts.
> Adding dimensions to emotions and settings, which will remain engrained in the memory.

(Continued)

Continued.

Thinking in holistic concepts and exceeding the client's expectations is one of the starting points for the Imagineer. Time, context, goals and the target group are other starting points. Overall direction is important. Arjan van Dijk started a full service event organizing company with different disciplines such as building decors, entertainment, catering, location and communication strategies.

Contemplation about the correct choice. What is the correct choice? Versatility is challenging.

All superlatives, run-down monumental properties were bought, restored and decorated in style. 'Designing, developing, conceptual thinking and executing all ideas have always interested me, this is where I differentiated'.

Creating expectations requires skills and knowledge,
To exceed these expectations is an art.

Once upon a time, Arjan van Dijk made a trip in order to do some soul-searching, and to discover the actual quality moments of his life. Additionally he wanted to give ample time to anyone or anything important in his life. He didn't want to die on the battlefield of striving for success.

The past is history, the future is a question, now is a gift.

He consciously looks for work–life balance, spiritual and philosophical deepened awareness. He enjoys anything that crosses his path, sports, spirituality, community service, long-haul trips, arts, and enjoying outdoor life.

Outstanding achievements are based on passion and inner need.

Part III

I, the Imagineer

Last week I met Skylar, a cute four-year-old boy. He was holding a plastic container with green, smelly slime in it and asked whether I would put my hand in it. Yuck, I thought, no way I want to get my hands dirty and smelly. Skylar's play corner in the living room was full of finger paint canvasses, dirty paint brushes, drawing materials, stamps and other building materials. He wasn't afraid at all to get his hands dirty in any way. He actually enjoyed it! Once upon a time we used to build all kind of things, we grabbed the opportunities to build a shed, and made a kind of pudding from leaves and little branches, secretly imagining this to be a the tastiest dish ever. When I was a child, I used to cycle with my neighbourhood friends, we used to imagine that each cycle was actually a car. The lamp-post served as a petrol station. It had a string with a piece of wood attached to it, which represented the hose.

'Ting-ting-ting' we used to say to re-enact the sound related to filling petrol. Every day I came home with dirty hands, we made hundreds of pieces of art, performed in improvised role plays (for which the other children in the neighbourhood voluntarily paid 10 cents to watch the plays).

Today I contemplate whether I should actually do something, 'maybe shouldn't be acting in a funny way' or 'I can't draw that well, so why should I start in the first place'. What triggers this 'self-censorship'? Moreover, how do you get rid of it?

WHY IMAGINEERING?

In part I, we showed you that we live in such a complex society that it requires meaning and communication in order to stand out – be unique – amongst the already existing communication inundation. This means that there is a need for Imagineers who can design this.

Unity is achieved by standing out with a simple (therefore conveyable) story, that is so unique and takes people by surprise; additionally, it is concrete and credible, and it touches people on a subconscious and emotional level.

When people are touched on a subconscious and emotional level by a story and the experience that is linked to it, this gives room and enables them to add their own ideas. Additionally, it educates, engages and enlightens them. The Imagineer is the person who can develop these meaningful stories, design and shape them (or he can have it done for him).

By initially focusing on the gatekeepers, the story will slowly spread through their networks. As a result, the whole **user group is engaged** and expanded. The goal is to get the user in a positive mood, which enables him to be open to communication and retention, he remembers the message. Communication is not only focused on characteristics ('the cheapest!'), however, the main focus is on **values**: the philosophy that unites and gives meaning to a fan club.

The Imagineer stimulates this by delivering a **consistent** message and **facilitates** by offering **means to connect** between user groups (social context).

There are three contexts that are influential and which need to be taken into consideration while designing an experience. These are the personal, social and physical context. Within these contexts, an offer is designed in such a way that it offers a correct story (**symphony**), at the same time, that is easily conveyable. It contains elements of game and play (**interactive**), it is desirable (**design**), it meets the person's needs (**empathy**) and gives meaning (**educational**). All this is done with the purpose of moving the user away from his daily routines and engaging him. Users are offered a platform within the experience. This platform facilitates users' exchanges about the experience and as a result the experience will be stronger and could last for a longer period of time.

IMAGINEERING: WHO AND HOW?

In Part II of the book we explained what an Imagineer does, what are his tasks and which skills are required. His roles are leader, connector, translator, motivator, researcher, designer and/or director. In case he is unable to fulfil any of these roles, he can appoint people or form a team in which these roles can be taken on by people who do possess these specific skills. Entrepreneurship, innovation, emotional intelligence, curiosity, the urge to create and creation of synergy are characteristics an Imagineer needs to have. An Imagineering team is strategically put together and consists of writers, orators, draftsmen, interaction designers and people with different skills.

The Imagineering process consists of four phases:

- **Information:** Why do we start, what are the conditions, what is the problem?
- **Inspiration:** What kind of knowledge, experience and imagines can we collect?
- **Implementation:** How can we move from abstract to concrete?

- This way of designing is focused on the human being, and therefore we refer to it as **people-focused design**. The reaction of people to the design can be tested through prototyping. The design process is **iterative**, which means that certain stages and steps will be repeated until it meets the correct quality level.

In the end, the Imagineer creates a **meaningful experience which serves as a solution of the management issue** as the user group is motivated to be engaged in the communication and offered experience. By using a dramatic build-up of the experience, The attention span is held for a predefined period of time by using a dramatic build-up of the experience. This results in a transformation of the user which was one of the Imagineer's predefined goals.

I, THE IMAGINEER

In Part III you will be searching for the Imagineering power within you. On the basis of a number of exercises you are stimulated to develop your own imagination and fantasies, and additionally the realization of your dreams.

Everybody has this power; however, it could be lost as a result of the current education system, which is particularly focused on development of the left, analytical, side of the brain, instead of the right, imaginative side of the brain. Part III will therefore start with a warm-up exercise for the right side of your brain (Chapter 9).

An Imagineer designs people and their behaviour. He therefore always tries to touch people on an emotional level and give them an image that leaves an impression for a longer period of time. This is why the exercises of Chapter 10 are focused to have you consciously look at your own emotions and behaviour of other people. This is a good way to understand how people 'work'. Which stories do they tell us? What do these stories mean? What do they notice and what goes unnoticed and disappears in the masses?

In Chapter 11, you will start training your skills as an Imagineer and develop your own signature by collecting images, ideas, games, experience, findings, discoveries and anything else that inspires you and makes you aware of the power of stories, metaphors, symbols, changing perspectives and giving meaning.

This part is mainly practising. The exercises you will encounter will help you quite a bit.

chapter 9

Warming Up for the Right Side of the Brain

Gabriëlle Kuiper

WELL…

That was fun, all that theory…
But how does it actually work for me?

Where to start?

Simply clear your mind…

IT IS ABOUT TREATING PEOPLE…

In groups as…

Individuals with a shared experience, which results in a more intense individual experience.

Individuals in a group …

Sharing an emotional experience…

… results in a more intense individual experience and a lasting memory.

chapter 10

I, the Imagineer, Learn to Understand People, their Emotions and Behaviour

An Imagineer designs experiences for people and steers their behaviour. He tries to touch people on an emotional level by giving them certain sentiments and visuals that will stick with the participant.

The exercises in this chapter intend to have you start becoming more conscious of your own emotions and behaviour and that of other people. This is a beneficial way of learning to understand how people function. What kind of stories do they tell? How important are these stories? What do they notice and what goes unnoticed?

We start by training your Imagineering skills by showing you ways to become empathetic and become conscious of the link between behaviour and emotions.

10.1 STEP 1: HAVE A CLOSE LOOK AT MYSELF

Fig. 10.1 A mirror. (Courtesy of Elizabeth/Table4Five.)

How are emotions triggered in you when confronted with daily events or exceptionally rare events?

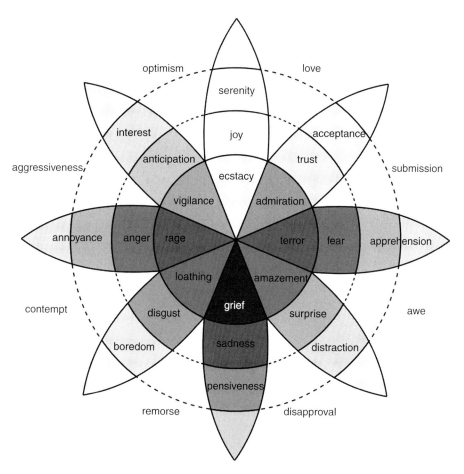

Fig. 10.2 Robert Plutchik's wheel of emotions.

10.1.1 Exercise 1: Keep an Emotion Diary of Each Weekday (and Weekend!)

Keep a diary in which you write down the emotions and thoughts you encounter on a daily basis (see example below). After a while, you write which one of these emotions or thoughts has made an impression and stuck with you; try to recall where this sentiment came from. After 2 weeks, have another look at your diary and try to remember each and every independent event and try to re-live the events. How do you feel now in comparison to the moment the event actually took place? Are you keen on doing the activity again? Why? Why not?

While reading, please pay attention to the differences between, for example:

- routine activities and brand new activities;
- creative and recurring activities;
- activities in a state of flow, or activities that seemed endless; and
- common activities or solitary activities.

Day	Activity	Description of emotion	Alone / together	Special	2 weeks later
Monday	Waking up	Hungry, happy, tired	Together (two people)		Don't remember
	Having a shower	Warm, comfortable, fresh	Together		Same feeling every day
	Making the bed, cuddle the dog	Comfortable, cosy, tidy	Alone		Don't recall
	Making breakfast	Enjoyable, nice, healthy	Together		Yes, special kind of bread roll
	Call the tax services	Scary, trouble, stuff	Alone		Yes, a nice tax advisor
	Driving the car	Stress, traffic jams, hurry	Alone Together with 1,000 other car drivers	BNR was funny concerning another country	
	Arriving in the office	Uneasy, unmotivated	Together with the receptionist	A bunch of flowers	Don't recall
	Meeting	Flow (time passed really quickly) happy	Together with three colleagues	Developed an idea for…	It was a fun activity with the colleagues, it was nice to spend more time together

- What did you notice specifically about yourself?
- Compare your emotion diary to someone else's. What are the differences and what could be the cause of this?

acceptance

Envy

Fear

Anticipation

Regret

Admiration

Hate

Hope

Jealousy

Love

Contempt

Shame

Guilt

Regret

Pride

Sadness

Bored

blame

Desperation

...

Primary emotions according to Aristotle's rhetoric	
Anger	Calmness
Love	Hate
Fear	Confidence
Shame	Impudence/shamelessness
Kindness	Unkindness
Pity	Malice
Pride	Indignation
Contentment	Envy

Source: Aristotle, 384–322 v. Chr.

10.2   STEP 2: HAVE A CLOSE LOOK AT OTHERS

Fig. 10.3 Observing others. (Courtesy of chase_elliott.)

Go to an event, shopping centre or theme park and observe other people.

- What are they doing?
- What is their body language telling you?
- Why are they doing this?
- Can you predict what they will do next?

10.2.1   Exercise 2: Threefold Observation

Choose three activities in which you will meet other people in a group setting. Visit the activities together with someone else and each make a list of observations. You could go and visit a:

- cinema;
- night club;
- supermarket or warehouse;
- festival; or
- street.

In this exercise you are consciously not a member of the group (stay sober on top of this!). You will observe other people's behaviour. How does the group react to certain stimuli? Do they react to sound, or a change of noise, music, lights or the physical environment? What are the logistics of the location, why is it the way it is? How do the individuals react, what do they say and what can you deduce from this in terms of their emotions? Why is this the case and what are the possible causes?

Compare your observations to the observations of your peer the following day:

- What are the similarities and what are the differences?
- What could have been done to change to an even more positive outcome for this group?

Yet another interesting exercise!

Enter a fast food restaurant or any other space where a minimum of six toilets are available. Check each toilet in terms of cleanliness and sufficient toilet paper. What do you notice?

Repeat the exercise but in a different location. Have you noticed something peculiar? Have a look at the location of the toilets: are they near the entrance or slightly further away, are they on the left or on the right, lighting, accessibility, etc.

- How does this influence the outcome of your observation?
- What does this teach/tell you about people?

When you consciously observe people, when you actually see what they are doing, particularly in terms of why, then…

- What is routine?
- What is what we call the comfort zone, when do you feel safe and when don't you feel safe?
- When does a group feel safe and when not?
- How do you establish the boundaries?

Too far out of the comfort zone means PANIC.
Just on the edge or just out of the comfort zone means GAINING EXPERIENCE.

10.2.2   How Does This Help Me as an Imagineer?

During this first step, you have become aware of your own behaviour and accompanying emotions and the behaviour of others and their emotions. You are aware of the fact that activities in a social and physical context have an influence on personal experiences. This means that you, in your capacity of Imagineer, can design a social and physical context in such a way that you simultaneously shape the personal experience. In case you would like to become an Imagineer, you will need to start observing your surroundings and realize what kind of emotional effects it has on yourself. You can use this information for simulation and use it strategically.

10.3 RECOMMENDED READING

Learn to observe others by looking through the eyes of guru Desmond Morris:

- Morris, D. (2004) *People Watching. The Desmond Morris Guide to Body Language*. Vintage, London.

Understand more about consumer behaviour:

- Solomon, M.R. (2012) *Consumer Behavior*. Prentice Hall Florence, New York.

chapter 11

Working Towards Your Own Signature

In this chapter we try to help you work towards your own signature. This is done through collection of your ideas and inspiration in such a way that you become conscious of the power of images, stories, metaphors, symbols, changing perspectives and creation of meaning.

- Collect by opening up…
- … fill your backpack with items that are just outside your comfort zone
- Just a bit different…
- Yet, not too different…

How can you achieve this?

- Make a list.
- Stack everything you see and bundle it.
- Make a collage.
- Keep a diary.
- Make a scrapbook with pictures, photos, drafts, drawings, articles, inspiration.

Fig. 11.1 A scrapbook. (Courtesy of Nate Steiner.)

11.1 EXERCISE: CREATE YOUR OWN SCRAPBOOK OF INSPIRATION

Over a period of 6 weeks you collect ideas, images, articles and anything that inspires you in a scrapbook.

	Design	Meaning		**Symphony**
Story				
	Play		**Empathy**	

Week 1: Design

Warm-up exercise

- Choose a consumer article that somehow irritates you, for example a toilet brush holder in which dirty water remains at the bottom.
- Meanwhile, have cup of coffee or tea and think for about 5 minutes on how you can improve the flaw of this particular product.
- Draw a design and make a description of your design and write it in your scrapbook.

Collect your emotions

During the second week you collect designs of items that emotionally affect you. Go out street-combing and take at least ten photos of unexpected items that make you smile, curious, sad, etc.

Fig. 11.2 Street-combing.

Tear or cut inspiring pictures or advertisements from different magazines. Stick them in your scrapbook and write one or two key words and the reason why these pictures caught your attention. Continue doing this for the next 5 weeks.

How does this information relate to me in my capacity as Imagineer?

It teaches you to become aware of your own taste and the way how you perceive the world. By comparing your findings with others who also do the same exercises, you will see that you already have your own signature, as well, your own world perception. Once you are aware of it, you can apply on the design process. Moreover, you collect ideas and inspiration that can serve a certain purpose at a later stage, when you might unexpectedly need it.

Week 2: Story

The essence of a story is the fact that it can be conveyed. This week you will be testing whether stories are conveyable.

What makes a story conveyable?

This week, collect a:

- fairy tale;
- newspaper article;
- magazine article;
- advertisement;
- product;
- episode of your favourite television series;
- poem; and
- good joke.

Rephrase the above-mentioned items in stories of three sentences.

- What is it within the stories that appeals to you? Why does it appeal to you?
- Which one of the stories can easily be conveyed? Why this story in particular?

What makes a good story?

Approach a friend and ask him/her a story about something s/he experienced and vividly remembers. Draw the story in your book as detailed as possible: what does it exactly look like? You can find out by asking many questions.

1. When you have finished, try to recall the story in three sentences. Are you looking forward to telling the story? When you feel excited about telling the story, it means that it is a good story. The same goes for jokes: a good joke is so appealing that you want to tell someone else.

2. What makes a story a good story; try to tell this to someone in three sentences only.

3. Can you even use one or two words to convey the story? This technique helps you to think of a catching title for the story. A title makes it even easier for people to convey a story.

> Brand Activity Agency 'Being There' had to come up with a brand concept for Unox. The purpose of this concept was to create an association between Unox smoked sausage and winter/cold. This concept became the event called Unox New Year's Dive. The concept was simple and could be easily conveyed, as the concept relayed what it was all about in just three words (Verrips, 2010).

What can I do with this information as an Imagineer?

An Imagineer is someone who recognizes stories, acknowledges them, produces or has them produced. As a result of this exercise (and repetition of it in the coming years) you will understand that a story has an essence, this essence determines whether it is conveyable, additionally you learn that a catchy title helps in this process.

Week 3: Empathy

Listen and tell

Ask someone to tell you the story of what it felt like to leave the family home and move out to a place of their own. How did s/he experience the first few months on his/her own?

You are only allowed to listen, you are not supposed to say anything or write down anything.

After the story, you can write it down and ask the other person to read it. Does your story actually convey the correct facts and does it give the right impression of his/her feelings? Does the other one 'feel' the story (recognize/relate)?

Subsequently, answer the following questions:

1. Have you been able to really capture the story teller's feelings?
2. Which essential facts were still missing in your story?

Collect feelings

In Chapter 10 you can find the primary emotions of Aristotle's rhetoric. Look at all the emotions and choose an emotion and connect this emotion to a story anyone has ever told you. Do this for each emotion. Describe in approximately 50 words what triggered the emotions.

- Is there anything you notice when you compare this story to your own emotion diary from exercise 1?

You now have to find a different context (with three or more people) for each emotion. You can do this by walking around and through observation (in a café, in the street, at school or work). Preferably, make pictures of the situation. Stick the photos in your book and describe the emotion and situation.

- What do you notice? Which particular emotions are easy to collect and which ones are more difficult to collect? How did you manage to read people's emotions and situations?

How does this information relate to me in my capacity of Imagineer?

By doing the exercises in Chapter 10, you learned how to consciously observe your own and other people's behaviour, furthermore, you learned to connect behaviour to emotions. The exercises in this chapter focused on linking design and stories to emotions. An Imagineer can design situations in which a certain behaviour will emerge together with the emotions that need to be evoked.

Week 4: Play

My favourite game and my favourite play

What is your favourite game? Why does it appeal to you? What does this game offer you on an emotional, intellectual, social and competitive level?

Game collection

- Collect as many as possible examples of games. Put an example of each game in your book. Use key words and describe the essence of the game. Assess each game in a few sentences in terms of mechanics, dynamics and aesthetics (see Section 7.3.3).

While playing a game, players will play by the rules and the game has a fixed outcome. This is quite different from play, whereby the outcome isn't fixed.

- Collect as many examples of different kinds of play. Again, describe each form of play in terms of mechanics, dynamics and aesthetics.

In your opinion, what is the difference between game and play?

Observe participants playing a game

By the end of the week you will observe a group of friends that will play a game of their choice. You don't participate in the game but you observe only. Make a log book of each friend who participates and write down what activates/motivates him/her during the game.

Additionally write down:

1. When do they actively participate?
2. When do they smile or become angry? What causes this?
3. What are the experiences everyone reacts to, and what seem to be the more individual experiences?

Summarize your log book and put it in your book. Preferably with a picture of your friends playing as well as an extra picture of the winner!

Television game shows

Look through the TV guide and find out how many game shows there are on TV, and what kind of audiences these shows have? Did you realize that there are all kinds of shows for all kinds of people?

How does this information relate to me in my capacity of Imagineer?

Game and play are valuable tools for your design. By incorporating interactivity in your ideas, you will be able to stimulate behaviour and its related thoughts and emotions. This does not mean that everyone will actively participate in the designed game/play: as long as spectators are part of the idea and story and can talk about it or convey it to someone else.

Week 5: Giving Meaning

Identity can be conveyed through arguments (why are you doing this?) or story (how are you doing this). Convictions can be persistent: when someone (or a group) has a conviction, he won't easily give them. When this person does change his convictions, this usually turns them into different people with different activities and priorities (e.g. when someone no longer believes in God and doesn't attend church anymore).

We are who we are based on our convictions, however, who we are changes by itself. We don't choose our convictions, they have formed over time and have become part of our character and behaviour.

You are your convictions.
Convictions can be conveyed through stories.

My Convictions

Describe in a few key words which convictions were handed down to you through your upbringing:

- Life and Death;
- Material and Spiritual;
- Body and Soul;
- Man and Woman;
- Human and Animal;
- Status and Failure;
- Left and Right.

'In Hindsight'

What kind of life do you lead? How would you like to live your life?

Make sure that you are alone and have access to something to drink and to nibble on. Imagine yourself as a ninety-year-old. Take about half an hour to imagine your life path till now. What kind of life did you lead? Have you achieved anything? How did you contribute? Whom did you contribute to and what did it mean to them? What does it mean to you? Do you have any regrets? Why?

Different People, Different Convictions

Find someone you don't know that well, and who has also done the exercise on describing their convictions.

In turn, name what you think are the other person's convictions and compare this to what the other person had previously written down.

How does this information relate to me in my capacity of Imagineer?

By becoming aware of what your user group finds important, you will be able to adapt your design accordingly. An Imagineer does this during the research stage by engaging the users in the process. Even when the 'users' are the audience it is important to know what their convictions are, what kind of behaviour is linked to these convictions and the thoughts that relate to it. When you as an Imagineer are aware of the conviction of your users, you can then attach emotions in such a way that the thoughts of the users become meaningful. They will attach more value to the experience by wanting to hold on to these thoughts and feelings, even after the experience. During the research stage, the Imagineer considers and thinks about all convictions, perspectives and giving meaning to the future user. What kind of meaning would you like to give to your users?

Week 6: Perspective
Perspectivism:
Try to understand someone's interests
And actually hear/listen to his story

Metaphors change perspectives

During this week, write down some interesting and surprising metaphors that you have encountered. After about a week, you will start to understand the purpose and power of this exercise. It will an inspiration for you to use metaphors in your writing, you will even come up with your own metaphors.

> METAPHOR
> - A human being can be compared to a wolf.
> - The chairman creates a smooth sailing meeting.
> - It looks like a pig sty!
> - This writer is the new Shakespeare.

A METAPHOR CHANGES PERSPECTIVES

I, the Imagineer

By changing perspectives
you can get people out of their comfort zone in a comfortable manner!

What can I do with this information as an Imagineer?

An Imagineer is aware of automatic thought processes and the emotions these evoke, which is basically a result of behaviour. By changing perspective, automatic thought processes aren't automatic anymore, but are guided towards a new direction by looking at it again, and looking at it from a different angle.

Perspectives can be changed by placing certain routines in different contexts. Perspectives can be changed by routinely placing something in a different context. As a result of this, something will stand out and out and catch the eye. When this new situation can be conveyed by means of a story, the Imagineer has reached his goal: the story remains in the memory of the person who has had the experience. This person will convey the story within his social group, or convey it within the group that was created by the Imagineer (for example by offering a platform or meeting place).

11.2 RECOMMENDED READING

Get inspired by design and creative advertising:

- Burtenshaw, K., Mahon, N. and Barfoot, C. (2006) *The Fundamentals of Creative Advertising*. AVA Publishing, Singapore
- Best, K. (2010) *The Fundamentals of Design Management*. AVA Publishing, Singapore.
- Dreyfuss, H. (1995) *Designing for People*. Allworth Press, New York.

More on stories and storytelling:

- Campbell, J. (1972) *The Hero with a Thousand Faces*. Princeton University Press, Princeton, New Jersey.
- Denning, S. (2000) *The Springboard: How Storytelling Ignites Action in Knowledge*. Butterworth-Heinemann, Maryland Heights, Missouri.
- Fog, K., Budtz, C., Munch, P. and Blanchette, S. (2010) *Storytelling: Branding in Practice*. Springer, Berlin Heidelberg.

On games and play:

- Rouse, R. (2001) *Game Design: Theory and Practice*. Jones & Bartlett Learning, Sudbury, Massachusetts.
- Saffer, D. (2010) *Designing for Interaction: Creating Smart Applications and Clever Devices*. New Riders, Berkeley, California.

On metaphors:

- Owen, N. (2001) *The Magic of the Metaphor*. Crown House, Carmarthen.
- Lakoff, G. and Johnson, M. (2008) *Metaphors We Live By*. University of Chicago Press, Chicago, Illinois.

Inspiration

Art offers us often different perspectives on things we normally tend to overlook …

Fig. 11.3 Banksy collage.

Just like Alice in Wonderland: 'Step through the looking glass' and change your perspective every now and then…

Fig. 11.4 Alice in Wonderland.

How can you use this as an Imagineer?

- Collect
- Take in
- Watch
- Observe
- Think
- Wonder

Show the world from your perspective

Fig. 11.5 Your way of perceiving the world?

`You decide …

| Your way to have others look at the world in awe is … |

Change context

Why are we afraid of a man wearing a Mickey Mouse suit at 10 at night, and not when we see him in Disney World at 3 in the afternoon?

Something quite ordinary can become something quite awkward in another context (imagine going to work wearing your pyjamas).

Make people believe

Why do we believe that it is possible in Disney World?

What story do you need to create to have other people act in it?

Have people participate

Just because of the fact that virtually anyone hugs Mickey Mouse in Disney World, it becomes kind of normal; moreover, maybe it encourages others to do the same. It might even cause a queue!

How can you make sure that even more people allow this and like what you have placed in a different context? What else is necessary do you think?

Allow and give them a platform and space to talk about with each other.

SO…

- In this book, we discussed the theory of why Imagineering creates added value.
- You have read how you as an Imagineer can structure your work in a process.
- You have done exercises to look at the world from different perspectives.

Are you an Imagineer by now?

No!

NOT YET!!

Imagineering is

DO COLLECT DO THINK COLLECT DO SEE OVERSEE COLLECT ANALYSE FEEL LEARN ASK COLLECT DREAM DO HEAR LISTEN DREAM DO COLLECT LISTEN DO THINK COLLECT DO DREAM SEE OVERSEE COLLECT FEEL LEARN ASK COLLECT ANALYSE LISTEN DO DREAM COLLECT DO THINK COLLECT DO SEE OVERSEE FEEL LEARN ASK COLLECT DO EXPERIENCE THINK OF WRITE DRAW TELL A STORY ENTERTAIN REALIZE DREAM DO COLLECT DO THINK COLLECT DO SEE OVERSEE COLLECT FEEL LEARN ASK COLLECT ANALYSE LISTEN DO DREAM DO COLLECT DO THINK COLLECT DO SEE OVERSEE COLLECT ANALYSE FEEL LEARN ASK COLLECT DREAM DO HEAR LISTEN DREAM DO COLLECT LISTEN DO THINK COLLECT DO DREAM SEE OVERSEE COLLECT FEEL LEARN ASK COLLECT ANALYSE LISTEN DO DREAM COLLECT DO THINK COLLECT DO SEE OVERSEE FEEL LEARN ASK COLLECT DO EXPERIENCE THINK OF WRITE DRAW TELL A STORY ENTERTAIN REALIZE DREAM DO COLLECT DO THINK COLLECT DO SEE OVERSEE COLLECT FEEL LEARN ASK COLLECT ANALYSE LISTEN DO DREAM DO DO COLLECT DO THINK COLLECT DO SEE OVERSEE COLLECT ANALYSE FEEL LEARN ASK COLLECT DREAM DO HEAR LISTEN DREAM DO COLLECT LISTEN DO THINK COLLECT DO DREAM SEE OVERSEE COLLECT FEEL LEARN ASK COLLECT ANALYSE LISTEN DO DREAM COLLECT DO THINK COLLECT DO SEE OVERSEE FEEL LEARN ASK COLLECT DO EXPERIENCE THINK OF WRITE DRAW TELL A STORY ENTERTAIN REALIZE DREAM DO COLLECT DO THINK COLLECT DO SEE OVERSEE COLLECT FEEL LEARN ASK COLLECT ANALYSE LISTEN DO DREAM DO DO COLLECT DO THINK COLLECT DO SEE OVERSEE COLLECT ANALYSE FEEL LEARN ASK COLLECT DREAM DO HEAR LISTEN DREAM DO COLLECT LISTEN DO THINK COLLECT DO DREAM SEE OVERSEE COLLECT FEEL LEARN ASK COLLECT ANALYSE LISTEN DO DREAM COLLECT DO THINK COLLECT DO SEE OVERSEE DO COLLECT DO THINK COLLECT DO SEE OVERSEE COLLECT ANALYSE FEEL LEARN ASK COLLECT DREAM DO HEAR LISTEN DREAM DO COLLECT LISTEN DO THINK COLLECT DO DREAM SEE OVERSEE COLLECT FEEL LEARN ASK COLLECT ANALYSE LISTEN DO DREAM COLLECT DO THINK COLLECT DO SEE OVERSEE FEEL LEARN ASK COLLECT DO EXPERIENCE THINK OF WRITE DRAW TELL A STORY ENTERTAIN REALIZE DREAM DO COLLECT DO THINK COLLECT DO SEE OVERSEE COLLECT FEEL LEARN ASK COLLECT ANALYSE LISTEN DO DREAM DO OVERSEE FEEL LEARN ASK COLLECT DO EXPERIENCE THINK OF WRITE DRAW TELL A STORY ENTERTAIN REALIZE DREAM DO COLLECT DO THINK COLLECT DO SEE OVERSEE COLLECT FEEL LEARN ASK COLLECT ANALYSE LISTEN DO DREAM DO COLLECT DO THINK COLLECT DO SEE OVERSEE COLLECT FEEL LEARN ASK

Am I going to be an Imagineer anytime soon? Maybe ...

- Enjoy everything you see
- Enjoy everything you do
- Enjoy people
- Enjoy beautiful things
- Enjoy designing
- Enjoy making
- Enjoy life
- Enjoy discovery
- Enjoy dreaming
- Enjoy fantasizing

But first ...

Rent a boat together with someone you love.

Don't speak to each other during the trip.

Look around you and enjoy.

Bibliography

LITERATURE

Aaker, D.A. (1991) *Managing Brand Equity*. Free Press, New York.

Aaker, J.L. (1997) Dimensions of brand personality. *Journal of Marketing Research* 34, 347–357.

Accenture Consultants (2007) Opkomende economieen steeds actiever op overnamemarkt. *Management Scope*, October.

Akerboom, M. (2002) *Gerichte communicatie op basis van segmentatieonderzoek*. Rijksvoorlichtingsdienst/Publiek en Communicatie, Den Haag.

Anderson, J.R. (2009) *Cognitive Psychology and its Implications*. Macmillan, New York, p. 519.

Bauman, Z. (2000) *Liquid Modernity*. Polity, Cambridge.

Beck, U. (1992) *The Risk Society*. Sage, London.

Best, K. (2010) *The Fundamentals of Design Management*. AVA Publishing, Singapore.

Bitner, M.J. (1992) Servicescapes. The impact of physical surroundings on customers and employees. *Journal of Marketing* 56, pp. 57–71.

Boswijk, A., Thijssen, J.P.T. and Peelen, E. (2006) A new perspective on the experience economy: meaningful experiences. The European Centre for the Experience Economy, the Netherlands.

Brown, T. (2008) Design thinking, *Harvard Business Review*, June 2008.

Brown, T. (2009) *Change by Design: How Design Thinking Transforms Organizations and Inspires Innovation*. HarperCollins, New York.

Byko, M. (2000) Aluminum Exhibits Its Versatility in Art, Life. *JOM* 52, 9–12.

Bytebier, I. (2002) *Creativiteit Hoe? Zo!* Lannoo, Tielt.

Cornelis, P. and Hover, M. (2008) *Imagineering en het Disney Brandweb*. NHTV Lectoraat Imagineering, Breda.

Covey, S.R. (2004) *The 7 Habits of Highly Effective People: Powerful Lessons in Personal Change*. Simon and Schuster, New York.

Csikszentmihalyi, M.C. (1990) *Flow: The Psychology of Optimal Experience*. Harper Collins, New York.

Csikszentmihalyi, M. (1996) *Creativity: Flow and the Psychology of Discovery and Invention*. HarperCollins, New York.

Cullman Banner (Alabama) (22/01/1942) *Behind the scenes of American business* [newspaper article].

de Jong, J. and Harkema, S. (2007) *Winst door innovatie*. Academic Service, Den Haag.

Delfos, M. (2010) *De schoonheid van het verschil*. Pearson Assessment and Information, Amsterdam.

Desmet, P. and Hekkert, P. (2007) Framework of product experience. *International Journal of Design* 1, 57–66.

Falk J.H. and Dierking, L.D. (1992) *The Museum Experience*. Howells House, Washington, DC.

Fennis, B.M. and Pruyn, A.T.H. (2007) You are what you wear. Brand personality influences on consumer impression formation. *Journal of Business Research* 60, 634–639.

Fog, K., Budtz, C., Munch, P. and Blanchette, S. (2010) *Storytelling: Branding in Practice*. Springer, Berlin, Heidelberg.

Franzen, G. (2004) *Wat drijft ons? Denken over motivatie sinds Darwin*. LEMMA, Utrecht.

Geursen, G. Hazewind op gympen. EPN, Nijmegen.

Galjaard, S., Bots, H. and Huynh, T. (2007) *Ideeën voor creativiteit*. SDU Uitgevers, The Hague.

Gardner, H. (1999) *Intelligence Reframed: Multiple Intelligences for the Twenty-First Century*. Basic Books, New York.

Gilmore, J. and Pine, J. (2007) *Authenticity. What Consumers Really Want*. Harvard Business Press, Boston, Massachusetts.

Godin, S. (2008) *Tribes: We Need You to Lead Us*. Little Brown, London.

Godin, S. (2005) *Purple Cow*. Penguin Books Ltd, London.

Heath, C. and Heath, D. (2007) *Made to Stick*. FT Prentice Hall, Amsterdam.

Herremans, R. and Rijnja, G. (2005) Grip op grillige doelgroepen. Meer bereik met meervoudige segmentatie. In: Andere media, nieuwe kanalen!? Den Haag: Rijksvoorlichtingsdienst – SDU Uitgevers, RVD-communicatiereeks, Platform 3, pp. 63–71.

Humphreys, A. and Grayson, K. (2008) The intersecting roles of consumer and producer: a critical perspective on co-production, co-creation and prosumption. *Sociology Compass* 2, 963–980.

Hunicke, R., Leblanc, M. and Zubek, R. (2004) MDA: A formal approach to game design and game research. In: *Proceedings of the Challenges in Game AI Workshop*, Nineteenth National Conference on Artificial Intelligence, pp. 1–5.

James, W. (1890) *The Principles of Psychology*, Volume 1. Henry Holt, New York.

Jensen, R. (1999) *De Droommaatschappij. Van informatie naar verbeelding*. McGraw-Hill, New Jersey.

Kahle, L.R. (1983) *Social Values and Social Change: Adaptation to Life in America*. Prager Publishers, New York.

Katz, D. (1960) The functional approach to the study of attitudes. *Public Opinion Quarterly* 24, 163–204.

Keller, K.L. (2007) *Strategic Brand Management*. Pearson Education, New York.

Kessels, J., Boers E. and Mostert, P. (2002) *Vrije ruimte, filosoferen in organisaties*. Amsterdam, Boom.

Keuning, D. (2003) *Grondslagen van het management*. Groningen, Stenfert Kroese.

Kolb, D.A. (1984) *Experiential Learning: Experience as the Source of Learning and Development*, Volume 1. Prentice-Hall, Englewood Cliffs, New Jersey.

Kotler, P. and Armstrong, G. (2010) *Principles of Marketing*. Pearson, New Jersey.

La Grand, D. (2010) *Co-creatie-de-klant-weet-het-altijd-beter*. Retrieved February 2010, from http://www.syntens.nl/Artikelen/Artikel/Co-creatie-de-klant-weet-het-altijd-beter.aspx

Levitt, T. (1983) Globalization of Markets. *Harvard Business Review*, May/June 1983.

Maslow, A.H. (1943) A theory of human motivation. *Psychological Review* 50, 370.

McGuire, W.J. (1976) Some internal psychological factors influencing consumer choice. *Journal of Consumer Research* 2, 302–319.

Mitchell A. (1983) *The Nine American Lifestyles: Who We Are and Where We're Going*. Warner, New York.

Mulder, R. and ten Cate, R. (2006) *Innovatief ondernemen*. Pearson, New Jersey.

Nijs, D. and Peters, F. (2002) *Imagineering, het creeren van belevingswerelden*. Boom Lemma, Amsterdam.

Osterwalder, A. and Pigneur, Y. (2010) *Business Model Generation: A Handbook for Visionaries, Game Changers, and Challengers*. Wiley, Hoboken, New Jersey.

Parasuraman, A., Zeithaml, V.A. and Berry, L.L. (1988) SERVQUAL: A multiple-item scale for measuring consumer perceptions of service quality. *Journal of Retailing* 64, 12–40.

Petty, R. and Cacioppo, J. (1986) *From Communication and Persuasion: Central and Peripheral Routes to Attitude Change*. Springer-Verlag, New York.

Petty, R.E. and Wegener, D.T. (1999) The Elaboration Likelihood Model: current status and controversies. In: Chaiken, S. and Trope, Y. (eds) *Dual-process Theories in Social Psychology*. Guilford, New York, pp. 41–72.

Pieters, R.G.M. and van Raaij, W.F. (1992) *De werking van reclame*. Stenfert Kroese, Leiden.

Pijnappels, C. (2009) *ZorgBasics Ondernemen en innoveren*. Boom, Den Haag.

Pine, B.J. II and Gilmore, J.H. (1999) *The Experience Economy: Work is a Theatre and Every Business a Stage*. Harvard Business School Press, Boston, Massachusetts.

Pink, D.H. (2005) *A Whole New Mind. How to Thrive in the New Conceptual Age*. Riverhead Books, New York.

Porter, M.E. (1985) *Competitive Advantage*. The Free Press, New York.

Postma, P. (2006) Neurologie berooft marketing van logica. Tijdschrift voor Marketing, March, 20–23.

Prahalad, C.K. and Ramaswamy, V. (2004) *The Future of Competition: Co-creating Unique Value with Customers*. Harvard Business School Press, Boston, Massachusetts.

Quinn, R.E. and Rohrbaugh, J. (1983) A spatial model of effectiveness criteria: Towards a competing values approach to organizational analysis. Management Science 29, 363–377.

Quinn, R. (1997) *Handboek Managementvaardigheden*. Academic Service, Den Haag.

Redeker, H. (1995) Helmuth Plessner *of de belichaamde filosofie*. Delft, Eburon.

Reynaert, I. and Dijkerman, D. (eds) (2009) *Basisboek crossmedia concepting*. Boom Onderwijs, Amsterdam.

Reynolds, T.J. and Gutman, J. (1984) Laddering. In: Pits, R.E. and Woodside, A.G (eds) *Personal Values and Consumer Psychology*. Lexington, Books, Lexington, Massachusetts, pp. 155–167.

Ries, A. and Trout, J. (1981) *Positioning: The Battle for Your Mind*. McGraw-Hill, New York.

Rijkenberg, J. (2006) *Concepting. Het managen van conceptmerken in het communicatiegeoriënteerde tijdperk*. BZZTôH, Den Haag.

Ritzer, G. (2008) *The McDonaldization of Society*. Pine Forge Press, Los Angeles.

Rokeach, M. (1973) *The Nature of Human Values*. Free Press, New York.

Roberts, K. (2005) *Lovemarks*. PowerHouse Books, New York.

Robinson, K. (2011) *Out of our Minds: Learning to be Creative*. Capstone, New Jersey.

Rogers, E. (1962) *Diffusion of Innovations*. Free Press, London/New York.

Russell, J.A. (1980) A circumplex model of affect. *Journal of Personality and Social Psychology* 39, 1161–1178.

Schultz, M. and Hatch, M.J. (2003) The cycles of corporate branding. The case of the Lego Company. *California Management Review* 46, 6–26.

Schwartz, S.H. and Bilsky, W. (1987) Toward a universal psychological structure of human values. *Journal of Personality and Social Psychology* 53, 550.

The Imagineers (2005) *The Imagineering Way: Ideas to Ignite your Creativity*. New York, Disney Editions.

Thijssen, T. (2009) Klantbeleving begrijpen, meten en bevorderen. *FMI* 12, 82–86.

Time Magazine (16/02/1942) *The place they do Imagineering* Advertisement Aluminum company of America, p.59.

Trout, J. and Ries, A. (2005) *Positioning: The Battle for your Mind*. McGraw-Hill, New York.

van Gool, W. and van Lindert, C. (2008) *Imagineering VTM*. NHTV Internal Publications, Breda.

van Neer, R. (1986) *Concentratie op school. Omgaan met het concentratievermogen van de leerling*. Zwijsen, Tilburhg.

Verrips, G. (2010) *Doe iets!* Being There, Amsterdam.

Vroom, V. (1964) *Work and Motivation*. Wiley, New York.

Wright, A. (2005) *The Imagineers:* The Imagineering Field Guide to Magic Kingdom at Walt Disney World. New York, Disney Editions.

Zukin, S. (1996) *The Cultures of Cities*. Cambridge, Blackwell Publishing.

WEBSITES

Branddating.nl last accessed June 2013

Brown, T. (2010) 'Creativity and Play'. Retrieved August 2010 from www.tedtalks.com

The Future Laboratory, Brandocracy. Retrieved May 2010 from www.thefuturelaboratory.com

Geursen, G. (2008) concepting. Retrieved August 2010 from www.bedrijvigheden.nl

Godin, S. (2008) on tribes that we lead. Retrieved August 2010 from http://sethgodin.typepad. com/seths_blog/2008/01/tribal-manageme.html

Mentality, http://www.motivaction.nl/en/mentality

Ozier, K. Who is this guy? And what makes him special, Retrieved August 2010 from www.kileozier.com

Pink, Daniel, on motivation. Retrieved August 2010 from http://www.youtube.com/watch?v=u6XAPnuFjJc

Win-Model TNS-NIPO. Retrieved June 2010 from http://www.tns-nipo.com

Index

Page numbers in **bold** refer to figures and tables